D1189395

Reading Susan Sontag

READING
SUSAN
SONTAG

A Critical Introduction to Her Work

Carl Rollyson

Ivan R. Dee
CHICAGO

READING SUSAN SONTAG. Copyright © 2001 by Carl Rollyson. All rights reserved, including the right to reproduce this book or portions thereof in any form. For information, address: Ivan R. Dee, Publisher, 1332 North Halsted Street, Chicago 60622. Manufactured in the United States of America and printed on acid-free paper.

Library of Congress Cataloging-in-Publication Data:
Rollyson, Carl E. (Carl Edmund)
    Reading Susan Sontag : a critical introduction to her work /
Carl Rollyson.
        p. cm.
    "Works by Susan Sontag": p.
    Includes bibliographical references (p.) and index.
    ISBN 1-56663-391-5 (acid-free paper)
        1. Sontag, Susan, 1933– —Criticism and interpretation. 2. Women and literature—United States—History—20th century. 3. United States—Intellectual life—20th century. I. Title.

PS3569.O6547 Z875 2001
818'.5409—dc21   2001028604

Contents

Susan Sontag: *Sui Generis*

Susan Sontag sparked national attention when she published "Notes on 'Camp'" in the fall 1964 issue of *Partisan Review*. That December, *Time* magazine heralded a fresh and bold new voice. Unlike an earlier generation of American critics, many of whom had also published landmark essays in *Partisan Review*, Sontag was not wary of popular culture. She embraced it. Although her article continually referred to great works of literature and art, stamping Sontag herself as an aesthete, she readily invoked Hollywood movies and rock and roll, branding herself as "hip"—to use the parlance of that time. A new kind of museum of her own creation had suddenly been established, and distinctions between "high brow" and "low brow" art had been blurred. She categorized camp as a playful style of response to art, a response that could be found everywhere in the culture. It was camp to enjoy a perfectly dreadful movie so long as one knew it was dreadful and enjoyed the work's consistent dreadfulness. It was camp to slum through contemporary culture if one maintained an arch awareness of that slumming. It was camp to enjoy the self-parodying performance of a Mae West. It was camp, in sum, to revel in all that popular culture offered, occasionally finding works of genius amidst the substandard, or at least appreciating the elements that high and low culture had in common. Unlike earlier *Partisan Review* critics, Sontag did not bother worrying whether a taste for popular or mass culture would deaden or crowd out the appetite for the classics and the masterpieces of modern culture.

Time thought Sontag particularly audacious when she traced the sources of camp to a homosexual sensibility. In 1964 there were no popular culture departments or journals, no gay studies courses or programs—the word "gay" had yet to be applied to homosexuals, who were regarded by the culture at large as marginalized figures and even as immoral and criminal threats to society. Although Sontag portrayed herself as an observer who was both attracted to and repelled by camp, the very density and comprehensiveness of her "notes" situated her as an advocate of what she herself would later call a "new sensibility."

Gore Vidal once pointed out that Sontag's embrace of the new made her the "Detroit" of critics. She had designed herself as the new-model intellectual, emphasizing form over content, arguing that art was art only when matters of style and structure, not message and meaning, predominated. Her rise to fame, he implied, depended on this idea that she was a trend spotter, that Susan Sontag could forecast the shape of things to come.

No one reads Susan Sontag today to spot trends, yet the name Susan Sontag remains a potent way to initiate cultural debate. Her signature essays, "Against Interpretation," "On Style," "The Pornographic Imagination," "The Aesthetics of Silence," and "The Imagination of Disaster," and at least two of her books, *On Photography* and *Illness as Metaphor*, are staples of the American curriculum, assigned in college courses in various disciplines. Her fiction has not achieved the same stature, although eminent critics such as Tony Tanner, Theodore Solotaroff, and John Banville have treated it with considerable respect. In November 2000, Sontag's novel *In America* won the National Book Award. Yet this prize did not settle the matter, for its announcement set off a fierce debate (initiated by Daniel Halpern in the *New Republic* and Laura Miller in *Salon*) about the merits of the novel, which had received mixed reviews. Sontag's fiction deserves a careful reading, if only as a way of tracing her development as a writer whose fiction and nonfiction have an essayistic quality. As she confessed to interviewer Jonathan Cott in 1978: "I've always thought of the essays and the fiction as dealing with very different themes. . . . It's only quite recently, because it's been forced on my attention, that I realized the extent to which the essays and the fiction share the same themes. . . . It's almost frightening to discover how unified they are."

Sontag's films have not stimulated much study, and they are the only part of her body of work that her publisher, Farrar, Straus & Giroux, has not kept in print. I have chosen not to discuss them here—except for brief synopses in Chapter 1, which provides a chronological overview of Sontag's career. I refer readers to chapters on the films in my book *Susan Sontag: The Making of an Icon.*

Unlike many writers of her generation, Sontag's eminence rests not only on certain key works but on her image. As Leland Poague points out in *Conversations with Susan Sontag,* "It is hard, at the end of the twentieth century in America, *not* to have some picture of Susan Sontag." Glamorous photographs of her continue to appear in glossy magazines such as *Vogue* and *Mademoiselle.* Irving Penn, Diane Arbus, Peter Hujar, Phillipe Halsman, Thomas Victor, Robert Mapplethorpe, Richard Avedon, Jill Krementz, and Annie Leibovitz—in other words a roll call of renowned fashion and celebrity photographers—have provided the culture with alluring Susan Sontag portraits. She has come to represent the idea of the seductive intellectual, the "Natalie Wood of the U.S. avant garde," as one commentator put it. A public that has not read her work may still have at least a vague idea of who she is, since Barnes & Noble has recently used her image to promote book sales, and she has even appeared in an advertisement for Absolut Vodka—not to mention various books and calendars featuring photographs of writers.

So this "reading" of Susan Sontag will include discussions of all her books and of the cultural figure she has become, with attention to her intellectual background and to her biography—mainly in Chapter 2, which also discusses her work as a theatre director and playwright. Where possible, I have also tried to let Sontag speak through the many interviews she has given, since she is a most articulate commentator on her own work, though also a most reluctant authority on her public image. Since this is a book about Sontag's reputation as well as her achievement, I will discuss reviews of her work to demonstrate how the public perception of Susan Sontag developed. Reviews are not necessarily a valid reflection of a writer's ultimate worth, but in Sontag's case they contributed significantly to the view of her as a celebrity writer and an embodiment of her times.

Susan Sontag: The Making of an Icon was the first biographical narrative to discuss Sontag's career in chronological order. But the biography was not intended to provide a detailed analysis of her work, or to delve into her intellectual roots as deeply as a work of literary criticism does. Analytical prose is often at odds with biographical narrative; the latter can only begin to suggest the sources and effects of Sontag's writing, which this book explores at greater length.

It is remarkable that there is no book-length orientation to Sontag's work for general readers and students. Sohnya Sayres's *Susan Sontag: The Elegiac Modernist* and Liam Kennedy's *Susan Sontag: Mind as Passion* contain many useful insights. But both books are revisions of Ph.D. dissertations which still seem aimed at the graduate school classroom and at other advanced scholars. Jargon predominates, especially in Sayres's book, and both critics tend to pursue themes, not the evolution of a career. A beginning student of Sontag needs a firmer grounding in her biography and in cultural history, in summaries and clear analyses of her work. This book is addressed to what Virginia Woolf called the "common reader." I do not begin by assuming that readers have read her work or that they remember the details of her novels. I do not take Sontag's importance for granted. Rather I want to show why she is important and deserves still to be read.

To the first-time reader of Sontag, and to someone not versed in the history of the arts, her constant parade of names and concepts will be bewildering. In my synopses of her work, I have tried to stay close to the main points of her argument. Even then, terms and figures referred to in the synopses may be unfamiliar to someone seeking an introduction to Sontag's work or wishing to trace the pattern of her references. Surprisingly, for a writer who invokes so many names and terms, none of Sontag's books is indexed. So I have included in Chapter 14 "A Susan Sontag Glossary," brief descriptions and reminders of the terms and cultural figures that she draws on.

With the publication of *In America*, Sontag voiced certain doubts about the critical work on which her reputation rests. Why this should be so is the subject of this book's last chapter, "Sontag Reading Sontag." As *Conversations with Susan Sontag* demonstrates, she has always read herself as a writer in process, disburdening herself of ideas that no longer seem useful or true. She can, without embarrassment, switch sides in an argument, rather like a performer enjoying a new role. She likes to think of herself as "self-invented," *sui generis*. Psychiatrist Arnold Ludwig has studied the illusion of self-invention—Sontag herself refers to it as an illusion—observing that the "belief in self-invention requires that we remain ignorant of the forces that let us feel we have the power to create ourselves anew." Since Sontag shows no evidence of wanting to write her own memoirs or intellectual autobiography, this book will attempt to bring those forces into view.

Reading Susan Sontag

ONE

A Chronological Overview

Susan Lee Rosenblatt was born January 16, 1933, in New York City. She would not acquire the last name of Sontag until after her father's death on October 19, 1938, and her mother's marriage in 1945 to Nathan Sontag. Her memories of her father, Jack Rosenblatt, are vague, though her powerful need to identify with him—a fur trader in China who died of tuberculosis—is apparent in her short story "Project for a Trip to China" (included in *I, etcetera*). In her fiction, stories, and interviews Sontag presents a highly ambivalent picture of her mother, Mildred Jacobson, an alcoholic and aloof woman but also a self-absorbed beauty who seemed at a loss as to how to raise her precocious daughter. Although Sontag has a younger sister, Judith, born February 27, 1936, the writer has said little about her sibling, leaving the impression that Judith did not share her intellectual interests or form a close emotional bond with her sister.

Jack Rosenblatt and Mildred Jacobson were the children of Jewish immigrants eager to assimilate into American life. Susan was not raised as a Jew. Indeed, the only religion she knew firsthand was Roman Catholicism, absorbed from attendance at mass with her Irish nanny. Susan once asked her grandmother Gussie (who died when Susan was seven) where she came from. "Europe," was the terse reply. Old enough to know that was not a very specific answer, Susan tried again, "But where, Grandma?" "Europe," Gussie repeated. "And so to this day I don't know from what country my paternal grandparents came," Sontag told interviewer Geoffrey Movius in 1975.

"Project for a Trip to China" expresses Sontag's need to reimagine a past her family has denied her. She pictures her parents crossing Russia by train. Mildred wants to stop in Bialystock to visit her mother's birthplace. But in Stalinist Russia, coaches with foreigners are sealed, and Mildred weeps in frustration at the Bialystock stop, where old women knock on the train windows hoping to sell their food. In fact, Sontag does not know if her mother cries, but it is a compelling story she feels the need to "see," and to complete. Mildred never forgave her mother for dying in Los Angeles when Mildred was only fourteen, and Sontag links that event to the loss of her own father (she is only five when he dies). She forgives him, although his death provokes in her a lifelong detachment—perhaps as a way of coping with pain, perhaps as a matter of pride. Sontag playfully wonders if her detachment might be prenatal and oriental, a result of her having been conceived in China, though she cannot be sure she was conceived there. This detachment links her with her mother, a bond she never acknowledges, except perhaps in the muted dedication of *I, etcetera*, "for you, M." Sontag finally deals with the immigrant experience in America—though not with her own family—in her novel *In America*.

Shortly after her father's death, Susan suffered her first asthma attack. Her mother decided to leave New York City in search of a better climate for her ailing daughter. After a brief stay in Miami (which proved too humid for Susan), Mildred Rosenblatt settled her family in Tucson, Arizona, where the arid environment alleviated Susan's symptoms. Already an avid reader, six-year-old Susan was placed in the third grade. Sontag recalls her Tucson period (1939–1945) as rather dull. Although she got along well with her schoolmates, nothing much in her surroundings interested her. In "Project for a Trip to China" she recalls digging a hole in her backyard and announcing that she was tunneling to China, which represented the world of her father, the world elsewhere that she longed to explore.

She found solace in classics such as *The Secret Garden*, which spoke to her need to fashion her own world. Travel books by Richard Halliburton and novels like *Les Miserables*, which made large political statements set against broad canvases of society, stimulated her imagination. "If you were a small kid discovering George Eliot or Thackeray or Balzac or the great Russian novels, little Indian dolls with turquoise beads sure couldn't hold a candle to the nineteenth-century novel," she said in a 1992 interview with Marian Christy.

Edgar Allan Poe made the earliest and most lasting influence on Sontag. His work creates a self-enclosed, literary world. His stories rarely have specific locales. It is the form of the words, the shape of the sentence or line, that is seductive in Poe. His heroines are dark-featured and intellectual; they suffer from wasting diseases and are mourned obsessively. His evocations of melancholy and mortality appealed to a solemn, book-besotted child grieving over her father. Poe contended that literature created its own reality; a poem is a poem is a poem, he insisted. His precepts would be reiterated in Sontag's signature essay, "Against Interpretation." Poe wanted to create beautiful literature, not to express himself. It was the body of work that mattered, he argued, as Sontag would in *Under the Sign of Saturn* and in countless interviews.

Louisa May Alcott's *Little Women* and Jack London's *Martin Eden* first introduced Susan to the idea of a writer's career. Jo and Martin Eden are assiduous authors, busily sending out manuscripts, corresponding with magazines, coping with rejection slips. That the odds against succeeding are tremendous (Martin Eden commits suicide) only made writing seem an even more ambitious project to Susan. The very arduousness of making a success aroused her ardor. She began her own neighborhood newspaper during World War II and realized early the satisfactions of publishing.

After Susan's mother married Nathan Sontag, an air force officer convalescing in Tucson, the couple decided to move to California, where in 1946 Susan entered North Hollywood High School. In her memoir, "Pilgrimage," Sontag presents a contemptuous picture of her stepfather, handsome but superficial, contented with his backyard barbecues. Her remote mother is treated just as derisively. And school is an exercise in mediocrity. Sontag remembered with disgust that one of her teachers assigned the class the *Reader's Digest.* At thirteen she had already discovered *Partisan Review,* the premier intellectual journal of her time. It published distinguished critics such as Lionel Trilling, Philip Rahv, Mary McCarthy, Dwight Macdonald, Clement Greenberg, and Hannah Arendt. She dreamed of going to New York City and "writing for them," she later told reporter Peter Grondahl.

The centerpiece of "Pilgrimage" is the journey that Sontag and her friend Merrill take to meet Thomas Mann. Sontag, still in high school, considers herself unworthy to meet the great author and is dragged along by Merrill. She is embarrassed about her Southern California background and that she has done nothing to merit Mann's attention. Meeting Mann is disappointing largely because he is not detached enough; that is, he does not match Sontag's picture of the great artist who exists on a plane far removed from ordinary people.

"Pilgrimage" thus reveals a good deal about Sontag's lofty sense of literature. Her theory of art depends on this sense of its autonomy. Art does not mirror or imitate reality; art supersedes the world as it is. She absorbs this belief in the supremacy of the aesthetic from the journals and novels of André Gide. They present a literary life that is all-engrossing. Jamake Highwater, one of Sontag's high school classmates, remembers that they read and argued about Gide's novel *The Counterfeiters,* just as Bernard and Olivier, characters in the novel, argue about a novelist (Edouard) writing a novel. *The Counterfeiters* is about the writer's need to leave home, to reject one's parents and any authority other than one's own: "The feelings one has for one's progenitors are among the things that it is better not to go into too deeply." A writer's pilgrimage, in other words, is always away from mundane, fixed reality, and from a sustained engagement with family origins. As young Bernard, a budding writer, puts it: "There's no better cure for the fear of taking after one's father than not to know who he is. The mere fact of inquiry binds one."

Susan Sontag graduated from North Hollywood High in January 1949 at the age of sixteen. She wanted to attend the University of Chicago, where the Great Books curriculum touted by its dynamic president, Robert M. Hutchins, seemed a suitable challenge. Indeed, the university specialized in admitting high-achieving younger students, and one of Sontag's high school teachers, a Chicago alumnus, encouraged her choice—a most unusual one, since most of Sontag's contemporaries chose California schools that did not, with the exception of Berkeley, offer such a daunting curriculum.

But Sontag's mother disliked the idea of her daughter living in what Mildred regarded as an urban, radical environment, and Susan reluctantly agreed to try Berkeley for the spring term. She did well, studying with the college's best professors. She was even allowed to take graduate courses. She liked Berkeley well enough, but Chicago remained her dream, and her mother relented. She enrolled at Chicago in the fall semester of 1949 and sped through the university curriculum in just two years. Her achievement was impressive if not singular, since other great minds (such as critic George Steiner) had achieved similar records at Chicago.

Chicago emphasized the mastery of texts, which students would demonstrate in final examinations. Sontag was not required to write papers. Writing per se was not her goal at this point; rather she wanted to absorb as much as she could from professors whom she regarded as authorities, as models of learning she could emulate. Her own opinions seemed almost irrelevant. Her first task was to comprehend the canon of literature and philosophy.

It is arguable that Leo Strauss, a European Jew who left Germany in 1932 to escape the impending Holocaust and settled in Chicago in 1938 after stopovers in France and England, provided Sontag with the manner and mystique she would later employ so dramatically in the cause of her own career. George Steiner remembers him entering a classroom: "Ladies and Gentlemen, good morning. In this classroom, the name of . . . who is, of course, strictly incomparable, will not be mentioned. We can now proceed to Plato's *Republic.*" *Who* was incomparable? the eighteen-year-old Steiner wanted to know. He had not caught the philosopher's name, and Strauss made him feel as if a "bright, cold shaft had passed through my spine." After class, a graduate student supplied Steiner with the reference: Martin Heidegger. At the library, Steiner began his struggle with the difficult Heidegger, understanding, it seemed, nothing, but caught up in an intellectual vortex that he would enter again and again until he mastered it. Leo Strauss, in other words, epitomized the Chicago experience, alluding to great thinkers, dropping names and the titles of great works that might seem esoteric even to gifted students like Steiner. Strauss exemplified in person the aura of the sages Sontag would extol in *Under the Sign of Saturn.* Like Strauss, Sontag would stud her essays with the names of important thinkers, so many names that only the best read of her readers could match her frame of reference.

Philip Rieff, a young sociology professor still working on his Ph.D., exuded the Chicago intellectual's air of command. Students knew that he was working on a ground-breaking study of Freud, and Sontag was advised to audit one of his classes. Rieff spotted her immediately. Sontag's classmates do not remember another young woman who had such dark striking looks combined with such an air of assurance. Rieff spoke with her the first day she attended his class. In ten days (December 1950) they were married. She was seventeen; he was twenty-eight. Terming herself an "unconscious feminist," she retained her maiden name. He was the first man who had ever treated her like an adult woman, Sontag later admitted. He was steeped in literature as well as in philosophy, sociology, and psychology. They became collaborators on his important book, *Freud: The Mind of the Moralist*, although she would realize, after only a year of marriage, that she had made a mistake. He did not have a great mind. In "Zero," the preface to *In America*, she compares Rieff to Dr. Casaubon, the dried-up pedant in *Middlemarch* (1872) who marries the intellectually vibrant Dorothea Brooke. As early as 1951 she seems to have discerned that Rieff was too stodgy for her. That year she read Simone de Beauvoir's *The Second Sex*, an influential text in which de Beauvoir observes: "Marriages, then, are not generally founded upon love. As Freud put it, 'The husband is, so to speak, never more than a substitute for the beloved man, not that man himself.'" But Sontag would not divorce her husband until 1958, commenting much later that it took her nine years to summon the conviction that she had a moral right to do so.

Sontag graduated in the spring of 1951 with a B.A. degree from Chicago. Rieff accepted an assistant professorship at Brandeis University for the 1952–1953 academic year. Sontag, pregnant by January (her son David would be born in Boston on September 28, 1952), enrolled in the graduate program at the University of Connecticut in the fall of 1953. But the program at Connecticut seemed mediocre, and by the next year she was enrolled in the philosophy department at Harvard.

There she earned a master's degree in philosophy in 1957 and won a fellowship to study at Oxford for the 1957–1958 academic year. Rieff was offered a fellowship at Stanford. Although the couple separated at this point (their son David went to live with Rieff's relatives), they did not contemplate a divorce. They were like the couple in Sontag's story "Baby" (included in *I, etcetera*) who say to each other that it will be good for their relationship if they split for a while.

At Oxford, Sontag found the school of analytical philosophy as practiced by professors such as A. J. Ayer uncongenial. She gravitated rather to Iris Murdoch, who in 1953 had published *Sartre, Romantic Realist.* Murdoch's second book, *Under the Net*, explicitly linked philosophy and fiction, observing how the existentialists pursued the theme of the self-seeking absolutes (goodness, love, morality) in an absurd universe. Whereas Ayer analyzed statements and employed logic, Murdoch engaged with narratives and symbolic actions. Sontag found the latter approach more congenial; it reminded her of the method employed by her great teacher at Chicago, the critic Kenneth Burke, whose novel *Towards a Better Life* would serve as a model for her first novel, *The Benefactor.*

Early in 1958 Sontag moved on to the Sorbonne and Paris, the city that had fired her adolescent imagination—as she wrote in her foreword to *A Place in the World Called Paris.* In Paris she discovered a French intellectual class that reveled in Hollywood movies and regarded all aspects of film with intense seriousness. She lived on the rue Jacob in the Latin Quarter. There, as the journalist Stanley Karnow notes, "theaters featured lengthy audience debates following their *séances*, and the weekly literary journals ran lengthy articles analyzing *le cinema* in tedious detail." She went to the Sorbonne to hear Simone de Beauvoir lecture; later she would become de Beauvoir's friend and secure gratis the screen rights to one of de Beauvoir's novels.

Sontag had begun to read André Breton and other surrealists who were interested in the figure of the artist, of the creator behind the work. They provided her a link with Walter Pater and Oscar Wilde—writers she had studied at Chicago—who created a style inseparable from the idea of the aesthetic personality. Or as Mark Polizzotti, Breton's biographer puts it, the "creator and the work were inextricably bound. . . . The artist's first and most important creation . . . was himself." Both the self and the work had to be extolled, to be advertised, argued Breton in one of his more Wildean moments. It is an appealing conceit for the writer with a *sui generis* conception of herself.

Writers such as Louis Aragon and André Malraux meticulously polished their images and created a mystique. Aragon and

Breton guided the avant-garde toward left-wing politics, fashioning a progressive and daring movement, even though fitful alliances between the Communist party and the surrealists, for example, were absurd and bound to break up. No matter. The idea, the platonic conception, of the artist *engagé* entranced Sontag. It excused any amount of contradictory and self-defeating behavior. As Tony Judt, a historian of this period concludes, to the French intellectual (with few exceptions) "there was thus an aura of romance surrounding the Communist adventure that gave to its failings and mistakes a truly heroic quality." Even Khrushchev's damning 1956 revelations of Stalin's camps were treated in what Judt calls "ethical parentheses." Sontag's later infatuations with Cuba and North Vietnam reflected this peculiar form of Gallic collaborationism with the "moral torture" of Stalinism, articulated in the "comforting thought that the path one had chosen was complex, painful, and perhaps even hopeless."

In France, in 1958, Sontag discovered a small, close-knit group of writers, intellectuals, and filmmakers who enjoyed an influence out of proportion to their size. They were an "elite caste." They were deified, as Stanley Karnow observed in 1950s France (he was married for a time to the daughter of Nathalie Sarraute, one of the experimental novelists whom Sontag emulated). But Karnow, never wanting to be an insider, and having no need for acceptance into avant-garde circles, noticed something else: "Most intellectuals, beneath their façade of individualism, were remarkably conformist." They were also remarkably ill-informed about America and anti-American to the core—not very troubling to Sontag who later rejected her own country and said that the only livable American place for her is New York City, which to her is not like the rest of America.

When Sontag returned from Paris to the United States, she announced to Philip Rieff that she wanted a divorce. As she told interviewer Jonathan Cott, she came home to America with the conviction that

I'd like to have several lives, and it's very hard to have several lives and then have a husband—at least the kind of marriage that I had, which was incredibly intense; we were together all the time. And you can't live with someone on a twenty-four-hour-a-day basis, never be separated for years and years and have the same freedom to grow and change and fly off to Hong Kong if you feel like it . . . it's irresponsible. That's why I say that somewhere along the line, one has to choose between the Life and the Project.

As early as 1950, Sontag had expressed in print her attraction to the idea of living several lives, which is a form of reinvention. In the winter 1950 issue of the *Chicago Review* she reviewed *The Plenipotentiaries*, a novel by H. J. Kaplan, then a young American writer living since 1945 in Paris. Kaplan's work attracted her notice, she revealed, because it was like *The Counterfeiters*, portraying a novelist writing the novel that the reader is reading. His characters were outsiders, "strangers in their own country," who were the only ones with "full powers." The figure of the writer alienated or exiled from his culture had obvious appeal for Sontag, who would befriend and model herself after emigrés like the novelist Danilo Kis and the poet Joseph Brodsky.

Kaplan's main character, Phineas Strauss, has trouble writing his novel, in achieving his "full powers"—the words he writes at the top of a blank page. Sontag's page was also blank, and Europe represented, as it did for Kaplan's characters, the quest for self-consciousness and maturity, the grand theme, Sontag's review points out, of James's "American-in-Europe" fiction. The self-conscious narrators of Sontag's *The Volcano Lover* and of "Zero," the preface to *In America*, have their genesis in Kaplan's figure of the narrator as foreigner.

Interviewed in *People* magazine in 1978, Sontag said she arrived in New York on January 1, 1959, with "6-year-old David, two suitcases, and $30." She had refused to accept alimony. She wanted to be on her own. "I was thrilled. I was like Irena in *The Three Sisters* longing for Moscow. All I could think was New York!

New York!" Joan Didion, a Sontag contemporary and another California writer who came to Manhattan to "make it" as a writer, recalled the exhilaration of feeling that "everything was within reach. Just around every corner lay something curious and interesting, something I had never before seen or done or known about." To the outsider, Didion observes, "the idea of New York" represents an "infinitely romantic notion, the mysterious nexus of all love and money and power, the shiny and perishable dream itself."

Sontag has been reticent about this aspect of her career building. But biographical research shows that she set about making herself known, cruising parties—as Didion did—and making connections with important writers, editors, and publishers. She taught classes first at City College, then at Sarah Lawrence, and finally at Columbia University. But she had abandoned the idea of an academic career. These positions earned badly needed income as she began to write her first publishable essays. She helped to form an informal writers' group in which manuscripts could be exchanged and critiqued. She was laying the groundwork for her first novel, tentatively titled "Dreams of Hippolyte."

When Sontag had completed two chapters of the novel she showed them to Jason Epstein, a powerful editor at Random House, the founder of Anchor Books, and a member of the editorial board of the *New York Review of Books*. Although he decided not to publish Sontag, he recommended that she seek out Robert Giroux, the legendary editor at Farrar, Straus & Giroux. He had edited T. S. Eliot, Flannery O'Connor, and many other great twentieth-century writers. Even better, he was well known for taking risks on first novels that he believed were of great literary merit. When Sontag approached him, mentioning Epstein and his comment that Giroux was the only editor in New York who would understand her book, Giroux was charmed and flattered. On the basis of reading Sontag's early chapters, he signed her to a contract in May 1961.

Roger Straus, the owner of the firm, soon became Sontag's

stalwart champion, the only book publisher she would ever have. He would work tirelessly on her behalf, securing her foreign publishers and even taking charge of her lecture dates and other publicity. He wrote to prominent authors and public figures to tout her work—all of which he kept in print. By the time her first novel was ready for publication in early fall 1963, Farrar, Straus had secured the written endorsement of two pillars of the New York literary establishment: Elizabeth Hardwick and Hannah Arendt. Publicity materials compared Sontag to Mary McCarthy, the reigning woman of letters. "We have discovered a major writer," wrote Lila Karpf of Farrar, Straus.

Reviews of Sontag's first novel—the title had been changed to *The Benefactor*—were respectful but mixed. She was not hailed as a promising new novelist so much as a provocative and puzzling purveyor of ideas. Roger Straus, sensing that Sontag's talent showed best in polemical essays, suggested that her next book be a collection of essays. Like *The Benefactor*, this book was published with a provocative jacket photograph that made Sontag look like a glamorous female out of a French *film noir*. Reviewers such as Benjamin DeMott in the *New York Times Book Review* commented not only on Sontag's ideas but on her aura as the "lady on the scene," attuned to the latest avant-garde art in New York and in Europe. As with *The Benefactor*, reviews were mixed, but no matter what the critics said, the impression conveyed was of a figure who could not be ignored because she had a formidable intelligence and curiosity about new art and was clearly making an impression on contemporary culture.

Essentially the same dynamic characterized the reception of Sontag's next two works, *Death Kit* (1967), a novel, and *Styles of Radical Will* (1969), a collection of essays. While the novel received a few enthusiastic responses—especially from the distinguished editor and critic Theodore Solotaroff—critical opinion began to harden around the notion that Sontag had little talent as a novelist but considerable merit as an essayist and promoter of new ideas. Gore Vidal, one of the preeminent critics and novelists of the postwar period, reviewed *Death Kit* and suggested that Sontag was an American trying too earnestly to fit her style into the form of the French *nouveau roman*. He quoted phrases from Nathalie Sarraute's work echoed in Sontag's novel that demonstrated how forced and factitious he found *Death Kit*.

Alfred Kazin, an equally distinguished critic, in 1973 assessed Sontag as thinker and novelist in his book *Bright Book of Life*. He called her a grim figure with a "startling esthetic . . . advancing new positions" in "surprisingly sustained novels." She wrote "irreconcilable sentences" and "provocations," for she lived in a world of assertions, not of traditions, in which the "new" was never natural but something willed, "a voice, a self, in a world so determinedly construed from the outset as totally without foundation." Her novels were a philosopher's suppositions "without the slightest touch of comedy." He could not understand why she did not see the character Hippolyte as comic. "She is proud, but her hero is a ninny." Thus he observed that *The Benefactor* "takes place not in Paris, where the characters are living, but in Susan Sontag's will to keep this up." Yet he insisted that the novel "works because its author really sees the world as a series of propositions *about* the world." Writing as much like a biographer as a critic, Kazin concluded that she was a fantasist about the world:

> Sontag writes about situations, is always figuring out alternatives to her existing ideas about them and thus works at situations in the way that a movie director works something out for an induced effect. But she is always in the book, visibly parallel to the scene she is writing. A book is a screen, as she is a mind visibly "projecting" her notion of things onto it. Screen and mind are separated by Sontag's refusal to tell a story for its own sake.

There is an air about Kazin's criticism of one who is trying hard to like a form of fiction and a mind that are quite alien to his own—and to what he takes to be the literary heritage.

Kazin is responding to a form of fiction, yet his criticism sounds like it is of a person—or at least of a sensibility. He has an image of the writer implicit in his criticism, just as Sontag was, to some extent, imagining her own life as she wrote novels like *The Benefactor.* (She became much more open about this process in her later interviews.) The critic Richard Kostelanetz, a graduate student at Columbia while Sontag taught there, observes that Hippolyte "appears to be very feminine, while Frau Anders [Hippolyte's lover] seems to be a very masculine woman." Then Kostelanetz remembers that Hannah Arendt's first husband was the German philosopher Gunther Anders: "Recognize that, and you can see that this book tells of unfulfilled and unrequited love for Hannah Arendt, which may or may not reflect personal ambition." Arendt was then the reigning intellectual/philosopher/queen in New York literary life. Mary McCarthy pointed out in a 1967 letter to Arendt: "When I last watched her [Sontag] with you at the Lowells' [the home of poet Robert Lowell and his wife, Elizabeth Hardwick], it was clear that she was going to seek to conquer you. Or that she had fallen in love with you—the same thing. Anyway, did she?" Arendt does not seem to have answered the question, but she and Sontag remained on good, if not intimate, terms.

Kazin portrayed a writer who was in love with ideas and characters who embodied those ideas, and Kostelanetz supposed that this phenomenon pervaded not just Sontag's work but her life—or rather that the life and work were of a piece. Sontag herself says in *Under the Sign of Saturn*: "One cannot use the life to interpret the work. But one can use the work to interpret the life."

By 1969 Sontag's stature as an essayist was secure, her standing as a novelist shaky. Her efforts to write more fiction resulted in several aborted novels that reflected a crisis of confidence in her creativity. There were other distractions: she was invited to make films in Sweden; she became involved in protests over the Vietnam War; she supported and wrote enthusiastically about new Communist regimes—such as Castro's—in a belief that they represented the alternative to capitalism that the old-style Stalinist regimes of Eastern Europe had failed to provide.

Although Sontag's essays took on a quasi-Marxist language, her films—especially *Duet for Cannibals* (1969)—projected a highly skeptical view of political life and of charismatic figures. Its main character, Bauer, seems to be on the left, yet his predominant desire is to manipulate people and to exercise power over them. Just as *Duet for Cannibals* is a kind of parable about power, *Brother Carl* (1971) is an allegory about making art. Sontag calls Carl, a retired dancer, a "holy fool." Carl's mentor/nemesis is the director Martin Ericsson, who has done something terrible to Carl (it is never divulged) but who is determined to redeem himself and to rescue Carl from his silence (Carl speaks very few words in the film) and from his withdrawal from the world. Ericsson is a kind of Bauer who regrets the way his wielding of power has damaged people, yet he seems, like Bauer, unable to reform himself.

The women in these films revolve in the orbit of these dominant men. In *Brother Carl*, Lena (Ericsson's former wife) and her friend Karen form a strong bond, which is perhaps why Sontag later referred to it as a feminist film. But their relationship hinges on their attitude toward the two males, Ericsson and Carl. When both men reject Lena, her tie to Karen is not enough to prevent her from committing suicide. In both films, female identity is subsumed in a male-dominated world. Although Sontag has in later years paid tribute to female influences on her work, the predominant pattern, as in *Under the Sign of Saturn*, reinforces the omnipresence of a patriarchal world.

Sontag's films received a mixed reception both in Sweden and in America, although *Duet for Cannibals* enjoyed a modest success at the New York Film Festival. The films owed an enormous debt to Bergman. Indeed, they seem derivative in both theme and technique, especially *Brother Carl*, which is virtually a remake of *Persona*, a film Sontag would write about brilliantly in *Styles of Radical Will*.

The exhausted state of Sontag's male protagonists in both films coincides with her view of contemporary Sweden, though at the time she did not claim she was making a comment on the country per se. Yet her "Letter from Sweden," published in the leftist magazine *Ramparts* in July 1969, reveals her dissatisfaction with a people whose socialism seemed too pat and staid for a writer determined to romanticize the revolutionary cultures of Cuba and North Vietnam. "Letter from Sweden," which she has never reprinted in her collections of essays, is a key document in the development of her sensibility.

Sontag wrote about her "profound quarrel" with the country that seemed at once so welcoming and so resistant to her advances. She saw a negative for every Swedish virtue she could tick off. Swedes had a "genuine gift" for self-criticism, yet it came too easily, causing her to suspect that the country harbored within a "vast self-satisfaction." She disliked the Swedish reluctance to scrutinize character. Why expend so much energy on trying to fathom motives? they seemed to say. Yet Sontag's own work was built on a refusal to psychologize and analyze human intentions. Her work seems all too Swedish in its refusal to probe personality. Similarly, it grated on her that the Swedes were so silent. Were they all like Greta Garbo, wanting to be left alone? she wondered. Her films are full of such silences, and two of the characters in *Brother Carl* are virtually mute. She deeply distrusted the even-tempered Swedes. Surely, she suspected, they were hiding defects. They were, indeed, inhibited, anxious, and practiced an "emotional dissociation."

Sontag admitted that she shared certain puritanical traits with the Swedes and that she was among a people who could "use more emotion." They suffered from a Protestant angst that she believed informed her two "Swedish" films as well. She did not claim to be a Swedish filmmaker, but by virtue of working in Sweden for a year and surrounding herself with a Swedish crew, she had had more than enough time to recognize the Swede in herself and to regret it.

Of course there was much that Sontag admired about Sweden. She liked the egalitarian mentality. It did not abolish class distinctions—as Swedes liked to think—but it did make for a more democratic culture, in which having a servant, for example, was a source of embarrassment. One of her profoundest pleasures consisted simply in being able to walk anywhere and never fear being accosted by men, and to go to work and never have it mentioned how remarkable it was that she, a woman, could direct a film.

Sontag's role as radical thinker has never been clearly recognized in the United States, in part because a few of her most important political articles have never been published here. During her stay in Sweden, for example, she published an article in *BLM*, a Swedish journal, about Herbert Marcuse's concept of "repressive tolerance." Marcuse had speculated that in Western societies tolerance was a method for maintaining the status quo. The powers that be in the United States, for example, allowed an inconsequential liberalism because they knew that such liberalism was self-defeating. Tolerance in the United States and other advanced European democracies, Sontag argued, was a kind of psychological safety valve, not a true index of how much freedom the society actually enjoyed. She went so far as to attack John Stuart Mill's idea of liberty, dismissing him because his idea of tolerance derived from laissez-faire capitalism. Mill did not understand the psychological dimension of tolerance, how it could be used as a sop in an otherwise repressive society. She ended "A Letter from Sweden" with "¡Hasta la victoria siempre!" and her piece on Cuban posters with a rousing "Viva Fidel."

In "A Letter to Sweden," Sontag undercut her revolutionary sloganeering with sober observations: If Sweden was not truly a socialist society—economic power was not only in private hands but in the possession of just a few families—it did seem truly tolerant. Sweden's devotion to the anti-Vietnam movement impressed her: "it seems a little forced to view the Swedish power structure, as consciously or in fact, that manipulative." Surveying everything Sweden had done to harbor U.S. deserters, to protest U.S. actions, and even to embarrass U.S. diplomats, she pronounced herself satisfied and praised the government for taking a vanguard role on the international scene. Indeed, the government had come so close to adopting the radical program that she admitted the Swedish New Left no longer had a "unifying cause."

In interviews and articles in the early 1970s, Sontag began to recast her intellectual development in terms of feminism, a movement she had previously ignored. For example, she described *Brother Carl* as about a working woman (Lena) enslaved to a bastard of an ex-lover, and a married woman (Karen) trapped in a boring middle-class marriage. In "The Double Standard of Aging" (1972), Sontag remarked on how long men can hold on to power, and how they can attract much younger women. Age and physical appearance were of little consequence to powerful men. Age was a "movable doom" for women, who kept expecting catastrophe when they reached twenty-one or thirty or forty or fifty. Sontag described a female friend's crisis at twenty-one: "The best part of my life is over. I'm not young any more," she wailed to Sontag. Yet Sontag thought her friend still beautiful, charming, vital, and "striking-looking" even at forty. Women compensated for the double standard of aging by pretending to be younger, lying about their age, using makeup and all the skills of an actress. Women decorated and costumed themselves. They had to be acutely conscious of style.

"The Double Standard of Aging" is a conventional article that breaks no new ground. On the other hand, "The Third World of Women," which appeared in the *Partisan Review* in the spring of 1973, expressed a radical, uncompromising, even strident feminism. Sontag reaffirmed her support for revolutionary socialism but declared that no government purporting to adopt Marxist principles had ever liberated women—which in her lexicon meant not merely establishing equality under the law but enforcing a power-sharing scheme between the sexes. She regarded women as a threatened species, vulnerable to attack on the street in virtually every part of the world. She scorned liberal panaceas. To simply work for equality under the law would always mean that women would lag behind men, for men had proven their unwillingness to part with power. And that was what feminism demanded: men must relinquish some of their power. What ruling class had ever voluntarily reduced its own strength? Sontag asked. True change would require women forcing men to change. The choice for change was just that stark, since the "very structure of society is founded on male privilege."

How would women achieve power? They would have to labor for it. Every woman should work, Sontag insisted: "It must be *expected* that most women will work." Until women had the means to support themselves, they would never be free. "Liberation means *power*," she reiterated.

Work also entailed, however, a psycho-sexual attack on the hegemony of "genital heterosexuality." A "nonrepressive" society, she explained, would be androgynous, for it would steadily subvert the differences between the sexes. This "depolarization" would lead to a redefinition of women's roles, so that they would no longer think of themselves first as "potential sexual partners." Instead, sexuality would be "diffused." Sontag next predicted that in a liberated society, "homosexual choices will be as valid and respectable as heterosexual choices, both will grow out of a genuine bisexuality." She identified the enemy: "machismo."

Sontag enjoined women to take to the streets in protest. No marching men, please. Women should learn karate, whistle at men, attack beauty parlors, organize campaigns against sexist toy companies, and "convert in sizeable numbers to militant lesbianism." They should run their own abortion clinics—Sontag was one of several prominent women who in 1972 signed the *Ms.* "Abortion Law Repeal" petition. Women should sue popular women's magazines, conduct male beauty contests, run feminist candidates for public office, deface demeaning billboards, retain their own names, renounce alimony, and in general raise hell wherever male privilege and female subordination were in evidence. No matter how extreme, how rude, how shrill they were considered, women should persist in a "guerilla theater" that struck at sexist standards. Reform could only ameliorate; radical agitation could fundamentally change the terms that determined women's lives.

Women must realize that the family by its very nature held women back. It incarcerated women in their homes, made them unfit to compete in society, and fostered a "guilt-producing factory, and a school of selfishness." Sontag was even opposed to every home having a washing machine. Even if every family could afford domestic help, it would not liberate women from an acquisitive, consumer society bent on devouring itself and everything else. The family was not a refuge but a prison, kept in line by the homogenized message of television sets that dominated living rooms.

Even as Sontag reiterated her radical views, she was coming to the conclusion that Castro's regime in Cuba had betrayed the revolution. She was one of sixty signatories to a letter (published in *Le Monde* and the *New York Times*) to Castro protesting Cuba's treatment of the poet Heberto Padilla. She appeared on the front page of the *Times*, her photograph placed next to ones of the signatories Jean-Paul Sartre and Alberto Moravia. She abandoned her projected book on the Cuban Revolution and sought another utopia in China, planning a trip that would also culminate in a book—another unfinished project. Like Antonin Artaud, whose writing on the theatre Sontag would later extol in *Under the Sign of Saturn*, she was drawn to "living through a revolutionary moment." Yet that moment kept eluding her as one promising revolutionary society after another proved to be a tyranny. In January 1973 she took a three-week tour of China. It remains a blank so far as her creative work is concerned. She never published a word about it.

A trip to Israel in 1973 for her documentary film *Promised Lands* yielded troubling insights. Just as Sontag had never made much of her feminism before the 1970s, neither had she explored her Jewish roots, yet her treatment of the conflict between Israelis and Palestinians—as reflected in her title—suggested a sense of tragedy that did not square with her radical phase. The politics of

Promised Lands contradicted the rather pro-Arab sentiments of many of her New Left associates. Stanley Kauffmann, the eminent film critic who had panned Sontag's earlier films, admired her presentation of the Israel-Arab conflict as "not a struggle between truth and falsehood but between two opposing, partial truths."

Sontag's documentary film and her essays on photography during the mid-1970s began to reorient her career yet again. She was moving away from radical causes and exploring in great depth individual subjects and writers. She was also carving up aborted novels into short stories. The short form in both nonfiction and fiction proved to be her strength, so that by the late 1970s she burst into print with three remarkable books: *On Photography, Illness as Metaphor,* and *I, etcetera.* Her work seems even more impressive considering that for more than two years—between 1975 and 1977—she was under treatment for breast cancer. Although doctors had given her little hope of surviving the disease, she opted for a radical mastectomy and an aggressive and prolonged period of chemotherapy with experimental drugs.

She made no mention of her own illness in her writing, though she discussed her own case in several interviews. Yet her fiction began to take on an autobiographical tendency. Her stories are often about the narrator's or writer's dilemma: how to be creative, how to find the proper structure for a story, a story that is often an account of the writer's own perceptions. "Project for a Trip to China," for example, reads like a diary of her feelings about her father and mother, and "Baby," she has admitted in interviews, is partly a reminiscence of how she and her husband responded as parents of their son David.

In the French journal *Tel Quel* in the summer of 1978, Sontag offered interviewer Guy Scarpetta her strongest repudiation of radical politics. She rejected Marcuse's thesis of "repressive tolerance." It was time to stop blaming bourgeois society because it was so adept at absorbing dissent. Intellectuals should face it: they were part of the ruling class; they should do the hard work of ameliorating bourgeois society, campaigning for "real issues" like health and justice. The idea of a "revolutionary project" was now passé; you could not change everything; when you tried, you were forced to "oppress." Sontag counseled against cynicism; there was still political work to do. She even wanted to remain a Marxist—whatever that meant. She did not spell it out, though her references to the contradictions of capitalism and its exploitative aspects have never wavered.

The *Tel Quel* interview began a series of recantations that would culminate in Sontag's controversial speech in 1982 at Manhattan's Town Hall, when she blasted the left for not confronting the totalitarian ethos of communism. It is always disconcerting when a forceful voice reverses itself. Composer Ned Rorem, a great Sontag admirer, voiced his own concern in a diary entry:

> Sontag remarks, "I think now, looking back, that I don't really believe all the things I said in the essays I wrote in the 1960s." Where does that leave those whose consciousness was raised by her once novel concepts? Sontag was not, after all, a warm romancer, but a cool cataloguer (catalogueress?) of opinions (many, of course—like those on music—sounding as though she'd come to them yesterday) which she shouldn't belittle, if only for the sake of her own converts. Or will the converts follow her bandwagon, not having learned from the early essays to think for themselves?

Rorem's categorization of Sontag's manner echoes Elizabeth Hardwick's June 1978 recollection in *Vogue* of the sixties young woman who had a "certain airy certainty of self requisite for difficult undertakings."

The cool catalogueress could shift direction with startling swiftness—a virtue for a thinker aiming to ride the latest fashion, as critic Benjamin DeMott thought in his November 1978 *Atlantic Monthly* piece, "To Outrage and Back." He had in mind the Rorem Sontag whose opinions seemed formed "yesterday." But both Rorem and DeMott acknowledged a second Sontag, the scholar. If she had been serious to begin with, how could she abandon positions so readily?

If one takes Sontag at her word—that she is inventing herself moment by moment—her program as quick-change artist is not so bewildering. The project is not what she is writing about; the project is Susan Sontag. Beginning in the mid-1970s, Professor Cary Nelson produced an engaging rationale for Sontag's reversals of position: "Sontag's frank need to distance herself from what she has written and to claim it as her own is not unusual." Her critical prefaces—such as the one to the paperback edition of *Against Interpretation*—revealed an ambivalence about her arguments. Prefaces, Nelson argued, were often the critic's way of taking back or qualifying or arguing with the book he or she had just written. The critic's "argumentative confidence" was never as high as readers supposed. This was why Sontag "assays the same issues again and again under different names. Everything is offered to be restated." One of these recurrent issues was the broad, inquisitive essay of definition—"On Style," "Theatre and Film," "On Photography." In these meditations she was really on an "often unconscious quest for the origins of her own critical consciousness. Each time she scrutinizes a work of art, she is seeking at the same time to know the nature of the critical act." This was why she said in her preface to *Against Interpretation*, "Writing criticism has proved to be an act of intellectual disburdenment as much as of intellectual self-expression." If writing was a means of collecting thought, it was also a way of shucking it off. Thus "virtually every sentence in her work becomes a mirror. Once the essays are examined as self-interrogations, their entire vocabulary turns back on itself." Essay writing, in other words, was "self-realization at a distance."

Nelson's argument accounts for an admirable honesty in Sontag, who does not pretend that she has settled the issues of her discourse. Her method in *On Photography* ensures, for example, that thinking about the subject cannot be foreclosed. But Nelson's approach does not absolve Sontag from a certain skepticism about her methods. For she is neither as consistently self-reflexive nor as rigorously conscious of her definitions as Nelson suggests. She does write flat declarative sentences that are not self-canceling, that do not wind back upon themselves. Essays such as "Theatre and Film" are more catchalls than they are explorations of the critical act itself. Her tone is often reflective, yes, but especially in her overtly political prose she is impassioned, sometimes arrogant, sometimes hysterical, and sometimes lacking in common sense—revealing little grounding in reality. DeMott points this out when he adverts to her comment about the white race being the cancer of history. Her grasp of the everyday, of material reality, is thin, DeMott remarks. Not until she becomes sick, he implies, and becomes a part of other sick people's experience, does she begin to revise her attraction to extravagant metaphors and extremist and violent thinkers such as Artaud. But even before her illness Sontag was capable—at least fitfully—of drawing back from the brink of extremism. Of Simone Weil she writes in *Against Interpretation*: "No one who loves life would wish to imitate her dedication to martyrdom, or would wish it for his children or for anyone else whom he loves."

In the summer of 1979 Sontag spent six weeks in Italy rehearsing Pirandello's play *As You Desire Me*, which she would direct as a modern feminist parable with operatic overtones. The play is about a woman whose identity is fought over by a writer, Carl Salter, and by her family and husband, who claim she is the lost Cia who was abducted and possibly raped and assaulted during the war. A decade after the war she has been returned, her family believes, to her home in Avilla near Udine. What was done to Cia is purposely vague—just as what has driven Carl to stop talking in *Brother Carl* is never divulged.

Cia is called "The Strange Lady," for she refuses to explain her past. She is both herself and a "fiction" the other characters make up, so to speak. She refers to herself in both the first and third persons—as Diddy, the main character in *Death Kit*, does. "We do not all see with the same eyes!" Cia exclaims. "Being? Being is nothing! Being is becoming!" she continues, attempting to keep open all her options and resisting the identity others would impose on her. Sontag wanted to emphasize the excessive, the emotional, the world of desires that had cut a woman loose from her home—or from a sense of home as the ground of her reality. To her, it was a play about "desperation, about the desperation of a particular woman." Pirandello happened to write the perfect Sontag ending, since Cia chooses to return to Berlin with Salter, the writer, and to create a life for herself as a dancer—a life, in other words, in which she is free to reinvent herself. She becomes like Sontag and like Sontag's characters in *I, etcetera* who cut themselves off from their homes, families, and communities in a quest for self-fulfillment.

In October 1981, in Toronto, at a conference on "The Writer and Human Rights," Susan Sontag told an audience, "There is not a day of my life when I don't think" about persecuted writers. She pointed out that "there is some reluctance to draw attention to the condition of writers and of people of conscience who are imprisoned in communist countries, particularly in Cuba." She contended that America's imperialism had so soured the left and human rights activists, and Cuba seemed so isolated and besieged, that the perfidies of its regime had been ignored. She thought it scandalous that a writer as great as Garcia Marquez should serve Castro's cause. Guilty of this double standard herself, she admitted, it was imperative that she speak out on behalf of all prisoners of conscience regardless of the ideology of their governments. She would appear in *Improper Conduct*, released in 1984, a documentary that not only excoriated Cuba for human rights abuses (particularly against homosexuals) but debunked the romantic aura of Castro as revolutionary leader.

A month after Sontag's Toronto talk, on November 13, 1981, Poland's Communist dictator, General Wojciech Jaruzelski, declared martial law and shut down the communications system so that his major opposition, Solidarity, found it virtually impossible to function. Of course there were imprisonments and other forms of repression, but what seemed so striking was the sudden silencing of Polish dissenters who had caught the world's attention with their demands for freedom. The very idea of Solidarity—a union of the working class and intellectuals, the city and the country, the Catholic Church and political activists, with more than ten million people protesting their lack of liberty—was an extraordinary phenomenon that exploded the conventional realities of cold war politics.

Sontag could no longer support any governmental form of communism, and she became increasingly dismayed as her friends on the left continued to engage in a long history of condoning Communist oppression, attempting to sustain the illusion that some kind of reformed Communist government would eventually fulfill their hopes of a more democratic future. In February 1982 in New York she addressed an audience of the left, brought together to protest the suppression of Solidarity but also to denounce the Reagan administration for its hypocrisy in condemning repression in Poland while engaging in union-busting in the United States (President Reagan had just fired the striking air controllers, effectively destroying their union).

Sontag's highly public denunciation of the left caused a storm of controversy, especially because of her provocative statement that "Communism was fascism with a human face." This paradoxical formulation confused commentators. If communism and fascism both resulted in tyranny, how could communism have a human face? But the phrase reflected Sontag's lingering desire to pay respect to those, like herself, who had once believed that communism was the hope of the future, and then believed that if it was not exactly the hope, it could at least be reformed.

Criticism of Sontag was so fierce that she gradually backed away from any involvement in political movements, fearing she had alienated her friends on the left and exposed herself to the charge that she was adopting a conservative position—perhaps because she claimed that readers of the conservative *Reader's Digest* had been better informed about communism than readers of the leftist *Nation*. Her criticism of herself and the left was couched in devastating terms: "We were so sure who our enemies were (among them, the professional anti-Communists), so sure who were the virtuous and who the benighted. . . . We thought we loved justice; many of us did. But we did not love the truth enough." Commenting in the *New York Times Book Review* on her Town Hall Speech several months later, Sontag told Charles Ruas:

> I said something I wasn't supposed to say, and I knew what I was doing. . . . The idea of it is you were supposed to be a good guy and be mobilized for the pro-Poland rally on Feb. 6 and the anti-nuclear rally on June 12. I didn't want to do that anymore. That was deeply resented, and that was the first wave of reaction on the part of the so-called left.

Sontag conceded that what she said was "obvious, but it's never too late to say the truth, and it's important to have people argue the truth."

Sontag's growing interest in writing about dance, first signaled in 1981 in "Dance and Dance Writing," was put to startling use in 1984 with the airing of "A Primer for Pina: Susan Sontag on Pina Bausch: A Television Essay" on Channel Four in Great Britain, and in New York two years later on Channel 13 and at the Museum of Broadcasting. Sontag had been an unremitting critic of television. To Roger Copeland in 1981 she had spoken of her "visceral dislike" of the medium. It had destroyed attention spans and corrupted human consciousness, so that even graduate students seemed less capable of digesting, let alone liking, the complexities of literature. Television had shrunk the world into a "tiny focus," and the pervasiveness of commercials fragmented everything presented. "I know this sounds terribly cranky and eccentric. . . . But I really think it's the death of western civilization."

So what provoked Sontag to both script for and appear on Channel Four? A nonprofit company that operates as a subsidiary of the Independent Broadcasting Authority (a rough equivalent of the Federal Communications Commission), it had earned plaudits for "Extending the Medium"—the title New York's Museum of

Broadcasting (now the Museum of Television and Radio) used to showcase Channel Four's programs. For a writer interested in form, this might be the one place to test television's resources. In 1984–1985 alone, Channel Four had commissioned three hundred independent companies to produce programs. This is a scale of production that American public television has never come close to matching. Channel Four's commissioning editors worked in tandem with authors in something like the supportive setting Sontag had experienced at Farrar, Straus. Editor Michael Kustow, for example, had come from Britain's National Theatre and from Robert Brustein's American Repertory Theatre at Harvard, where Sontag would direct a play the following year. Kustow had produced programs with John Cage, Philip Glass, and other artists whom Sontag respected.

Like all her work, Sontag's television essay was shaped entirely by her sensibility—free of editorial interference. In retrospect, her choice of dance seems inevitable. In "Dancer and Dance," a 1987 essay, she posited: "There is a mystery of incarnation in dance that has no analogue in the other performing arts." In other words, one had to see the dancer and the dance. Although she conceded that in the history of dance there had been a shift from the nineteenth century's almost exclusive focus on the dancer to the twentieth century's prizing of the choreographer, one still could not separate the dancer from the dance, as one could separate, say, the actors who played Hamlet from *Hamlet*. Every movement in dance was judged (by the dancer) against a standard of perfection that was not quite the same in the other arts. Hence "one cannot be just the best performer of certain roles but the most complete exhibit of what it is to be a dancer." Even the greatest dancers whom she had befriended—such as Baryshnikov—seemed incapable of believing they had executed perfection. Whereas actors relished compliments, dancers often rejected them, bemoaning their inability to perfect this step, that jump. Of course there were perfectionists in all the arts, but dancers performed in much physical discomfort and even pain, employing their bodies to somehow transcend the physical—like the great Baryshnikov jumping higher and landing lower than any dancer before him. The dancer's involvement with the dance seemed to Sontag a "higher order of attention where physical and mental attention become the same." She repeated the great dance historian's description of dance, which her friend, the dancer Merce Cunningham, had ratified: "a spiritual activity in physical form." In other words, dancers were the perfect platonists, fixated on the idea, making themselves into exemplums. (Reviewer Marvin Murdrick made fun of how many times Sontag employed the word "exemplary" in *A Susan Sontag Reader*, but art for her is precisely this: a self-contained model, a utopia of consciousness.)

Dance spoke to an all-encompassing conception of art that Sontag could not find within the bounds of literature, as precious as writing was to her. Dancers were serving an infinitely demanding master: "the god Dance." That formulation exactly expressed Sontag's own quest for masters, for the god of art, for that transformation of environment into pure aesthetic pleasure which she had first found in Poe's evocation of a realm beyond words and beyond the physical envelopes of his characters and the redundancy of his plots.

In Part One, Sontag sets up her television essay in the manner of *Under the Sign of Saturn*, immediately linking her own sensibility to her subject's—in this case, explaining to viewers how three years earlier she had become interested in Bausch at the recommendation of a friend who had encouraged a reluctant Sontag to attend a theatre festival in Cologne. There she realized that the German-born Bausch, a dancer, choreographer, and director, was a "major artist in the performing arts" in a decade that marked a great moment for the performing arts.

Sontag then describes the location of Bausch's dance theatre in Wuppertol, a small town in north Germany, and her twenty-six-member company who had come from fifteen countries. Like director Peter Brook, Sontag observes, Bausch is attuned to the "internationalist modernist traditions." Very much a creative group, "there are no stars," Sontag notes, although Bausch "is the creator."

Sontag quickly gives Bausch's background, her training as a classical dancer, her resumé of principal works. Sontag says she has befriended several of Bausch's dancers, drawn not only to their talent but to their way of incorporating their own personalities into their work. They improvise around certain emotions, but once they set their material, it remains highly structured. As part of the autobiographical thrust, dances such as *1980* are set in "real time," with a dancer making fifty to seventy revolutions around the stage, feeling the exhaustion he or she is supposed to be acting. Sontag points out that 1980 was Bausch's year of depletion, when she lost the "person who is most important to her, a man who was an important collaborator in her work." The dance then performs her grief.

Dance also seems to communicate to Sontag on an elemental level that she has never been able to express in her own art and criticism, for she is drawn to Bausch's choreography of childhood, of adults who play childish games and reveal their fears and other "naked states of emotion." (The closest Sontag has come to this kind of art and to Bausch's collage technique is "Project for a Trip to China.")

Sontag cherishes Bausch's longer dances, linking them to the Wagnerian tradition of lengthening the work of art to four and five hours and more, capturing again the sense of "real time," as director Rainer Werner Fassbinder did in his fifteen-hour adaptation of Alfred Doblin's novel *Berlin Alexanderplatz*. Bausch aims at a "total theatrical experience that would synthesize many different elements." Like the balletomane or opera buff, Sontag seeks an overwhelming experience that is beyond words, music, or dance but partakes of them all—as did her childhood reading of Poe, in which music, movement, and words all point toward an all-encompassing realm that envelops his grief-stricken souls.

Sontag uses Bausch to point to tensions in the modernist tradition between the striving for impersonality (as in T. S. Eliot's

"Tradition and the Individual Talent") or for emotion in a "transpersonal form" (she cites the work of theatre directors Robert Wilson and Peter Brook as well as dancer Lucinda Childs) and the expression of emotion as the focus of art. Bausch's work is about "hidden, shameful emotions," Sontag observes, and about the relationship between the sexes, courting rituals, and romance. No other contemporary dramatic work, Sontag insists, is so centrally and painfully about the "couple relation."

In Part Two, Sontag begins: "It's interesting to speculate that this is work done by a woman." It is women, Sontag notes, who "took women off point" and depolarized sexual roles. Although Sontag says she loves the dance tradition, in which the polarization of sexual roles is central—she is "happy to see another movement vocabulary." She singles out Twyla Tharp and Lucinda Childs for promulgating a unisexual style of movement, so that their male and female dancers do not enact sexually specific roles. Bausch, on the other hand, clearly marks her work off as done by a woman, Sontag believes. Men appear in groups, women appear in groups, and they must reach across a painful sexual barrier. Rather than overcoming the rigid distinctions of the classical tradition, Bausch dwells on them, emphasizing both the "possibilities of tenderness and the possibilities of frustration."

One feature of Bausch's choreography that fascinates Sontag is her use of repetition, the same movements and gestures reiterated as in a musical structure against a pattern of alternation, so that the work is decentered, with a sense, again, of "real life," of simultaneity, of action that is too much to take in in one performance but that must be seen again and again.

The real time of Bausch's dances is paralleled by a sense of real places, so that in *Sacre du Printemps* the dancers move on a surface of "real damp, brown earth"; in *Bluebeard* the stage is covered with leaves; in *1980* the audience can smell the real grass.

Sontag also considers Bausch within the German tradition, relating her work to Max Reinhardt's in pantomime and tableaux—the words Bausch employs to describe her art. Her work marks a return to the expressionist tradition—the portrayal of extreme emotions in a "convulsive style"—cut off by Hitler's regime, Sontag concludes.

As reviewer Alan Kreigman observed in the *Washington Post*, Sontag's television essay was no "ordinary 'talking heads' documentary." He credited director/producer Jolyon Wimhurst for structuring the piece, "using a Godardian, collage technique that itself helps prepare the viewer for Bausch's multilayered stagecraft and choreography—the form of the video is one with its message"—a judgment that had to please Sontag, since Godard is one of her exemplary artists. Calling Sontag a "polymath and critic" and an "ideal guide to Bausch," Kreigman marveled at how Sontag's "iridescent mind leaps across centuries, styles and personalities, making insightful connections all the way." In the *New York Times*, Jennifer Dunning suggested that "Ms. Sontag's soothing voice and distanced manner will doubtless calm the anxieties of die-hard abstractionists in the audience," but Dunning judged that the program "seems more act of devotion than esthetically revealing observation." Perhaps, but Sontag had stretched the medium, and it is a great loss to American television that she has not had the opportunity to write for it. Her sixty-minute essay is a miracle of compression and insight, belying Sontag's fears about the television eye's "tiny focus." Like her work in *Under the Sign of Saturn*, "A Primer for Pina" carries, in Sontag's words to Amy Lippman, "a lighter cargo of ideas." It is a portrait, not a densely reasoned essay.

In early 1985 Sontag directed a play, *Jacques and His Master*, an adaptation by Czech writer Milan Kundera of *Jacques le Fataliste*, a Diderot novel. She had been invited to work at Harvard's American Repertory Theatre by its director, Robert Brustein. Kundera is perhaps best known for *The Unbearable Lightness of Being*, a work that conflates the essay and the novel in a manner somewhat reminiscent of *The Volcano Lover*.

In the printed introduction to the play, Kundera explains that Jacques and his master are on a journey which is trisected by the love stories of Jacques, of his master, and of Madame de La Pommeraye. Each story, Kundera points out, is a variation on the other, just as his play is a variation on Diderot. The stories interrupt each other, repeat each other, and complete each other—very much like a Pina Bausch dance about the "couple relation." *Jacques and His Master* might be considered Act II in Sontag's career as a director, with her work on *As You Desire Me* representing Act I, and her subsequent work on Samuel Beckett's *Waiting for Godot* the culminating Act III. In retrospect it is possible to see that she needed this grounding in dramaturgy to write her own experimental play, *Alice in Bed*. She would also pursue the theme of "couple relations" in her most successful novel, *The Volcano Lover.*

Like the characters in *As You Desire Me*, the characters in *Jacques and His Master* are unsure of their destination and include the audience in their uncertainty:

> Enter Jacques and his Master. *After they have taken a few steps,* Jacques *gazes at the audience. He stops short.*
> JACQUES (*discreetly*): Sir . . . (*pointing out the audience to him*) why are they staring at us?
> MASTER (*a bit taken aback and adjusting his clothes as if afraid of calling attention to himself by a sartorial oversight*): Pretend there's no one there.
> JACQUES (*to the audience*): Wouldn't you rather look somewhere else? All right then, what do you want to know? Where we've come from? (*He stretches his right arm out behind him.*) Back there. Where we're going? (*Philosophically.*) Which of us knows where we're going? (*To the audience.*) Do you know where you're going?
> MASTER: I'm afraid, Jacques, that *I* know where we're going.
> JACQUES: Afraid?
> MASTER (*sadly*): Yes. But I have no intention of acquainting you with my painful obligations. . . .
> JACQUES: None of us knows where we're going, sir, believe me.

What is real, what is an illusion? the play asks. And who really is the master? The same questions bedevil the characters in Sontag's film *Duet for Cannibals*, in which the power figure, Bauer, seems to submit to his disciples and yet, paradoxically, puts them under his spell.

Reviews of Sontag's production were mixed. Frank Rich in the *New York Times* appreciated the "Pirandellian" devices, but he found that "Miss Sontag's staging lacks the requisite velocity and fizz." On the other hand, Jack Kroll in *Newsweek* reported that "Susan Sontag and her actors have caught this mood of defiant melancholy and rueful comedy."

Gerald Rabkin provided the most thoughtful commentary on the play and its director in the *Performing Arts Journal*, suggesting that it remained caught somewhere between a provocative literary exercise and a not entirely successful theatrical experience. Rabkin's article, "Milan and His Master," consisted of a dialogue between a literary critic (LC) and a theatre critic (TC), the latter imploring the former: "Slow down. Less theory, more description, please." LC astutely notes that the play is about exile, for whom (LC quotes the play) "forward is anywhere." This is why the stage is stark, bare. Echoing Frank Rich, TC notes the production lacks "the forward surge of a strong theatrical reading." Sontag's problem is compounded, TC adds, because Kundera does not provide her with enough opportunities to break the conventional theatrical frame. His style is still neoclassical for all his aping of Beckett. The play's faults seem less obvious on the page, which is perhaps why LC remains resistant to TC's criticism. (Breaking the conventional theatrical frame will become a strong feature of *Alice in Bed*.)

Except for *AIDS and Its Metaphors* (1989), Sontag published little new work after *Under the Sign of Saturn* (1982). She devoted much of her time in the 1980s to the cause of human rights. From 1987 to 1989 she was president of the American PEN Center, a branch of the international writers' organization founded in 1922 to foster international solidarity among poets, playwrights, essayists, editors, and novelists. She received worldwide press for her defense of Salman Rushdie, whose novel *The Satanic Verses* had been declared blasphemous by Iran's Ayatollah Khomeini. She campaigned not only for the lifting of the *fatwa*, the sentence of death, on Rushdie but for a recognition that the threat to him was a threat to civilization itself. Sontag emphasized that Rushdie stood for pluralism and tolerance—the values that were also under attack in the 1990s in Bosnia.

In the early spring of 1993 David Rieff, Sontag's son, urged her to visit Sarajevo when it was under siege. He was writing a book about the war in Bosnia, and he assured her that the people of the city would be heartened by her visit. Deeply moved by Sarajevans who wished to maintain their secular and pluralistic way of life, Sontag made visit after visit into the war zone.

In a piece in the *New York Review of Books* entitled "Godot Comes to Sarajevo," Sontag explained her decision to stage Samuel Beckett's *Waiting for Godot* as an act of solidarity, a "small contribution" to a city that refused to capitulate to "Serb fascism." During a conversation in April 1993 with Harris Pasovic, a young Sarajevo-born theatre director, she asked if he would welcome her coming again to the city to direct a play. "Of course," he replied. "What play will you do?" Sontag impulsively answered, *Waiting for Godot*, perhaps thinking of the opening line from the play that prefaced her *New York Review of Books* article: "Nothing to be done." The play seemed perfect for Sarajevo because the characters persisted even in the face of their despair, just as Sarajevans waited and waited for deliverance—for their Godot, for the West, for the Americans, to bomb the Serbs back to Belgrade. The minimal stage setting reflected exactly the state of a city stripped bare by a siege. Sontag believed, moreover, that "there are more than a few people who feel strengthened and consoled by having their sense of reality affirmed and transfigured by art." David Toole, in *Waiting for Godot in Sarajevo: Theological Reflections on Nihilism, Tragedy, and Apocalypse*, comments that staging the play became a form of facing suffering with dignity.

Critic Thomas Akstens points out that in *Against Interpretation*, Sontag characterizes Beckett's and Genet's plays as "a nightmare of repetition, stalled actions, exhausted feeling." The phrase

closely matches what she observed in Sarajevo: the seemingly futile yet unstoppable agony of Bosnian suffering and the will to resist—or at least to keep going.

Sontag opted for a "gender-blind" production, picking a ro-
bust older actress to play Pozzo (normally the play's dominating
male), and then cast three sets of actors simultaneously to play
Vladimir and Estragon, "three variations on the theme of the couple"—a theme, she might have added, that pervades her other
works as director in the theatre and in film. To cinch the tie between this allegorical play and Sarajevo, these parallel couples
were composed of actors from Muslim, Serb, and Croatian families. To tether the couples to her internationalist and universalist
ethic, Sontag made one relationship a "buddy pair," another a
mother/daughter duo, and another a contentious husband/wife
partnership. Situated in clearly demarcated upstage and down-
stage areas, the couples implicitly commented on each other and
sometimes functioned as "something of a Greek Chorus," Sontag
explained.

As David Toole observed, by expanding the cast and making it
so representative, she had made the play a "collective enterprise."
Vladimir and Estragon no longer seemed so isolated. The people
of Sarajevo could see themselves represented on stage, the "lives of
the individuals in the theater attained an aesthetic justification that
the world itself did not."

The verdict among reviewers and the world press was mixed,
some observers chiding Sontag for grandstanding and manipulat-
ing the text of Beckett's play. Others praised her for her courage
and artistic boldness. Foreign correspondents, however, testified
to the moving rapport Sontag was able to establish with her audience, even though some Sarajevans remained suspicious of her
motivations.

Sontag produced three important works in the 1990s: a play, *Alice
in Bed* (written 1991, published 1993), and two novels, *The Volcano
Lover* (1992) and *In America* (2000). All three feature female pro-

tagonists and other strong female characters. All three are historical and depend on the documented past, though Sontag refused to call her reading in her sources "research," preferring instead to think of the past as a launching pad for her explorations of human character.

Like *As You Desire Me, Alice in Bed* is about a woman tormented by and yet escaping male perceptions. The play reflects an anger at men that Sontag had rarely expressed so openly. "You are like all men, libertines and murderers, all, all!" said Sontag, speaking as Dona Ana in scenes from George Bernard Shaw's *Don Juan in Hell*, directed by Norman Mailer in a benefit for the Actor's Studio in February 1993 and reviewed in the *New York Times*.

References to Virginia Woolf proliferate in Sontag's later interviews, and it is not surprising to learn from her author's note to *Alice in Bed* that she had in mind Woolf's provocative book *A Room of One's Own*. In the book Woolf speculates that if Shakespeare had had a sister she would not have had the "inner authority" (Sontag's words) to write, for (Sontag continues) the "obligation to be physically attractive and patient and nurturing and docile and sensitive and deferential to fathers (to brothers, to husbands) contradicts and *must* collide with the egocentricity and aggressiveness and the indifference to self that a large creative gift requires in order to flourish." All the "ands" convey the impossible demands of the woman's role, which she expatiates on in her introductory essay to Annie Leibovitz's book *Women*.

Alice in Bed is about Alice James, the brilliant sister of William and Henry, diagnosed with breast cancer at forty-two (the same age as Sontag when she received *her* probable death sentence). Alice died at forty-three, and in the play she is presented as living in a room of her own. In Sontag's view Alice is also the "Victorian girl-child" who suppresses her aggressiveness, or who is allowed an active role only in fantasies such as *Alice in Wonderland*, the other key text for Sontag because it speaks to the world of imagination that saved her from a dull and demeaning childhood. *Alice in Bed* becomes a kind of mad tea party, Sontag explains, and a work she has been "preparing to write" all her life. . . . A play, then, about the grief and anger of women; and, finally, a play about the imagination."

Alice in Bed invents dialogue for Alice James, treating her invalidism not only as a feminist issue but as one of the central problems of humanity. What are we supposed to do when we get out of bed? Take the world by storm, as the nineteenth-century feminist Margaret Fuller did? She is one of the characters in the play who give Alice advice. Or do we stay at home, creating a world just as adventurous through the medium of language, as another of Alice's advisees, the nineteenth-century poet Emily Dickinson, did?

In her play, Sontag seems to ponder everything: what it means to be a woman in the distinguished James family; the nature of language ("tenses are strangely potent aren't they"); the patterns of history; class structure (Alice has a talk with a Cockney burglar); and the paradox of Alice herself, who does not get out of bed and yet says, "My mind makes me feel strong."

Productions of the play in Germany, at Harvard's American Repertory Theatre, and in New York received mixed reviews. Critics were divided by the play's overt feminism; some found it pretentious and others provocative. No production as yet has overcome the judgment that the essayist predominates over the dramatist.

The dramatic monologues that conclude *The Volcano Lover* are all by women who comment on a world shaped by men, a world that Sontag finds attractive in the figure of Sir William Hamilton, the connoisseur, and repellent in the figure of Lord Nelson, the hero of the reactionary forces that crush the revolutionaries in eighteenth-century Naples.

Viewed in the context of *Alice in Bed* and *The Volcano Lover,* Sontag's essay in *Women* is another dramatic monologue, a disguised autobiography since Sontag does not speak of her own experience as a woman. She notes the "tremendous changes in women's consciousness" and the "arrival of women's *ambitions*," a word she emphasizes because she believes that traditionally the ambitious woman has been conceived as an aberration. It is difficult not to imagine Sontag thinking of herself in such sentences: "It's still common to begrudge a woman who has both beauty and intellectual brilliance—one would never say there was something odd or intimidating or 'unfair' about a man who was so fortunate—as if beauty, the ultimate enabler of feminine charm, should by rights have barred other kinds of excellence."

Certainly one of the inspirations of *In America* is to explore the life of a beautiful and intelligent woman who is allowed to earn her fame because she is an actress and only acting the part, so to speak, of an ambitious woman. As Sontag notes in *Women*, America has been regarded "since the nineteenth century by foreign travelers as a paradise for uppity women."

The reception of *In America* was clouded by charges of plagiarism. In the *New York Times*, Doreen Carvajal reported that Sontag had taken at least a dozen passages verbatim from several works of history and journalism about Helena Modjeska, the Polish actress on whom she based her main character in *In America*. Moreover, other than acknowledging that her novel was based on real people, Sontag did not specify her sources. She responded that in a work of art it was not necessary to provide footnotes or acknowledgments: "All of us who deal with real characters in history transcribe and adopt original sources in the original domain," Sontag emphasized. "I've used these sources and I've completely transformed them. I have these books. I've looked at these books. There's a larger argument to be made that all of literature is a series of references and allusions." Sontag also made a distinction between writers and sources, the latter being simply fodder for the writer (artist) to use as she or he likes. But Carvajal reported that many novelists were concerned by Sontag's contention that she could simply appropriate the words of others without attribution. Russell Banks, author of a novel about John Brown, commented: "The contract with the reader is that I'm telling a story. I'm not writing a history, so I will tell you things that may not have happened. But the assumption is that the language is mine, and if I have taken language from elsewhere, I feel obligated to make that evident." As others whom Carvajal interviewed put it, the distinction was between information and language. The writer could use the information but not the language without giving credit to its source. Certainly there is a long tradition in the historical novel of acknowledging sources. From Sir Walter Scott to Joyce Carol Oates (her novel *Blonde* specifies her research on the life of Marilyn Monroe), authors of historical fiction have acknowledged their sources. A nettled Sontag expressed disappointment at the criticism of her resurrection of an obscure historical figure: "I actually thought they would be quite thrilled. Modjeska was quite forgotten. She was a great figure. I made her into a marvelous person. The real Modjeska was a horrible racist."

Inadvertently Sontag identified the major weakness of her novel: she had not come to grips with the full complexity of the past. She had idealized her heroine, making her less interesting and less complicated in an effort to make her more admirable. "Ms. Sontag certainly tries to make her heroine marvelous by propping her up with period dialogue, letters, journals and aphoristic musings," observed Margo Jefferson in the *New York Times*. "But I would much rather read about a woman of great talent and charisma—a marvelous creature indeed—who was also a woman with monstrous beliefs. I want to feel and understand all of this. I don't want things to be prettified and simplified in the name of literary uplift."

Asked to draw her self-portrait for *Who's Writing This?*, Daniel Halpern's collection of autobiographical essays by prominent authors, Sontag sketched a female head perusing a book—or rather just part of a head, because the large book blocks a view of the lower half of the face. It is the perfect self-portrait because it describes a life given over to books, a life half hidden behind books. Sontag has said that she enjoys the physical act of holding a book and that she needs the satisfaction of owning her own volumes. Library books have never appealed to her. It is the pleasure of possession that she craves. As a child she brought the world to herself in the form of books, and in the form of books she will take charge of the world, refashioning it in her image. Yet such a romantic image disturbs her, and she is quick to call herself "literature's servant." For she has tried to write as an apostle of the great books she has most admired.

In *Who's Writing This?* Sontag conceives of literary tradition as a series of arguments with itself, just as she conceives of herself as shaped by disputation:

> I say *this* when you are saying *that* not just because writers are professional adversaries, not jut to redress the inevitable imbalance or one-sidedness of any activity that has the character of an institution (and writing is an institution); but because the practice—I also mean the nature—of literature is rooted in inherently contradictory aspirations. A truth about literature is one whose opposite is also true.

Or as she says even more recently in *Women*: "We want now to know that for every *this* there is a *that*. We want to have a plurality of models."

TWO

The Benefactor

(1963)

SYNOPSIS

In certain respects, "Dreams of Hippolyte" is a more satisfying title for Sontag's first novel. For it is a book of dreams, a reverie reminiscent of Poe. In the first chapter, Hippolyte, the narrator, declares in French, "I Dream Therefore I Am." He takes a retrospective tone, contrasting the difference between "those days" and "now." He has written an article that excites comment in the literary world and gains him an invitation to the salon of Frau Anders. In retrospect, it is difficult not to see in Hippolyte the emerging figure of Susan Sontag, about to attain fame for an essay, "Notes on 'Camp,'" even as she enters the literary circle centered on *Partisan Review*. But in the novel autobiography becomes allegory, and New York City is displaced by a foreign capital similar to Paris but not named as such. True to her aesthetic, Sontag does not wish to make her novel a report on reality but rather a counterweight to it.

In the second chapter, Hippolyte relates his dream of two rooms that imprison him. He is ordered about by a sadist in a black wool bathing suit. The sadist limps and carries a flute. Hippolyte tells his dream to Jean-Jacques, a writer, homosexual prostitute, and former boxer, who tells him to live his dream and go beyond it. But to Hippolyte, the dream is an end in itself, or rather, it is a prelude to more dreams. In other words, rather than attempting to connect his dreams (imagination) to the outer world, he prefers to invert Jean-Jacques's advice—Hippolyte moves away from the world and further into his dreams.

In Chapters Three and Four, sexually charged versions of the "two rooms dream" lead Hippolyte to begin a new project: the seduction of Frau Anders. More dreams with pornographic and religious connotations prompt Hippolyte to discuss them with Father Trissotin, who considers whether they are inspired by the devil. Like Sontag, the essayist who resists critiquing art in moral terms, Hippolyte steadfastly refuses to reduce his dreams to psychological or moral terms. Rather, he desires to expand the experience of his dreams by seducing Frau Anders. The sex in his dreams is just that—sex—which Sontag later calls (in "The Pornographic Imagination") a form of pure pleasure that should be immune to moralistic debates and assessments. Just as literature should be appreciated in its own terms, so Hippolyte's dreams are not to be reduced to an interpretation of their contents. Hippolyte insists that his dreams are a dialogue with himself. He declares he wants to "rid my dreams of me"—implying, apparently, a desire to dissolve himself into his creation, just as Sontag would later argue in her essays that the work is the writer, that no writer is separable from the work. To expunge himself, then, is to attain a "silence," a kind of state of perfect equilibrium, apart from words, that Sontag will later name, in an important essay, "The Aesthetics of Silence."

Debating his quest for silence with Jean-Jacques in Chapter Five, Hippolyte announces that he hopes to fashion dreams like silent movies. Although Jean-Jacques has been a kind of model for Hippolyte, the men split on the subject of silence, since Jean-Jacques is very much a man of the world and a believer in theatricality and role playing. He is a participant, Hippolyte is an observer. Hippolyte treasures the sheer sensuousness of images in silent film; Jean-Jacques is a man of the word.

In Chapters Six and Seven, the logic of Hippolyte's dreams drives him to kidnap Frau Anders, to drug her, to share his dreams with her, and then to sell her to an Arab barman in an Arab city. Returning to the capital in Chapter Seven, he has dreams of an old man who becomes his patron, who makes him dig a hole and throw a cat in it. Like other similar dreams, Hippolyte abases himself to an authority who degrades him. Although he awakes cursing the "captivity of his dreams," a conversation with Professor Bulgaraux convinces him that the dreams are a form of psychic cleansing. Rather than feeling ashamed or humiliated, he appears liberated—evidently because he has divested himself of his worldly personality and submitted himself to the power of his dreams.

To submit to the dream is to relinquish the craving for interpretation, Hippolyte implies in Chapter Eight. He recounts his last role as an actor. Playing the part of a father confessor to a child-murderer, Hippolyte argues with the director who wants to explain the psychology of the criminal. Hippolyte objects to the director's belief that the criminal is passionate. Just the opposite is true, Hippolyte argues: the murderer is supremely indifferent to his crime. Psychology is only a form of exoneration, Hippolyte implies.

When Frau Anders's daughter, Lucrezia, receives a ransom note, Hippolyte agrees to pay the sum for Frau Anders's return. He discusses with Lucrezia, his lover, his theory that dreams are perpetually present—unlike real events which vanish after they occur and are, in a sense, revocable.

In Chapter Nine, Herr Anders, anticipating his wife's return, seeks Hippolyte's help in obtaining a divorce, since he wishes to remarry. Hippolyte's friend, Monique, delivers a letter from Frau Anders, who then appears. She has been maimed by the Arab and demands that Hippolyte tell her what to do. Hippolyte dreams of a piano lesson in which he crawls into a piano played by a Mother Superior in the garden of an ice palace. Inside the piano he meets "a young man with a tiny mustache" and advises him to crawl into a hole in the floor while students attack the piano. Hippolyte then shoots the Mother Superior and everyone in the room. Then he is pulled out of a tree by the man in the black bathing suit. Noticing that the Mother Superior resembles Frau Anders, Hippolyte sets fire to her apartment.

Suspecting that he has murdered Frau Anders, Hippolyte visits Monique in Chapter Ten. She is jealous about his relationship with Frau Anders. He tells her that he is guilty of "real murder." With Jean-Jacques he explores the concept of individualism, which can be creative or destructive. Hippolyte then leaves the capital to visit his sick father, with whom he discusses marriage and murder. When he returns to the capital, Monique has married, and Frau Anders tells him: "My dear, you're no better as a murderer than as a white-slaver." When he inherits his father's estate, Hippolyte decides to surprise Frau Anders by refurbishing a town house for her, thus becoming her benefactor.

In Chapter Eleven, Hippolyte takes Frau Anders on a tour of the house and is relieved and delighted to see that she accepts his gift. When he obeys her command to make love to her, he discovers, as in a dream, that in his "erotic fury" he has healed her. The "dream of the mirror" follows in Chapter Twelve. Hippolyte is standing in a ballroom trying to remember a name. When he strips naked and encounters a footman, he announces that he is a "potential amputee" and rips off his own left leg. He then struggles into an operating theatre where he is among volunteers waiting to have their eyes put out with knitting needles. He proposes to donate his body and worldly goods to the man in the black bathing suit if his leg and his sight are restored to him. When he is told to run, he finds himself in the street watching his own house burn. Rescuing his journal, a book of ancient history, and a tray with cups, he confronts his father. What will Hippolyte call his wife? his father asks. This long sequence of dreams involving dismemberment, destruction, and reunification, and the fact that Hippolyte seems to be waking up to see his dream in the mirror, suggests that perhaps the world of waking and dreaming are coming together. He goes back to his country home, marries an officer's daughter, and returns to the capital.

In Chapter Thirteen, Hippolyte seems content with his happy

wife, even though Jean-Jacques suggests that Hippolyte expresses his guilt by being a benefactor to Frau Anders. Hippolyte tells his wife the story of a nearly blind princess who marries a talking bear that decides not to talk. They live happily ever after, perhaps because she cannot see whom she has married. Hippolyte's wife makes friends with a Jewess who is being pursued by the authorities. The Jewess turns out to be Frau Anders. Meanwhile Hippolyte thinks about how self-love so perfectly contains the lover.

Hippolyte discovers in Chapter Fourteen that his wife is dying of leukemia. He attends her and they play with tarot cards. Jean-Jacques appears, masquerading as an officer who dies in a fight with Hippolyte, who then delivers (with the assistance of a delivery boy) an unconscious Jean-Jacques to his flat. Hippolyte's wife dies after three days in a coma. Professor Bulgaraux performs a private service, delivering a sermon entitled "On the Death of a Virgin Soul." Like the criminal, the virgin discovers innocence in the act of defiance, Bulgaraux declares. A tense Hippolyte feels the need of another dream.

Although increasingly estranged from Jean-Jacques, Hippolyte renews their friendship in Chapter Fifteen after learning that Jean-Jacques has been accused of collaboration (the novel is vaguely set during the years of the Spanish Civil War and World War II). The two men argue, with Jean-Jacques accusing Hippolyte of being a "character without a story." Hippolyte dreams again, and this time he is dismembered several times by three acrobats. He then retires to his town house to live with Frau Anders.

In Chapter Sixteen, Hippolyte reaches the end of his story and suddenly doubts its veracity. What has he been dreaming? What has been "real"? Have the two rooms of his dreams been an expression of his two modes of existence? Apparently evicted from his house, Hippolyte considers that perhaps he has been confined to a mental institution. Has his story been only the outline of a novel he finds in his notebooks? How can he separate his waking from his dreaming?

SONTAG READING SONTAG

The Benefactor, as Sontag admitted in 1974 to interviewer Joe David Bellamy, contains "systematically obscure elements . . . because I want to leave several possible readings open." On the one hand, the novel is the "dreams of Hippolyte," and like all dreams his contain unresolvable elements and events that cannot be reduced to a definitive interpretation. Sontag seems to have set out to construct a novel that defies or is "against interpretation." Even Hippolyte cannot say for sure what his dreams mean and how much he has dreamed. As Sontag told Jonathan Cott in 1979, Hippolyte is a "kind of Candide who, instead of looking for the best of all possible worlds, searches for some clear state of consciousness, for a way in which he could be properly disburdened." The idea that he can jettison reality, Sontag suggests, is ludicrous, and she means for some of his apparently solemn statements to be taken comically and ironically. He cannot abolish the waking world any more than he can stifle his dreams. The novel's ending, then, is ironic. By attempting to live entirely in his dreams, Hippolyte has no basis for comparison; he cannot know how much he has been dreaming because he has not kept careful track of his waking moments. His problem is not psychological; it is ontological. Like a Poe narrator, his problem is not that he is insane; it is that he has lost a standard or objective by which to measure himself. This is perhaps why Sontag told Edward Hirsch in 1995 that she "thought I was telling a pleasurably sinister story that illustrated the fortune of certain heretical religious ideas that go by the name of Gnosticism." She seems to have in mind the notion that Hippolyte's Gnostic search for esoteric or privileged knowledge is ironic because in his desire to be unique he destroys any way of grounding his uniqueness.

Sontag also told Hirsch that in retrospect she realized that the model for her first novel was Kenneth Burke's *Towards a Better Life*. He had given her a copy of the novel when she was at the

University of Chicago. Years later he would say that she was his best student, and not surprisingly he wrote to her later to tell her how much he enjoyed *The Benefactor.* Burke, more renowned for his literary criticism than his fiction, had published a work, Sontag explained to Hirsch, full of "arias and fictive moralizing. The co-quetry of a protagonist—Burke dared to call the novel's hero [John Neal]—so ingeniously self-absorbed that no reader could be tempted to identify with him." Similarly, Sontag had picked a narrator who was a Frenchman in his sixties to forestall any identification between herself and Hippolyte. (Burke's novel and its relationship to *The Benefactor* is discussed in the next section.)

Sontag resisted any autobiographical reading of *The Benefactor,* insisting to James Toback in 1968 that "I'm *nothing* like Hippolyte: at least I certainly *hope* I'm not. He fascinates me, but I dislike him intensely. He's purposeless and wasteful and evil."

CRITICAL COMMENTARY

Reviews of *The Benefactor* were respectful but mixed. In the *New York Times Book Review,* Daniel Stern commented, "It has been said of the French that they develop an idea and then assume it is the world. Hippolyte has decided that *he* is the world, and has proceeded to explore it." He compared Sontag's work to the *nouveau roman.* In *Against Interpretation,* she would secure her status as the foremost interpreter of the French new novel, selecting the work of Nathalie Sarraute and Alain Robbe-Grillet for her admiration. What her novel had in common with her French colleagues was a style that "concentrates . . . on itself," noted reviewer John Wain in the *New Republic.* She repudiated the American tradition of psychological realism. James Frakes in the *New York Herald Tribune* was perhaps the novel's greatest advocate, calling it "a very special book, written with care, polish, daring, and certainty. Very sure. Very tough." Yet he took note of *The Benefactor*'s "frustrating precise design." Though it reminded him of Kafka, to other readers

Sontag's absolute exclusion of psychological insight squeezed life out of the novel. What she gained in purity of form, she lost in chapters that became monotonous. In the *New York Review of Books*, Robert Adams appreciated Sontag's original depiction of a "mind lost in its own intricate dialectic." He thought of *Candide* but complained that Sontag did not have Voltaire's wit or gift for comedy.

Later critics, drawing on Sontag's essays, perceived that Hippolyte resembled her culture heroes such as E. M. Cioran (an alienated Romanian exile who lived and wrote in Paris) and Antonin Artaud (a great writer about the modern theatre's need to explore extreme states of mind, who himself went mad). Sohnya Sayres pointed to Sontag's comment that these writers' "uninhibited display of egotism devolves into the heroic quest for the cancellation of the self." Although Sontag told interviewer James Toback that she was nothing like Hippolyte and that she found him wasteful and evil, Sayres suspected that Sontag was "hiding from a complex set of feelings." She was ambivalent about the aesthetic view of the world—the one in which Hippolyte's dreams have first claim on him—because it seems to lead to a solipsism that negates the idea of the individual's ethical obligation to others. Ultimately Hippolyte's devotion to his own vision results in his self-disintegration. Yet the Sontag of the early essays she was soon to include in *Against Interpretation* extols precisely those artists who favor the beauty of form over the urgency of the message, the content. *The Benefactor* seems to subvert as much as it supports Sontag's essays. Sontag's first novel has buried in it the seeds of doubt about her aesthetic position that would begin to surface in interviews she gave to coincide with the publication of her most recent novel, *In America*.

No critic spotted the resemblance between Kenneth Burke's *Towards a Better Life* and *The Benefactor.* Burke's protagonist, John Neal, laments, rejoices, beseeches, admonishes, moralizes, and rages against the world, the status quo. He is a Hippolyte, a narcissist concerned with perfecting himself. As critic Merle Brown points out, Neal's language is "pure artifice"; that is, it does not arise out of character development or plot. Instead, he is his arias as much as Hippolyte is his dreams. Both Neal and Hippolyte are fashioning narratives that represent themselves, not the world. In his preface to *Towards a Better Life*, Burke favors the essayistic over the narrative, admitting that in the books "I had especially admired, I had found many desirable qualities which threatened them as novels." This is, no doubt, why he taught Joseph Conrad's novel *Victory* during one of Sontag's semesters with him. In Conrad's narrator, Marlow, Burke seized on the intruding figure—the writer who reminds the reader that stories are artifice.

Burke argues in his preface that the verisimilitude of the nineteenth-century novel that has come to dominate fiction is but a blip in the history of literature, which has traditionally prized form over lifelike content. Here he is foreshadowing Sontag's soon-to-be-published essays fulminating against content, psychologizing, and so-called realism in literature. Her key term will be "artifice" as she argues for an art that is enclosed in its own language—as Neal and Hippolyte are enveloped in theirs. Rejecting the value of pure story, Burke concludes that his hero's bewilderment "charts a process, and in the charting of this process there is 'understanding.'" Of what? Apparently of how the self construes an identity through words—or, in Hippolyte's case, through dreams.

Sontag seems to acknowledge Burke in Hippolyte's assertion: "I am interested in my dreams as acts, and as models for action and motives for action." That key phrase, "motives for action," alludes to Burke titles such as *A Grammar of Motives* and *A Rhetoric of Motives*, both of which reveal a sensibility interested in why people or characters in literature act as they do, but which also treats the idea of motives dispassionately—as separate from the notion of a unique personality that must be understood in biographical terms. In his novel, as in his criticism, Burke is simply not taken with the project of analyzing—really psychoanalyzing—the self. Like Sontag's Hippolyte, he explores the range of action open to the individual, which Hippolyte says constitutes his freedom. Otherwise, to inspect his dreams in order to understand himself would be "considering my dreams from the point of view of bondage." To Sontag, as to Burke, the idea that one is bound to a psychological matrix established in childhood is deeply offensive; it is a provocation to the *sui generis*.

The denouement of Burke's novel reads like a stencil for *The Benefactor*, for as critic Merle Brown concludes, "Toward the end . . . Neal talks to others who are only projections of himself and who reply to him in his own voice. He has lost all sense of an outer world." Hippolyte, who has been, he thinks, moving toward a better life, suddenly discovers journals and a novel-like narrative similar to the one he has been relating that call into question whether his present account is fiction or fact, a history of what has actually happened to him or simply a delusion. Friends treat him as though he has been in a mental institution. And Hippolyte concedes there are six years of his life about which he is doubtful—his memory wavers. The consequences of choosing himself—as Hippolyte puts it—include not merely narcissism but solipsism.

This impasse of the self-involved is precisely what modern novels have tended toward, Sontag observes in "Demons and Dreams," her review of an Isaac Singer novel. Why not, then, as in Burke, make that solipsism not just denouement of the novel but its subject? Why not suggest that Hippolyte's desire to become his dreams is the equivalent of the modern novel's desire to free itself from the world, from mimesis, and to become what Poe said a poem is: "a poem and nothing more—this poem written solely for the poem's sake."

What can be attractive as well as off-putting about this kind of self-contained fiction is that it is so *ouvre*. Critic Malcolm Cowley admired the virtuosity of Burke's style, its finished quality, but that very *rondeur* also robs the novel of vitality. Burke tried in *Towards a Better Life* to return to more "formalized modes of writing," to what he called the "structural" sentence, the "Johnsonese" manner as opposed to the modern, informal, conversational style. Sontag affects a Johnsonese grandeur in her passive constructions, which she tries to offset by quaint, teasing chapter headings reminiscent of eighteenth-century novels. But, like Burke, she turns away from what he calls the "impromptu toward the studied." At best such fiction has the alternation of excitement and depression that characterized, in Poe's view, the poetic principle. So much of Poe seems to take place in a dream—or rather, the nightmare that Sontag evokes in her Singer review. Poe's stories, like Hippolyte's dreams, have a redundancy that is both compelling and alienating. Poe wisely measured out his aesthetic in small doses; to string his short story structure into a novel is enervating. If Hippolyte is going mad at the end of the novel—as many critics have supposed—just as Neal appears headed for insanity, both Burke and Sontag confound their readers by insisting on narrators who write, as Merle Brown puts it, in the "same well-rounded, periodic sentences." Brown is applying this judgment only to Burke, but it holds for his pupil as well; she, like him, remains a "verbalizer and analyst."

Although Sontag would publish another novel, *Death Kit*, closely related to *The Benefactor*'s exploration of a disintegrating self, she was already writing herself into a dead end. It would take her twenty-five years to reverse her theories of fiction and to recoup her confidence as a writer of fiction. Roger Straus, an astute observer of her developing talent, suggested that her next book be a collection of essays. He recognized that Sontag's nonfiction was bold and provocative. Compared to the attentive but not exactly enthusiastic reviews of her first novel, the reception of *Against Interpretation*, Straus seemed to foresee, would be intense and wide ranging, so that the name of Susan Sontag would become a cynosure for controversy.

THREE

Against Interpretation

(1966)

Against Interpretation collects twenty-six essays Sontag wrote between 1962 and 1965. The work had appeared in such leading
journals, magazines, and newspapers as *Partisan Review*, *Commentary*, *Evergreen Review*, the *Nation*, the *New York Review of Books*,
and the *New York Herald Tribune's Book Week*. One essay had been
published in the glossy magazine *Mademoiselle*, which had also run
a glamorous photograph of Sontag. By the time her collection of
essays appeared, she had been written up in *Time* for "Notes on
'Camp'" and had fast acquired the attention of both a broad general readership and of academia.

In her introductory note to the book, Sontag disavowed the
label of critic. She wrote as a "partisan" and an "enthusiast." In
retrospect, it seemed to her the essays revealed a "certain naiveté."
It had been her ardor that had attracted certain readers—though
Sontag did not admit as much. She wrote for herself, she implied,
to test certain ideas that she came to believe only in the act of writing about them. Now she had come to disbelieve "some of these
same ideas again. . . . Writing criticism [in the end she could not
avoid the word] has proved to be an act of intellectual disburdenment as much as of intellectual self-expression." She had not resolved certain problems but used them up. Or had she? She
admitted her conviction was "no doubt illusory."

In her note Sontag sounds rather like Hippolyte who writes an entire narrative and then casts doubt upon it. Sontag disburdens herself of ideas the way he disburdens himself of people. Writing is a process, Sontag implies, that can both foster conviction and destroy it. What lives on is the writing itself, she emphasizes. She does not wish to be caught by her words. For some readers her position comes perilously close to admitting that she did not mean what she wrote. Her vision of writing as a provisional act, not a permanent one, has disturbed others who require from Sontag a greater degree of commitment to her ideas or a clearer repudiation of those she no longer holds.

SYNOPSIS

The book's signature essay is divided into ten sections which function as essays within the essay and miniatures of the work in its entirety. The first section contrasts views of art as explanatory (containing a message, i.e., content) and "incantatory" (evoking an experience). In the second section Sontag suggests that to opt for explanations or interpretations of art is to ignore the artwork itself. In the third section she argues that interpretation is never satisfactory because it can never grasp the artwork as a whole. Interpretation is reductive, accounting for only part of the work's existence. In the fourth section, coining one of the phrases she would become famous for, Sontag claims that interpretation is the "revenge of the intellect upon art." In the fifth, sixth, and seventh sections she concedes that certain artists invite criticism but that is hardly to say that their work's importance derives from interpretations of it. Sontag favors arts such as film because it can have such a direct ("unified and clean") impact which eludes criticism. In the eighth section she contends that the role of the critic should be to provide an "accurate, sharp, loving description" of the artwork. (Here she sounds like the "enthusiast" of her introductory note.) In the ninth section she declares that in a mercilessly analytical culture, critics must return to rendering the "sensory" quality of the work of art. Finally, Sontag concludes her essay with the oft-quoted call for an "erotics of art."

Sontag was writing in an era of the "New Critics," of the symbol hunters, myth critics, and adepts in psychoanalysis, who surrounded a text with a parade of learning and who relentlessly probed works of art for their "hidden meaning." In response to these critics, Archibald MacLeish wrote "Ars Poetica," a poem that declared a "poem should not mean but be." The poem for its own sake is what he had in mind. Similarly, in one of her epigraphs to "Against Interpretation," Sontag quotes a letter from Oscar Wilde: "The mystery of the world is the visible, not the invisible." Pay attention to the work itself—as Poe had advised a century earlier. Art was not message mongering, Sontag implied in her other epigraph from an interview with painter Willem de Kooning: "Content is a glimpse of something, an encounter like a flash. It's very tiny—very tiny, content."

Sontag deplored criticism that had an "overt contempt for appearances." She attacked Freud's idea of latent content as opposed to manifest content. This modern, aggressive, imperialistic usurpation of the artwork dismayed her because it depleted the world by attenuating the fullness of the aesthetic experience, the "luminousness of the thing itself." She spoke of the need to "recover our senses."

There is a kind of missionary, therapeutic zeal in this essay that is evocative of Sontag's best work—her argument against the imperialistic designs of photography in *On Photography*, and her battle against the use of the cancer metaphor in *Illness as Metaphor*. The militancy of her polemic is invigorating. She is doing battle with the Pharisees of modern criticism; she is banishing the Philistines.

"On Style," the companion piece to the opening essay, constituted Part I of *Against Interpretation*. Sontag argues in the first three sections of this twenty-four-section essay that style is not a separable part of a work of art. In sections four through eleven, Sontag writes that critics acknowledge as much, yet in practice they treat style as though it were a distinctive quantity, a value added to a work of art. By treating style separately, critics have set up a false dichotomy between style and morality, so that the pleasure taken in an artwork is held hostage to its morality or message. In the next three sections, Sontag insists that the aesthetic experience of a work of art is not to be equated with the world of action because the aesthetic experience expands consciousness to a degree that is "wider and more various than action." Style then, Sontag continues in sections nineteen through twenty-one, is actually an all-encompassing term, the artist's "idiom" deployed in the "*forms* of his art." Ultimately, she concludes, style is the artwork's way of presenting itself, of focusing on the "ineffable," on the silences that are beyond words.

"On Style," seems less original than "Against Interpretation"—in part because the ideas of form and content are recycled from the earlier essay, in part because "style" becomes a rather nebulous term; it is just what a work of art is. But Sontag's gift for phrasemaking is intact: "our manner of appearing *is* our manner of being. The mask is the face." This variation on Oscar Wilde leads to her denial that the aesthetic and ethical are "independent sorts of response" to artworks. Even Leni Riefenstahl's Nazi-propaganda epics, considered as art, merit the term "masterpieces" because their "grace and sensuousness," their beautiful forms, compel the aesthetic response. Presumably what makes Riefenstahl's films art is that they are exemplary objects which "return us to the world in some way more open and enriched" in spite of their evil ideology. (Sontag would later reconsider this argument in "Fascinating Fascism.")

Part II of *Against Interpretation* consists of eight essays that expand Sontag's notion of art and the artist, beginning with a piece on Cesare Pavese, "The Artist as Exemplary Sufferer." She comments on the "modern preoccupation with psychology" which is given full attention in Pavese's diaries, which are at once egotistical and desirous of (shades of Hippolyte) "self-cancellation." Pavese speaks to himself as "you," assessing his accomplishments as a writer (much as Gide did in his journals, which Sontag read as a teenager) and contemplating the possibility of suicide. The artist becomes exemplary because he expresses both the creative and destructive aspects of the human condition.

The next essay, on Simone Weil, presents an even more extreme case of the exemplary sufferer since Weil starves herself to death during World War II in protest over the extermination of the Jews. The martyrdom of Weil provokes Sontag to make one of those challenging and all-encompassing polemical statements that made her famous: "Ours is an age which consciously pursues health, and yet believes only in the reality of sickness." It is not her "gnostic theology of divine absence" that has won Weil readers since her death but rather her "personal authority," her willingness to sacrifice herself for her convictions.

A good deal of personal history lay behind this short essay. The quest for gnosis—the intuitive apprehension of spiritual truths, which led to an esoteric form of knowledge sought by the Gnostics—had been a subject Sontag had explored at Harvard under the tutelage of Jacob Taubes, a charismatic professor who cultivated a mystique that in itself might be called Gnostic. His wife, Sontag's best friend, wrote a dissertation entitled "The Absent God: A Study of Simone Weil." Susan Taubes writes in Nietzsche's wake, the Nietzsche who proclaims the death of God and who seeks a heroic vision of man—an "overman" Taubes calls it—to replace God's absence. The poet Richard Howard, another Sontag friend, later spotted on a Sontag manuscript this marginalia: "Nietzsche, my hero!" Similarly, novelist Edmund White, attending one of Sontag's classes at the New School for Social Work, recalls her outburst: "Isn't Nietzsche great!" The artist, and writers such as Simone Weil, become for Taubes and Sontag sacrificial figures in their quest to invent themselves, alienated seekers after a truth that eludes the many and attracts those few willing to practice the "self-cancellation" Sontag refers to in "The Artist as Exemplary Sufferer."

Weil labored in a factory in support of the workers and bore witness to the republic's agony in Spain, and as a theologian and philosopher she became a cynosure for both Sontag and Taubes, articulating the position of the intellectual *engagé*. Susan Taubes explored Weil's acceptance of Nietzsche's announcement that God is dead. To Weil, the death of God promoted the paradoxical idea of seeking salvation in a hopeless world. Or as Taubes wrote: "Without hope the cross becomes the equivalent of a stoic resignation to the order of the world." That stoicism is written all over Sontag's descriptions of her childhood, yet it had to be countered by a more active, aggressive faith in her own sense of order. "Simone Weil took the Christian symbol of the cross as the point where gnostic revolt against the world and stoic resignation to the world converged," wrote Taubes in her dissertation.

Revolt and resignation, exuberance and melancholy, mark the extremes of the Sontagian temperament, often projected in sentences taut with a worldly tension. Sontag's essay on Weil evinces ambivalence; she admires Weil's energy, her "scathing originality," and above all her seriousness; yet Weil also offends the aesthetic voluptuary in Sontag. Actually to espouse Weil's ideas is tantamount to suicide—a fate in store for Susan Taubes, which Sontag later explored in her story "Debriefing."

Like Weil, the subjects of Sontag's next four essays—Albert Camus, Michel Leiris, Claude Levi-Strauss, and Georg Lukacs—appeal to her sense of the writer as alienated exile. In Camus it is the solitary nature of the writer's work that draws her attention; in Leiris it is his attack on the idea of literature itself; in Levi-Strauss it is his argument that anthropology is a form of "homelessness," and that the anthropologist has a "fascinated *repulsion*" toward his subject; in Lukacs it is his turning away from modernist literature in favor of what he calls the "critical realism" of the nineteenth century. The juxtaposition of these essays is like an oscillation between extremes—from Camus's sense of moral beauty to Leiris's assault on the very idea of literature as exemplary. Levi-Strauss seems closest to Sontag's sensibility in that he expresses, as she does in "Notes on 'Camp,'" an ambivalence to the subjects of his study. Leiris, on the other hand, attacks himself, as if to deprive himself as author of the very authority that most authors wish to establish by writing. This "anti-literature," as she terms it, paradoxically makes literature itself more valuable apparently because it arouses in her a greater consciousness of what literature is. Camus is less appealing to her because he tries so earnestly to fuse himself with what he writes. The connection between the author and his work, and between the work and "reality" (in Lukacs's writing), troubles Sontag because literature seems subsumed into the personality or into society so that literature itself is deprived of its autonomy. She is extending, by implication, her argument in "Against Interpretation" and "On Style": literature is not a container for something else; it is not merely a reflection of ideas, of society, or of the self. In her view, artists who express alienation are actually close to the nature of art itself, since art is not reducible to psychology, history, or any other kind of explanation.

In "Sartre's *Saint Genet*," Sontag buttresses her argument for art's autonomy by observing that both Sartre and the Genet of Sartre's biography engage in the "imaginative annihilation of the world." Sartre the existentialist creates a biographical subject reflective of the biographer—that is, a self whose own actions create meaning even as he finds that the world itself lacks meaning. The self seeks knowledge "out there," but he can find it only in himself—in the process of realizing he must turn from the world to the literature he creates. Once again the effort of a Sontag essay is aimed at liberating literature and striking the reader with the potency of literature's self-sufficiency.

"Nathalie Sarraute and the Novel," the closing essay of Part II, echoes Sontag's emphasis on the sensory value of art. She explores Sarraute's advocacy of immersion into the "direct and purely sensual contact with things and persons which the 'I' of the novelist's experiences." Yet Sarraute's view of the novel ultimately disappoints Sontag because she believes Sarraute still holds literature hostage to what Sarraute calls "truth" and "reality." Consequently Sarraute still maintains the form/content distinction that Sontag believes is inimical to literature, for "truth" and "reality" imply some kind of extraliterary standard, a "content" that the "form" of the novel is meant to capture. More satisfactory, in Sontag's view, is Alain Robbe-Grillet's contention that the novel, "so far as it belongs to the domain of art, has no content."

The five essays on the theatre in Part III explore, for the most part, Sontag's disappointment with 1960s mainstream theatre. "Ionesco" expresses her skepticism of the avant-garde playwright with banal ideas about the banality of his characters. Although it would seem that the way he depersonalizes and de-individualizes his characters might appeal to the anti-psychological Sontag, she dismisses him as intellectually complacent. She does not object to his disgust with life but rather to his disgust with ideas, which she believes is indefensible.

Although Sontag is more sympathetic to Rolf Hochhuth's play *The Deputy* and admires his dogged documentary approach to depicting Pope Pius XII's tacit complicity in the Holocaust, she criticizes the work's form. The "undigested exposition" destroys the drama. The New York production makes the mistake of accentuating the play's realism, whereas Sontag believes that an "ingeniously stylized" production performed in a ritualistic manner would emphasize the play's affirmation of honor and decency. Yet it is difficult to imagine how such a play, which carries the authority of fact, could be given a more figurative and less literal production. Sontag attempts to evade the problem by observing that a director would need an "unusual kind of moral and aesthetic tact."

In "The Death of Tragedy," Sontag reviews Lionel Abel's influential book, *Metatheatre: A New View of Dramatic Form*. He argues that modern playwrights can no longer write tragedy because of their self-consciousness. She agrees that this self-consciousness is already apparent in Shakespeare's plays, which are about "characters not *acting* so much as *dramatizing themselves* in roles." But she doubts some of his more sweeping ideas about Western culture—that it is as liberal or skeptical as he suggests—and takes issue with his way of lumping modern playwrights together: "Brecht has as little in common with Beckett, Genet, and Pirandello as Augustine's exercise in self-analysis has with Montaigne's."

In "Going to the Theatre, etc.," her roundup of theatrical productions, she is especially hard on Arthur Miller's *After the Fall.* Quentin, the play's narrator, ranges in subject matter from his personal marital and familial agonies to the Holocaust to the anti-Communist debates and McCarthyism of the 1950s. Sontag deplores this "quasi-psychiatric approach to guilt and responsibility." It "elevates personal tragedies, and demeans public ones—to the same dead level."

Sontag's role as theatre critic appears rather forced. She did not like to see herself in the role of judgmental reviewer, she later admitted. Although her interest in the theatre was genuine enough, these essay reviews demonstrate that she is more at ease promoting a way of looking at art, a means of perception, than in assessing the quality and effectiveness of productions and of books. At *Partisan Review*, where "Going to the Theatre, etc." appeared, editor William Phillips wanted Sontag to assume Mary McCarthy's mantle. But Sontag had none of McCarthy's biting wit or ruthlessness. She offered her unfavorable opinions with regret and disappointment, not with McCarthy's desire to demolish the second-rate or middlebrow. Thus even in her weakest, least interesting pieces, Sontag writes in a therapeutic tone. She wishes to improve what she sees in the theatre.

Only in the last essay in Part III, "Marat/Sade/Artaud"—Sontag's discussion of *The Persecution and Assassination of Marat as Performed by the Inmates of the Asylum at Charenton under the Direction of the Marquis de Sade*—is she able to fully release her affection for the theatre. "My admiration for, and pleasure in, *Marat/Sade* is virtu-ally unqualified," she announces. The play's dialectical structure—the debate between Marat in his bath and Sade in his chair on the significance of the French Revolution—exhilarates her. The songs of the insane asylum inmates, the inventive use of makeup, cos-tumes, and props earn her approbation of a "theatre of the senses," an all-encompassing art that she called for in her title essay. At the same time the play's intellectual grappling with ideas and com-plexes of emotions involving several characters at once remind her of Antonin Artaud, about whom she would later write a major essay. Artaud argued for a theatre freed from an enslavement to the psychological maladies of individual characters, for he wanted a theatre that was more universal, more philosophical, and more attuned to the problems of existence itself than he thought possi-ble in realistic drama. For Sontag, *Marat/Sade* fulfills the Artau-dian imperative by making all of the characters mad—not to say that the world is insane, but to obviate the concern with the per-sonalities of individuals. Since the characters' sanity cannot be an issue, only what they say, paradoxically, can be taken seriously. Their forms of expression, like the play's form itself, succeed in transcending the conventions of the realistic stage. The play's lan-guage, Sontag contends, is "used . . . primarily as a form of incan-tation, instead of being limited to the revelation of character and the exchange of ideas."

In Part IV, Sontag's essays on filmmakers, she is clearly more com-fortable finding contemporary examples of artists whose use of form makes their work especially immune to message hunters who extract content from art. She praises Robert Bresson for charting the "physics of the soul," eschewing psychology, which she deems superficial. Human character is not so easily understood; indeed it is opaque, a mystery, his films imply. He deliberately employs un-dramatic effects so that viewers do not identify with his characters. He is not interested in creating suspense or indulging in the other conventions of filmmaking. As Sontag will suggest in more than one essay in *Against Interpretation*, these techniques of distancing the artwork from its audience invite boredom, yet she positively relishes the abandonment of conventional, professional standards—touting Bresson because he uses amateur actors. Similarly, Jean-Luc Godard is "anti-psychological." He defies the concept of normal film narrative, dissociating words and images, and fragmenting the action. Such techniques thwart the desire to become lost in a story; instead the viewer is led to see the film *qua* film, as a construct, a form that has its own sense of completeness.

In the essays on Bresson and Godard, as in many of Sontag's earlier discussions of works of art, she does not describe plot— probably because she would then lapse into seeing art as content. The meaning of art, she implies throughout *Against Interpretation*, is best understood in terms of an attempt to describe how it unfolds as form. Thus what "happens" in a film is only of interest to her in so far as it helps show the shape of the art. "The Imagination of Disaster," for example, her classic account of science fiction films of the 1950s, does dwell on the basic plots of the genre precisely because the plot is the form, the "sensuous elaboration" of the "extraordinary," the evocation of destruction on a cosmic scale. Her attraction to these science fiction films clearly arises from their "aesthetic view of destruction and violence." For once her description seems to be done with deadpan humor. Thus her account of the model scenario: "(1) The arrival of the thing. . . . (2) Confirmation of hero's report [of alien invasion or act of destruction]. . . . (3) In the capital conferences between scientists and the military take place, with the hero lecturing before a chart, map, or blackboard. . . . (4) Further atrocities. . . . (5) More conferences. . . ."

Sontag describes other scenarios in an effort to capture the "cinematic charm" of these naive yet compelling movies. They may be "unintentionally funny" and therefore an object of campy pleasure, but their reliance on the fantastic seems to attract her precisely because they challenge the status quo and elaborate a form of art that is not simply a replication of what is considered to be reality. Another such challenge is Jack Smith's *Flaming Creatures*, a kind of tribute to transvestites that Sontag praises for the beauty of its images. In a typical Sontag judgment, she observes that if the film has the "sloppiness, the arbitrariness, the looseness of pop art," it also embodies pop art's "gaiety, its ingenuousness, its exhilarating freedom from moralism." She praises the artificial elements of the film, its "invented landscape of costume, gesture, and music," which creates an "aesthetic space." She does not deny that such a film could be condemned from a moral point of view, but she insists that there is a "space of pleasure"—especially in regard to sex—that can exist independently of ethical standards.

"Renais' Muriel" continues Sontag's exultation in film that disorders narrative, breaking it up into a sequence of images, a montage that strikes her as a way to "decompose" the story. Thus the viewer is distanced from the narrative and has to learn to read it rather than become absorbed in it. It is how shots are composed, the form of the story, that again takes precedence. History cannot simply be recalled or given an exposition in films such as *Last Year at Marienbad*. It has to be reconstructed, composed just as the film is composed.

The distinctions Sontag has made in her film essays between the psychological and the anti-psychological artist are elaborated in her "A Note on Films and Novels." Both genres have their vulgar and sophisticated practitioners; both attract artists who probe human motives and others who concentrate on the interactions between people and things, revealing human character as "opaque" (one of Sontag's favorite terms).

In the last section of *Against Interpretation*, Sontag begins with an attack on Walter Kauffman's collection, *Religion: From Tolstoy to Camus*. She objects to his conflating the term "religion" with writing that does not posit a God or a belief in divine revelation, or advocate the practice of religious ritual. The effort to locate religious conviction in modern writers is, she argues, the "backwash of broken radical political enthusiasms." It is the pursuit of "piety without content," a "religious fellow travelling" that stops short of commitment to a creed.

Behind Sontag's skepticism about using modern writing as a substitute for religion is her own dedication to the sacredness of writing as its own form of inquiry. Just as she does not want to reduce art to a message, she does not want to violate the integrity of writing. To her Kauffman is "soft-headed." In effect, this kind of Sontag essay is therapeutic, an effort to clear the intellectual air of cant.

A variant on this Sontagian severity is expressed in her next essay, "Psychoanalysis and Norman O. Brown's *Life Against Death*": "We are not tenacious enough about ideas, as we have not been serious enough or honest enough about sexuality." In this essay she is contemptuous of American psychoanalysis, which has made of Freud's ideas a bland concoction that can be dispensed by Park Avenue psychiatrists. She also attacks disenchanted American intellectuals, many of whom she deems "lazy" for equating atrocities like the failure of the Hungarian Revolution with the bankruptcy of communism itself. (Twenty years later she will reverse herself, conceding that the failure of Communist governments did confirm the bankruptcy of their ideology.)

Although Sontag has reservations about Brown and about Herbert Marcuse, whose book *Eros and Civilization* tried to reconcile the conflicting ideas of Freud and Marx, she lauds Brown for exploring the nature of sexuality in more depth, extending not only Freud's insights but also D. H. Lawrence's perceptions of how the human body, sexuality, and human consciousness are irrevocably linked. "The truth is," she announces, "love is more sexual, more bodily than even Lawrence imagined." The flourish of such statements accounts, in good part, for why Sontag was hailed and denounced, for they carry the weight of revelation and prophecy. For all their boldness, however, her proclamations sound terribly earnest and perhaps, as she herself suggested, somewhat naive. Brown's thinking has a utopian quality that Sontag shares, for she is attracted to his idea that human consciousness will be expanded through an increased consciousness of our bodies, and therefore of our sexuality.

In her welcoming of writing and of other arts that expand consciousness, Sontag is willing to forsake her concern with form. This explains her attraction to "Happenings," those impromptu events and actions that attracted small audiences to lofts, galleries, backyards, and small theatres in 1960s Manhattan. Sontag calls these spontaneous, chaotic events the "art of radical juxtaposition," justifying their formlessness by fostering the idea that Happenings are extensions of surrealism, a "mode of sensibility which cuts across all the arts in the 20th century." This sweeping definition allows her to praise Happenings as "animated collages," a combination of drama and art exhibit. "New meanings or counter meanings" emerge as a scene is created through music, silent actions, dialogue—in short through whatever seems appropriately shocking for the moment. A Happening might be something like those eighteenth-century tableaux in which people assumed the poses of works of art, though a Happening might also feature people behaving like objects in still lifes. The spontaneity of Happenings thrills Sontag, who extols "sensuous properties." Happenings are designed to thwart interpretation. Certainly to the traditionalist, to the classically minded, her advocacy of an art on the run, so to speak, is anathema, since Happenings would seem to annihilate the very quest for form that Sontag prizes in "Against Interpretation" and "On Style."

Yet Sontag's own loving and meticulous descriptions of Happenings convey the tone of a strict, incisive observer—a tone that carries over to her next essay, the famous "Notes on 'Camp,'" where she proffers herself as the first writer to describe the term "apart from a lazy two-page sketch in Christopher Isherwood's novel *The World in the Evening*." "Notes on 'Camp'" is nothing if not industrious. Not only does it detail a series of definitions of the term, it provides long lists of examples—the apparent result of years of research and reflection. Camp works of art and camp performances are "corny and flamboyant." Camp is the art of stylization, of artifice, of art calling attention to itself as art. Camp is extravagant. A movie such as *King Kong* is camp because it is so exaggerated, so over the top, but also true to its own principles, its own way of perceiving the world, which may be ridiculous, ludicrous, but also consistent and in its own way sincere. The camp sensibility is aesthetic—that is, it admires style in and of itself. Anyone, anything can be campy if it is recognized as "too much." Figures such as Greta Garbo, Jayne Mansfield, Mae West, and the "public manner and rhetoric of de Gaulle" are "pure camp." Such figures verge on becoming all style, devoid of substance.

Like Happenings, camp becomes important for Sontag because both represent the defeat of content, of the message mongering that she feels has debased the very notion of art in contemporary culture. Both camp and Happenings prepare for her assault on C. P. Snow's conception of the "two cultures": the world of science, which is rapidly changing and developing, and the world of art, which remains static. Only certain forms of art, like the modern American novel, seem moribund to Sontag. In other forms and literature, and certainly in the other arts, there are developments that Snow does not perceive. Like science, art expands and modifies human consciousness. There are not two cultures, Sontag rejoins; rather, there is one sensibility, a modern one that is for the first time linking art and science and the activities of singular minds with the masses. The crowdedness and speed of the contemporary scene is best incorporated, she suggests, in the cinema. Artists address problems and do research just as scientists do. An aesthetic position can be as rigorously worked out as a scientific one, she concludes. Only when art is reduced to a series of moral judgments does it seem inferior to science. Modernist art, like science, tests the mind: "Having one's sensorium challenged or stretched hurts," Sontag observes. Popular art may embody a beauty of form that is as elegant as any scientific equation, she implies. Of course, she concedes, there is inferior avant-garde art and trashy popular culture. But cutting across all categories of art and science is one sensibility that is "pluralistic" and appreciates the "beauty of a machine" as much as a painting by Jasper Johns, a film by Godard, or a Beatles song.

SONTAG READING SONTAG

By 1969, when interviewer Edwin Newman asked Sontag about "Against Interpretation," she admitted to a certain embarrassment, saying the essay was not as relevant then as when she wrote it. The context had changed: "Obviously, if nobody were paying attention to content or meaning or message, then probably I would be talking about that." Similarly, by 1972 she acknowledged to critic Joe David Bellamy that an explosion of talent in the American contemporary novel had overturned her low opinion of American fiction seven years earlier. By 1988 she admitted that she had been attracted mainly to the *idea* of the *nouveau roman*. The novels of its practitioners, Nathalie Sarraute and Alain Robbe-Grillet, were not actually that appealing. "I was not being entirely honest with myself in the 1960s," Sontag confessed to Stefan Jonsson. In general, Sontag was inclined to see her own work in historical terms, with her positions evolving along with her era. In 1975 she summed up her development for Maxine Bernstein and Robert Boyers: "I've come to appreciate the limitations—and the indiscretion—of generalizing either the aesthete's or the moralist's view of the world without a much denser notion of historical context."

CRITICAL COMMENTARY

Reviewers greeted *Against Interpretation* with considerable enthusiasm, curiosity, and animosity. David Hayman, in *Books Abroad*, liked Sontag's zest and clear diagnoses of contemporary culture and current trends. Burton Feldman, in the *Denver Quarterly*, called her a nag and found her emphasis on form and method overwrought. Richard Sullivan, in the *Chicago Tribune*, dismissed her as "dogmatic" and "condescending." Peter Brooks suggested in the *Partisan Review* that she overstated the role of interpretation in Anglo-American criticism. It was far more descriptive than she supposed. She was most successful in talking about form when it related to less discursive media such as film.

Richard Freedman remarked in the *Kenyon Review* that *Against Interpretation* "occupies the same place in criticism that *Vogue's* latest pronouncements on the miniskirt occupy in another, apparently related, world of fashion." Benjamin DeMott, in the *New York Times Book Review*, discussed what was already Sontag's well-burnished image as the "Lady on the Scene." He captured the paradox she represented—that of the self-lacerating Puritan full of strictures and the hedonistic *au courant* sybarite. The title of Elizabeth Stevens's review, "Miss Camp Herself," acknowledged that Sontag had become a symbol of "Making It New"—a reference to Norman Podhoretz's book *Making It*, which detailed his ambition to be a successful writer in New York and which suggested just how competitive and image-conscious New York writers were. In "The Sensational Susan Sontag," Mary Ellmann observed that Sontag's descriptions of the newest sensations and sensibilities had made her—for all her sober-sided prose—sensational herself.

Academic critics such as John Cawelti in the *American Quarterly* argued in Sontag's favor that "breaking down the walls of snobbery, elitism and status" justified "any threat to the great tradition of the arts." John Justus, in the *Southern Review*, lauded her for taking the moralizing out of criticism. In an otherwise sympathetic essay in *TriQuarterly*, Stephen Koch expressed skepticism about Sontag's brief for a "new sensibility" that unified the developments in science and the arts. Indeed, his argument weighs strongly when viewed in the context of Sontag's rejection of religion as defined by Walter Kauffman. Was she not guilty of his intellectual presumptuousness when she so easily conflated the arts and the sciences?

Yet whatever faults of judgment and logic, and lapses of taste are to be found in *Against Interpretation*, there is a compelling dialectical quality in Sontag's best essays and a pleasing form that is likely to attract new generations of readers. As critic Ihab Hassan observes, "Against Interpretation" and "On Style" are essays that "refuse dating, refuse obsolescence, because they address a timeless human impulse: to interpret and appropriate the world." The internal dialectic of these essays is also at work in the structure of *Against Interpretation*. Thus critic Elizabeth Bruss maintains: "The positions that one essay embraces are held at a distance in another. The distance itself seems to be achieved by pursuing a program of deliberate overgeneralization until the novelty of a claim has been exhausted and its hidden weakness exposed."

In 1996, in an essay commemorating the thirtieth anniversary of the publication of *Against Interpretation*, Sontag chose to emphasize the perennial quality of her project: "I saw myself as a newly minted warrior in a very old battle: against philistinism, against ethical and aesthetic shallowness and indifference." She might have added that to a certain extent she was aping such New York intellectuals as art critic Harold Rosenberg, a *Partisan Review* stalwart celebrated, like Sontag, for his epigrams (he coined the term "action painting" for abstract expressionism). As J. Hoberman reminds us, "one should never lose sight of him, or any of the New York intellectuals, as performers."

At various times and in different moods, Rosenberg shifted his positions—sometimes going with the fashionable flow, sometimes arguing against it, abusing pop culture, then espousing it in a *Partisan Review* symposium, declaring "both the alienation of the artist and the antagonism of public opinion to art have been successfully liquidated." Reports of his attitude toward Sontag were similarly conflicting: he adored her, he hated her, he felt ambivalent about her.

Sontag had grown up absorbing the pronunciamentos of New York intellectuals, but she was also the Westerner, the outsider, who had studied intellectual fashion like an anthropologist. Indeed, she was its Levi-Strauss. Critic Liam Kennedy notes that before Sontag, no New York intellectual showed her range. Literature as such figured in only a minority of her essays in *Against Interpretation*, and she would develop still further as a music and dance critic, and a film and theatre director. The only missing ingredient, soon to come with the Vietnam War, was her appearance as a politically engaged writer. As Sontag herself put it in her 1996 preface to *Against Interpretation*, the sixties were a delightful decade for opportunists: "there were new permissions in the air, and old hierarchies had softened, had become ripe for toppling."

FOUR

Death Kit

(1967)

Death Kit is ostensibly related by an omniscient third-person narrator, though internal evidence suggests that the novel's main
character, Dalton Harron (Diddy), is viewing *himself* in the third
person. Like Hippolyte exploring his dreams, Diddy seems to be
exploring the contents of his own imagination, which perhaps accounts for the perplexing repetition in parentheses of the word
"now," as if to suggest that "events" are only events occurring
"now" in the narrator's mind. The "now" is parenthetical because
it is provisional, tentative. Also like *The Benefactor, Death Kit* seems
to be about the burdens of consciousness and the narrator's efforts
to disburden himself of his thoughts even as he comes to terms
with them.

SYNOPSIS

Diddy is on a business trip, traveling by train from Manhattan to
Albany. Yet there are also references to a hospital scene, a Negro
orderly, a stomach pump, and Diddy's "hope of being born" as
well as his "wish to die." Apparently, Diddy has attempted suicide,
and the following narrative may be an attempt to come to terms
with his life, though it also has the phantasmagoric impact of a

dream, with the same events, or versions of those events, occurring again and again. Although more obscure, the effect of this opening is like the story of a dead man told from the dead man's point of view—as in Billy Wilder's film *Sunset Boulevard*, which Sontag mentions as an example of camp in *Against Interpretation.*

In his train compartment Diddy observes his fellow passengers, especially a fetching girl wearing sunglasses whose name is Hester. The train comes to a halt in a tunnel. An impatient Diddy leaves the train and encounters a menacing workman. Reacting to the man's insults with rage, Diddy seizes a crowbar and kills the man.

Returning to the train Diddy beckons Hester, who is blind, to join him in the corridor, where he confesses that he has committed a terrible crime. But Hester tells him the train never stopped and Diddy did not leave the compartment. An aroused Diddy conducts Hester to a lavatory where he proceeds to make love to her. Returning to their compartment he contemplates whether Hester might be right and that his crime is only an illusion.

Frustrated with his own behavior, Diddy takes Hester to the club car and questions her about her own life. Does she love anyone? Does she love him? He presses for a detailed accounting of all her feelings. But he remains quiet about his own feelings and seems trapped within his own story.

Back in the compartment, Diddy converses with Mrs. Nayburn, Hester's aunt and companion on this trip. Diddy suffers from the stress of his encounter with the workman, and he is drawn to Hester because she seems so forthright and unburdened by conflicting emotions.

At the train station Diddy decides to accompany Hester and her aunt to the Warren Institute, where she is scheduled for an operation that will attempt to restore her sight. Checking in later at his hotel, he watches television for reports of the workman's death. The first edition of the morning paper also carries no item about the murder. Diddy ponders confessing his crime. He muses or perhaps dreams about Raggedy Andy, a doll he played with as a child, then mistreated, blinded, and threw into a Halloween bonfire. Now the doll returns to him, an emblem of "his first suicide attempt." Searching a later edition of the newspaper, Diddy finds an item about Angelo Incardona, "apparently struck" by the train Diddy traveled on. While still contemplating a confession of the crime, Diddy becomes hungry and orders flowers for Hester.

Diddy has breakfast with business colleagues, then visits the factory—the site of his business meeting—while thinking all the time about Hester. His optics company is worried about competition from a Japanese manufacturer, but Diddy misses much of the discussion, still thinking about Hester.

Visiting the hospital, Diddy has to put up with Mrs. Nayburn's questions about his personal life. She hints that Hester could be his for the asking. Watching Hester, Diddy is entranced by her face, which cannot look at others. He watches her mouth during their awkward conversation. Should he tell Hester about the newspaper reporting Incardona's death? he wonders. But he does not, and Hester asks him to leave, sensing there is "danger" in the room.

Diddy returns to the hotel, has an unsatisfactory dinner with one of his business colleagues, and retires to his room, where he dreams about Raggedy Andy and of a story involving a seashell. He gets involved in a confusing sequence of events concerning the seashell. It becomes lost, and he returns to the tunnel where he hunts for the seashell. But the shell is not to be found because Diddy is "already inside it."

Diddy considers whether he should go to Incardona's funeral. Perhaps actually seeing his widow or son would convince Diddy of the reality of what he has done. But he cannot decide what to do, except that he puts off seeing Hester again.

Although Diddy realizes he has to keep his mind on his work, he calls the funeral home and is told that Incardona was cremated. He is disappointed because he had vividly imagined Incardona's autopsy.

After visiting Hester, Diddy, posing as an insurance investigator, goes to see Mrs. Incardona. Myra Incardona is a buxom woman with bad teeth living in a rather disorderly home. Yet Diddy seems attracted to her, and she begins to flirt with him. Then he admits he is not from the insurance company, but Mrs. Incardona is now angry and says, "You people are gonna pay and pay plenty." Diddy now believes in the reality of the murder, and he imagines marrying Mrs. Incardona. At a bar he meets a girl named Doris, has sex with her, and thinks about his brother.

Two days later Diddy spends a distracted day at work thinking about Mrs. Incardona while a vote is taken among the staff of his company to try to improve the microscope that is in direct competition with a Japanese product. Diddy resists the temptation to tell one of his fellow employees about Incardona. Skipping the rest of the day's work, Diddy returns to the hospital and tries to relieve Hester's suspicion that the operation has failed to restore her sight. When he makes a sexual overture to Hester, she rejects him. But when she makes love to him, he leaves.

Diddy ponders binocular vision, using it to symbolize the one eye of health (his love for Hester) and the other of disease (his murder of Incardona). He sends Hester a love letter via a telegram, visits sex shops, puts on a mask, and plays arcade games. Then he shows up at a television station for a program featuring his company. Afterward he returns to his hotel and dreams of Hester, their lavatory sex, and her denial that he has committed a crime. He dreams of Hester's operation and watches the surgeon using a laser on her. The whole scene appears as if on television. Diddy thinks of the dead Incardona's corneas as a replacement for Hester's. Then the dream switches to Diddy in Manhattan rushing to catch his train to Albany.

Depleted by his dreams, Diddy attends his company's morning meeting. He tells Hester's aunt he will help pay for the hospital bills. The operation has been a failure, and Hester consents to live with Diddy. At a company banquet, Diddy can only think of Hester.

Unable to tolerate work anymore, Diddy concocts a story to

obtain sick leave. He makes all the arrangements concerning Hester over a dinner with her aunt. Diddy now learns from Mrs. Nayburn that Hester was blinded by her own mother, who threw lye in her eyes. Diddy speculates on Hester's sexual experience and what she did during her two years at a special school in Chicago. Back in his hotel room he fantasizes about a whole group of Hester dolls and then sweeps them off his "dream shelf." He turns instead to a life-size mannequin in the window. Hester, he hopes, will restore him to sanity. She has a kind of sanctity about her. Hester may have much to teach him, he concludes. He hopes that she is the beginning of his new life and that he can jettison the memory of Incardona. Perhaps she can lead him out of the "labyrinth of his own consciousness." When Diddy arrives at the hospital to take Hester away, she warns him that he cannot expect to be like her. But he is excited about taking care of her and believes it is not too late to "unlearn" his self-destructive tendencies.

In New York City, Diddy and Hester settle into his apartment. She cooks and cleans. Their isolation is broken by the ringing of a doorbell. It is Diddy's brother Paul, drunk and demanding to see Diddy. After Paul leaves, Diddy and Hester quarrel. Diddy interrogates her about her reactions to her blindness and to her mother. Hester replies that she hates both and Diddy as well when he indulges in his "powerful desire to destroy" himself. When Diddy then insists that Hester meet Paul, Hester presses Diddy to have sex.

But Diddy and Hester remain isolated in the apartment. Diddy dwells on his unfinished novel, *The Story of the Wolf-Boy*. The draft of the book is lost but fragments remain that tell the story of a creature who weeps because he wants to be something more than an animal. He tells the story of his life, his adoption by a sword swallower who claims the wolf-boy is actually the offspring of two giant apes. He tells Diddy about the period when he lived in a cliffside cave outside Tucson, where a teenage girl with long dark hair visited his lair and tempted him to become a "real animal." But the girl does not actually meet the wolf-boy because she is interrupted in her climb to the lair by her dog and her anxious parents. Yet the experience with the girl had been "unbearably intimate." The story of the wolf-boy is intertwined with Diddy's thoughts about his brother Paul, a famous musician who has won the Chopin Prize. Suddenly the image of Incardona returns to replace the image of the wolf-boy's cave. Diddy is wary of recounting this sequence of events to Hester.

It appears that the love between Diddy and Hester is weakening. Diddy, in fact, begins to fail physically. Yet he rouses himself from his bed and finds himself once again in the train tunnel—this time with Hester. Or is it the same tunnel? Diddy is not certain. Once again he confronts Incardona; once again Incardona mocks him; once again Diddy raises the crowbar and kills him. "He's really dead (now)," Diddy says. He also shouts to the blind Hester: "I want to be seen!" Then he makes love to her, and he feels as though he is a sea creature rising "out of its shell." Leaving Hester behind, he explores the tunnel. He finds corpses, a crypt, and then more charnal rooms, decaying bodies in a nightmarish vision, which ends the novel, Diddy having "perceived the inventory of the world."

SONTAG READING SONTAG

Although Sontag has been reluctant to be explicit about how she views the events of *Death Kit*, she has conceded that, in Joe David Bellamy's words, the narrative can be read as the "contents" of Diddy's "final coma." Thus Hester and Incardona are figments of Diddy's imagination. Diddy's is a "fictional world," Sontag told Bellamy. The novel is a "death kit" because Diddy has "assembled the elements of his death" in the voice of a "disguised first person." But Sontag also insisted that the novel can be read as a "straight narrative in which certain magical events take place on exactly the same level as those events which are convincing in terms of everyday life." Like a film, Sontag continued, she wanted her novel to seem real simply because it was *"there."* She wanted both levels of experience to be "real"—that is, the dream itself and the experience of the dream as an actual event. To James Toback, Sontag revealed that she did not "know what Diddy is or even *that* he is. . . . I guess he's many things, and he learns about them through his fantasies. He's brutal and bitchy—but he's a poor slob, too."

Sontag also observed that her novel was written during the Vietnam War: "I've often thought that *Death Kit* could have been called *Why Are We in Vietnam?* Because it gets into the kind of senseless brutality and self-destructiveness that is ruining America."

CRITICAL COMMENTARY

The anonymous reviewer in *Time* and Eliot Freemont-Smith in the *New York Times* were representative of critics who found the novel tedious and irritating. Others, such as Doris Grumbach in *America* and Stanley Reynolds in the *New Statesman*, praised its ingenuity, beautiful form, and disturbing resonance. Gore Vidal lamented Sontag's "well-known difficulties in writing English." Similarly Denis Donoghue in the *New York Review of Books* observed: "She is not a natural writer, certainly not a natural novelist. She writes by insistence, the will doing the work of the imagination." Yet Vidal conceded her formidable "will to understand" and her impressive reading in European literature, an activity that most American novelists seemed to avoid. "More than any other American," Vidal wrote, she was a "link to European writing today." He saluted her sincerity yet turned it against her in a mortifying verdict:

> her moral seriousness is considerably enhanced by a perfect absence of humor, that most devastating of gifts usually thrust at birth upon the writer in English. Unhindered by a sense of humor, she is

able to travel fast in the highest country, unafraid of appearing absurd, and of course invulnerable to irony.

There was enough talent and intelligence in *Death Kit*, Vidal thought, to expect that Sontag would one day be able to create literature.

On balance, there were far more negative and mixed reviews than positive ones. Critics tended to see the novel as an illustration of Sontag's theories about literary form, and as such they deemed it too academic and lacking in the drive that made for first-rate fiction. A decade later Larry McCaffery's careful consideration of the novel in *Contemporary Literature* concluded that it was "one of the most interesting and successful experimental novels to appear in the 1960s." Yet he conceded that it is "not particularly interesting or original for *what* it says, and this may explain why it has received so little attention." McCaffery's article provides a helpful reading of the novel's style and structure, its "formal ingenuity."

Another way to read *Death Kit* is as a novel that deals with "unfinished business," a term with a specific meaning in gestalt therapy, a form of psychology that Sontag was drawn to as an alternative to the Freudianism she rejected in her essays. In January 1968 she gave a lecture and seminar on what she called "psychotechnics" at one of the hubs of the Human Potential Movement in the 1960s, the Esalen Institute in Big Sur, California, which specialized in gestalt therapy workshops. To the author of "Against Interpretation," who emphasized the formal properties of a work of art (its shape and surface), seeing psychology in terms of a gestalt—a figure or pattern against a background or field of perception—was appealing: to be conscious of the pattern—"dynamic awareness rather than introspection" is the goal, states one of the classic texts on gestalt therapy, written in part by Paul Goodman, to whom Sontag pays tribute in *Under the Sign of Saturn*. Whereas the Freudian analyzes a "repetition-compulsion," a behavior reproduced because the patient cannot bring it to a satisfactory conclusion, the gestaltist identifies "unfinished business" that the patient should act out (repeat) until there is an awareness of the whole out of which this obsessive behavior originates.

The constant references to "now" in the novel mark Diddy's desperate efforts to create himself anew, to engage in the self-invention that Sontag has always sought for herself. "Now" also echoes the gestaltist's emphasis on the present, focusing the patient—in this case Diddy and the reader—on the present, asking "What are you feeling now? What are you doing?" The book is Diddy's artifice, but the irony is that he is putting himself together for death, which, in a sense, everyone does, sooner or later. Thus Diddy's lapsing into "we" occasionally can be taken as both his dialogue with himself and with all human beings who compose themselves for death. In both life and art, Sontag favors a focus on visible form, on happenings. Part of Diddy's problem is that he is burdened by a past that he cannot let go, and his dreams reenact the past rather than free him to live.

Diddy is, after all, a failed novelist. He recovers the wolf-boy story in his dreams (which are dreams within the dream he is having in his dying moments). The story is obviously a commentary on Diddy's own estrangement from society and from his animal nature, his instinct for survival. If Diddy could only become more aware of how his fictional episodes, or dreams, are the pattern of his life, he could save himself, a gestaltist might propose. In fact, Diddy's death-dream is an attempt to repeat his life and to get it right the second time. His tragedy, like ours, is that there are no second chances.

The writer as a self-made construct thrills and intrigues Sontag. To say that her novel is forced is no criticism in her eyes, and the critics who tend to like the book praise its formal properties—its ingenious dream-within-a-dream properties while admitting the main character, Diddy, is deathly dull. (See Theodore Solotaroff's insightful review in his collection, *The Red Hot Vacuum*.)

Not only is Diddy dreaming, making the whole novel unreal,

Sontag implies that he *is* unreal, merely a confection of literature, a Diddy, or Didi—as Tony Tanner points out in reminding us of the nickname for Vladimir in Samuel Beckett's *Waiting for Godot*, a major text for Sontag. Like Didi, Diddy seems paralyzed. He wishes to move but he stands still—or his life does, at any rate. He is a man of action only in his dream, which is itself, ironically, brought on by his final act of suicide.

What Sontag will not allow to happen is mimesis—that willing suspension of disbelief that would throw the reader right into the novel as if it were not a novel but life—or the next best thing, a copy of life. In a talk Sontag gave at the New York Library Association in October 1965, she contended that no "serious literary tradition issuing from Joyce's work" had evolved. "The critically respectable novel has returned to essentially the aesthetic premises of nineteenth-century realism. That is, the novel is understood not so much as a work of art but as a mirror of reality." The Sontag project, then, entailed wresting her novels away from outmoded—if still prevalent—notions of verisimilitude.

As Hippolyte says in *The Benefactor,* "I am crawling through the tunnel of myself," which is his dreams, which is his novel, which is his death. The structure of *Death Kit,* in other words, is a House of Usher, with the last scene a depiction of a charnel house stock full of nineteenth-century images. As Tony Tanner suggests, environment proves to be intractable, "closing in on Diddy like the walls on Edgar Allan Poe's prisoner." Ultimately, Tanner concludes, the "centre of consciousness is the house of death."

Gore Vidal was as impressed with the novel's ending in the catacombs/charnel house. But as Theodore Solotaroff observes, Diddy is never quite believable as an "experiencing subject." Critic Elizabeth Holdsworth calls Diddy and his predecessor Hippolyte "existential abstractions of modern man." We do not care enough about them. Even in formal terms, Sontag's strength of structure is not enough. "It is more figure than carpet," Solatoroff judges. The gestalt (the whole, figure and pattern) does not cohere. *Death Kit* is merely tautological: it is what happens inside of one head and denies us, in critic Cary Nelson's words, "any sense of historical or social context."

It is not as if Sontag had chosen a peculiar theme. Tony Tanner convincingly relates *Death Kit* to the "American delight at feeling free from external control and shaping," the quest for a reality "sealed up in the self." There is an instinct, he observes, to "cultivate and protect an area of inner space" that recurs in contemporary American fiction. It is only inwardly that the hero or writer experiences freedom, but sooner or later there has to be some kind of confrontation with an outer world—not just a dream of such a confrontation. Diddy's entropy, in other words, has no objective correlative in the novel.

Long before Sontag would write about Elias Canetti in *Under the Sign of Saturn*, Tanner presciently noted that *Death Kit* resembles *Auto-da-Fe*. Canetti's Professor Peter Kien lives in a hermetic world that is a death kit. Indeed, Sontag has admitted that *Saturn's* studies of writers such as Paul Goodman, Elias Canetti, and Walter Benjamin are a form of disguised autobiography. To say so is to drop the disguise, of course, to self-criticize, as Sontag believes Canetti did in his only novel. Critic Sohnya Sayres identifies the key passage in *Under the Sign of Saturn*:

> *Auto-da-Fe* depicts the stages of Kien's madness as three relations of "head" and "world"—Kien secluded with his books as a "head without a world"; adrift in the bestial city, "a world without a head"; driven to suicide by "the world in the head." And this was not language suitable only for the mad bookman; Canetti later used it in his notebook to describe himself, as when he called his life nothing but a desperate attempt to think about everything "so that it comes together in a head and thus becomes one again," affirming the fantasy he had pilloried in Auto-da-Fe.

Such passages in Sontag support Sayres's contention that in *Death Kit*, Sontag is pillorying herself. In the *New York Times Book Review*, Benjamin DeMott shrewdly observed that Diddy was a self-portrait of the writer "bent on transforming self-hatred into an instrument of objective analysis." *Auto-da-Fe* proved to be a dead end for Canetti. He never wrote another novel. Sontag would not publish another novel for twenty-five years.

The burden of writing novels and of her own consciousness became too difficult to balance for Sontag, because for her the creative act of writing was tantamount to the creation of a self. Or as Diddy laments: "No one should be burdened with inventing his own nature from scratch."

FIVE

Styles of Radical Will

(1969)

SYNOPSIS

Styles of Radical Will is divided into three parts, beginning with one of Sontag's most important essays, "The Aesthetics of Silence." She describes how contemporary art has become a metaphor for the "spiritual project." Art, the aesthetic impulse, she suggests, is the main conduit for transcending the painful conflicts of existence. Yet art is, of course, a human product, a material object, and it is this recognition that drives certain artists to silence, so that they can free themselves of their ties to this world. Paradoxically she finds their very "reluctance to communicate" a way of engaging with art itself by defining the space between the artist and his audience.

Silence has taken many forms: suicide, rejection of the world, madness, and a censorship of expression. Whatever form the silence takes, however, can have the effect of making the work of art more central, more sensuously present, Sontag argues. Harpo Marx, for example, derives his silent power from his association with manic talkers. In literature, the inescapability of using language means that the work of art communicates and takes its place in the history of human consciousness regardless of the silences of the writer and his writing.

Sontag surveys how silence has been made visible. The silent person is opaque, refusing to interpret, clearing the air so to speak or provoking others to interpret the silence. Thus the character of the actress in Bergman's film *Persona* is eloquent in her silence and stimulates her nurse to take on the burden of talking. For the actress, as for other artists, silence may be a way of seeking a "cultural clean slate."

Thus silence provokes further thought even as it renders speech itself suspect. Silence, paradoxically, can be a means of redeeming language by calling attention to its limitations. Silence, as Rilke recommends in the *Duino Elegies*, is a kind of "emptying out," a therapeutic voiding of language, a language that can be perceived as layers of words that need to be peeled back, allowing "'things' themselves to speak." (Sontag's notion here is reminiscent of William Carlos Williams's injunction: "No ideas but in things.") John Cage's musical experiments with silence, in which he allows the natural sounds of the world to dominate, is another example Sontag uses to create a picture of the artist who wants to clear a new conceptual space for art. Cage and artists like him seek a new openness.

The use of silence in writers such as Samuel Beckett repels conventional searches for "meaning" in works of art. Although writers like Beckett and Kafka often seem to be writing allegories that entice a search for meaning, in fact their dramas and narratives resist interpretations that try to extract content from their work. Silence aids the modern artist by ensuring that the artwork expresses only itself and is not an expression of the world outside itself. Sontag suggests that composers like John Cage, painters like Jasper Johns, and novelists like William Burroughs create silence in their work to thwart the inroads of what she calls a bourgeois capitalist culture. Silence is one of the ways that art can maintain its autonomy.

In her conclusion Sontag returns to the idea of art as a spiritual project, noting that this type of art tends to exhaust itself. Since this is an art about raising consciousness, consciousness itself tends to become unraveled, and new works of art in the same vein must be created.

In "The Pornographic Imagination," Sontag views pornography as a social, psychological, and aesthetic phenomenon. She is mainly interested in the extent to which pornography can be examined as a literary genre. To do so, however, is to argue against the view that pornography is single-mindedly aimed at arousing sexual feelings and thus questions of style, motivation, and human complexity and characterization, it is thought, cannot arise. But critics have not looked very closely at pornography, largely because they take realism as their standard, and most works of pornography are not meant to be realistic. Indeed, if pornography is viewed as a form of fantasy akin to a genre like science fiction, there is no reason why pornography as such may not be deemed literary. In other words, only when critics make sexuality a special case can pornography per se be excluded from literary discussion. While few pornographic works may qualify as literature, Sontag insists that there are some, such as *The Story of O*, that meet the criteria involved in discussing a literary work. Like certain works of surrealistic art, *The Story of O* is about states of consciousness—which often verge on madness. A work of pornography, like any work of art, can be examined in terms of its "originality, thoroughness, authenticity and power of that deranged consciousness itself." Pornography can be said to excite the reader the same way a religious narrative may seek to entice converts, Sontag proposes.

Sontag then treats pornography as a genre of literature in its own right, observing that "sexual objects in pornography are made of the same stuff as one principal 'humor' of comedy." Thus the Marquis de Sade's Justine is like Voltaire's Candide—that is, both are rather vapid or empty characters who submit themselves to various ordeals; both characters are there for the reader's delectation. It is Candide's adventures that are paramount, not his feelings, and the same standard should be applied to pornography—which must suppress any complex exploration of character in favor of the events that arouse sexual appetite.

Viewed outside the context of Christian morality, which has condemned an exclusive focus on the body and on sex, pornography becomes an exploration of the demonic, or uncontrollable, forces that reside, as Sontag puts it, "beyond good and evil." Thus Sontag sanctions a work of literature that has O "progress simultaneously toward her own extinction as a human being and her fulfillment as a sexual being." *O* stands for a literature that is an "invocation of the erotic in its darkest sense and, in certain cases, an exorcism." Indeed, some writers—such as Georges Bataille—explore the possibilities of pornographic literature in order to expose the "limits of pornographic thinking."

The appeal of pornography to Sontag is that it is a complete universe; its autonomy appeals to a critic who seeks an art that is not an imitation of reality. Pornography is an assault on conventional standards which liberates one's thinking about sexuality. This aspect of the genre prompts Sontag to claim: "Ideally, it should be possible for everyone to have a sexual connection with everyone else." Linking pornography with "visionary obsessions," she criticizes modern capitalist society for not providing more outlets for people to transcend themselves.

Sontag does not quarrel with those who find most pornography brutalizing and coarse, yet she finds the worry about the spread of pornography "misplaced," since she regards it as just another kind of knowledge that will be counteracted by a "wider scale of experience." Any knowledge can shock the innocent, she suggests. And arguments against pornography may, in part, be arguments against knowledge. If knowledge is found disturbing, then what may be at stake is a far greater prospect of censorship than just campaigns against pornography. Like all forms of knowledge and art, pornography must be judged by its quality, not quantity.

"'Thinking Against Oneself': Reflections on Cioran," the last essay in Part I, considers the Romanian exile's place in the history of philosophy. He represents the personal, aphoristic, and anti-systematic kind of thinking that has emerged since the death of Hegel, one of the last great system builders in philosophy. Actually the Hegelian dialectic is built into Cioran's essays (as it is into Sontag's), so that she concludes "it is the destiny of every profound idea to be quickly checkmated by another idea, which it itself has implicitly generated." There, in a nutshell, is Hegel's exposition of the thesis-antithesis-synthesis paradigm. (It will account, in good part, for Sontag's willingness to contradict herself in the later stages of her career.)

Sontag acknowledges that Cioran's intellectual progenitor is Nietzsche, who dramatized the complex mind in conflict with itself. Cioran's true subject is, like Sontag's, an exploration of consciousness itself and how it operates. Thus he is most concerned with how humans construct the world—the world as human artifice. He may be politically reactionary, Sontag acknowledges, yet his willingness to explore how the mind overturns itself is implicitly a radical approach to thought.

Sontag also associates Cioran with the "Gnostic-mystical tradition"; that is, his probing of consciousness takes him away from the mainstream and toward the esoteric—knowledge that inheres in the Gnostic, not in his culture. Or as Sontag puts it, Cioran as Gnostic mystic engages in a "polemic with himself." What attracts Sontag is his role as exile writing in France, and the way that exile separates him from environment: "We must sever our roots, must become metaphysically foreigners," Cioran argues. It is a contention that intrigues the self-invented Susan Sontag, for it allows for the fullest freedom to improvise and invent. Thus she also emphasizes how devoted Cioran is to the "*will* and its capacity to transform the world." This is precisely the thinking she will endow her heroine with in her novel *In America*.

In "Theatre and Film," the first essay in Part II, Sontag canvases the distinctions between cinema and stage that critics have emphasized. While maintaining that film is a medium that can include representations of stage plays, she also suggests that a rigid separation between plays and films cannot be sustained. Thus while the camera may indeed open up space for the audience, many films such as *Les Enfants Terribles* are claustrophobic and as intense as any stage production. Kurasawa's filming of Gorky's play *The Lower Depths*, which takes place in one large room, is as cinematic as the director's *Throne of Blood*, a version of *Macbeth*.

Thus Sontag takes issue with Erwin Panofsky's view that the theatre space is "static" and cinematic space is mobile. All art is artifice, she insists, so that one art cannot be deemed more realistic than another. If film can establish through close-ups and camera angles an intimate relationship with the audience, it cannot match the rapport a stage play can establish with a live audience. Theatre is a means of "exchange" that film can never be. But there is no reason why a film cannot be theatrical.

Sontag does see one absolute difference between film and theatre. Whereas the former uses discontinuous space, the latter can only exist in continuous space. Montage, or the arrangement of screen images, is not available to the theatre, in which the actor must coexist with the single space available: the stage. But this divergence of cinema from theatre does not imply the superiority of film. One art should not be viewed as an advancement over the other—especially since both aim at a simultaneity of effect, which she likens to painting.

"Bergman's Persona" applies Sontag's anti-psychology bias to a reading of what she considers a cinematic masterpiece. The film is not about states of mind but about ontology, questions of being. Alma, one of the two main female characters, does not just hallucinate certain scenes, for Bergman does not mark off her fantasies from the "real" scenes in the film. Her illusions have the "look of objective reality." The film explores the fact that we hallucinate the "real." Alma and Elizabeth, her nurse, can be viewed as "two mythical parts of a single self." Alma and Elizabeth are doubles of each other, watching each other, so to speak, perform themselves. That Bergman is concentrating on the ontology of selfhood is evident to Sontag because he makes the viewer so conscious of the camera. Just as the two women violate or expose each other, so the film violates and exposes itself by using sequences such as the one in which a close-up yields a composite face—part Elizabeth, part Alma. The film's ultimate subject, Sontag concludes, is the "violation of the spirit." In other words, Alma's problems that have led to her silence are not merely personal; rather, they reflect the agony of existence, which no therapy can cure. They can only be shared or, in a sense, transferred to another personality as a form of "vampirism."

In "Godard," Sontag admires the French director's willingness to appropriate literature and the essay form into his films, his use of popular culture (Hollywood musicals), and his "juxtaposition of contrary elements." The result is an anti-narrative, a breaking up or fragmenting of the action, and once again an artifice that calls attention to itself. This playfulness with cinematic form enhances Godard's control over his own material, preventing him from succumbing to the conventions of filmmaking, especially to the psychologizing of character. By refusing to maintain the distinctions between past, present, and future, and by organizing his material as a continuous present, the director thwarts the idea of "depth" or "innerness." Rather, "each film is a provisional network of emotional and intellectual impasses." And it is Godard's refusal to resolve conflict that Sontag most admires. His films or stories are never resolved because there is no illusion established that they are taking place at another time. Instead the viewer is suspended within the art and unable to judge it from without.

Part III marks a departure in Sontag's work in that it concentrates exclusively on writing that is entirely political. "What's Happening in America" is her response to a *Partisan Review* questionnaire. She decries America as the "arch-imperium of the planet," holding the world hostage in its "King Kong paws." Sontag sums up American history by citing the "genocide" against native populations and its "culturally deprived, uprooted people." It is a land of "crude materialism" fed on the "fantasy of Manifest Destiny." She speaks of a "national psychosis" and of the country's "denial of reality." In Vietnam, President Johnson has simply expanded the country's "genocidal expeditions." For it is a "passionately racist country." The only sign of hope is young people. She approves of their interest in "Oriental thought and rituals" and their drug taking. At least they are dissenting from the status quo, realizing that there is "something terribly wrong with Western white civilization." Indeed the "white race *is* the cancer of history." It has "upset the ecological balance of the planet" and threatens its very existence. It is a "doomed country," though she takes heart in a new generation who are "alienated *as* Americans."

In "Trip to Hanoi," the last essay of *Styles of Radical Will*, Sontag mentions her previous inability to articulate her political convictions in print and her doubts that she could add much to the anti–Vietnam War movement by writing about her trip to Hanoi. She visited Hanoi without the intention of writing about it. Only on her return did she realize she had to write about it. But she writes filled with doubt about the validity of her "culture-bound" reactions. The fact that she and her two companions are treated like children bothers her. The Vietnamese are not only controlling, they speak in a simplistic, uniform style that is the antithesis of her own sophisticated manner. Vietnam seems to lack texture and nuance.

Sontag knows that she is expected to play a role as one of the "American friends of the Vietnamese struggle." This two-dimensional world reminds her of an earlier generation of intellectuals who took friendship trips to the Soviet Union and after tightly supervised tours extolled the superiority of the Communist system. Indeed, Sontag reveals that she was influenced by such fellow travelers but that she later was turned off by Communist rhetoric precisely because it was so rigid and philistine. Now with the war in Vietnam, she finds she can use terms such as "imperialism" and "capitalism" without embarrassment. Now Marxist vocabulary is in accord with her aesthetic sensibility, her "historical memory," and her vision of the future. Although she still finds it difficult to adopt the absolutist morality of her Vietnamese hosts, she confesses to an inclination to "assent" to it. If she cannot wholeheartedly embrace what she sees, in part it is because she is worried about "patronizing" it.

Sontag also finds that she misses the Western "world of psychology" in Vietnam's "monothematic" culture. She does not want to be "ironed out." Lacking the variety and sexiness of the Cuban Revolution, the Vietnamese cause seems stiff, formal, and devoid of irony. Yet Sontag constantly questions her authority to make such judgments, conceding that she might very well look "spoiled, corrupt, decadent" to the Vietnamese—just another soldier in the "armchair army of bourgeois intellectuals." Whatever her limitations, though, she finds herself happy in her hosts' company. She begins to admire their ingenuity, their public spirit and cheerful ethic of self-sacrifice which she regards as a valuable form of democratization. It is truly a "people's war," she concludes.

From her initial impression that the Vietnamese are simplistic, Sontag moves to the idea that Vietnam is a genuinely simple culture. "Existential agony" is not a term recognizable in such a society. Because they are united in a great cause, war is not, as in the West, a dehumanizing experience for individuals. There is not even any sign of bitterness, Sontag observes. American pilots, for example, are given better food rations than the Vietnamese themselves, she reports.

Now Sontag wonders if she has succumbed to a "phony sentimentality," indulging herself in the "ideology of primitivism" and creating a pastoral ideal that Westerners have sought in other cultures since the eighteenth century. No, she decides, North Vietnam "*deserves* to be idealized," for Sontag formed her impressions out of her "direct experience." In spite of the apparent endorsement of North Vietnam, Sontag spends a paragraph insisting it is not a "model of a just state." She acknowledges the brutalities of the system—such as forced collectivization and persecution of political dissidents. But almost immediately she concludes that North Vietnam is a "genuine substantive democracy much of the time." What is more, the North Vietnamese are "'whole' human beings, not split as we are."

In the last part of this long essay, Sontag returns to an assessment of America that is identical to her remarks in "What's Happening in America."

SONTAG READING SONTAG

Sontag explained to interviewer Edwin Newman that "The Aesthetics of Silence," the lead essay in *Styles of Radical Will*, was "Against Interpretation Revisited." She thought the latter work better because it explored the view not of the interpreter of art but of the maker of art. She presented the modern artist as deeply aware of art's limitations; the artist's recourse to silence was a kind of anti-art, or rather an art that exposes its own inability to fulfill the traditional claims of art: to be perfect, complete, whole. Her essay was also intended to counteract the romantic notion that all art is about self-expression. For Sontag, much of twentieth-century art is about making art, not about the artist's psychology. To Newman, she did not so much deny the connection between the artist's personality and art as to suggest there were better, more fruitful, and fresher ways to respond to art.

As with her previous books, Sontag saw reasons to change her opinion or approach. She wanted to write a better essay on science fiction, she told Maxine Bernstein and Robert Boyers. She found her juxtaposition of Cioran and John Cage "sophistical," she confided to Roger Copeland. She would take a more "historicist" approach, she continued, signaling an interest in history and historical context that would begin to dominate her work in *Under the Sign of Saturn, The Volcano Lover,* and *In America.*

Going to North Vietnam changed Sontag's view of the "possibilities of community," a view that had atrophied in the disillusionment of middle-class, urban life. It had stimulated her desire to be patriotic, even to wave an American flag, though she felt constrained not to do so because the flag had been co-opted as a symbol by "rightwingers." Still, when confronted with Newman's pressing questions about her politics, she sounded more hopeful than did her essays about the prospects for positive change. Nearly ten years later she told Jonathan Cott that her writing about North Vietnam was not only "true but helpful to people in a very immediate, practical way."

Twenty years later, Sontag viewed her role as critic and her trip to Vietnam quite differently. To Frances Kiernan, Mary McCarthy's biographer, Sontag described her visit to American prisoners of war: "I was really dumb in those days. But I still had my instincts and I thought, This is a terrible situation. I don't understand it and I don't know what's right. So I didn't deal with it in my book." The "terrible situation" Susan Sontag did not want to confront was the torture of American prisoners of war. Frances FitzGerald, author of the much acclaimed *Fire in the Lake*, a historical study of Vietnam, commented to Kiernan that neither McCarthy, who also wrote a book on Vietnam, nor Sontag "understood the Vietnamese very well."

CRITICAL COMMENTARY

Although *Styles of Radical Will* embodied Sontag's effort to fuse her aesthetics and her politics, very few reviewers or critics thought she succeeded. In the *New York Times*, Christopher Lehmann-

Haupt noted how fastidious Sontag was about metaphor when writing literary criticism and how glibly she used metaphor when describing the white race as the cancer of history. Emile Capouya, in the *Saturday Review*, deplored Sontag's effort to detach art from morality. On the other hand, Peter Berek, in *Commonweal*, lauded her for probing so deeply the experience of reading literature. Similarly Jonathan Raban, in the *New Statesmen*, praised the breadth of Sontag's writing, likening it to Emerson's "casserole style of essay writing." In *Encounter*, Martin Dodsworth observed a disjunction between Sontag's avidity for avant-garde art and the sober, traditional style of her essays. In the *Michigan Quarterly Review*, Gary Houston dramatized the paradox of the Sontag persona—at once a participant and aloof observer of the contemporary scene:

> I can picture her attending a performance of *Paradise Now*: A rabid, screaming actor, not knowing who she is, rushes up to her. He . . . demands that she not be afraid to *be herself*, violate the norms of the system, take off all of her clothes, and fornicate in the aisles—all expressed in saltier terms, of course. She patiently takes him aside to a corner and says, a bit amused but earnestly, "Look, I'm Susan Sontag. I know the Becks [founders of The Living Theater] and have followed their career for years. I know what you're trying to do and I congratulate you for it. But of course in my case it isn't necessary. Keep up the good work.

In fact, Houston's fantasy was not far wide of the mark. When Andrew Kopkind, a journalist and disco enthusiast, tried to engage Sontag in the music scene of the late 1970s, she did the obligatory tour but retained a cool, almost stiff attitude.

If Houston was amused by Sontag's attendance at spectacles of extremity and shrewdly imagined how she always stuck by her sense of self-control, Vernon Young in the *Hudson Review* saw her sponsorship of the avant-garde as self-serving and contemptible. Every essay in *Styles of Radical Will* was a "*ruse de guerre*, an ordering of her little circle of friends, a strenuously argued attempt to hold an untenable position," he wrote. She had all the "secondary attributes" of the revolutionary:

> an irreparable want of humor, a sweeping disregard of the nuances of history, a hatred of elites over which she does not personally preside, a faculty for translating all data into propaganda—and underneath it all, barely concealed, a private thirst to be devoured by something bigger, more forceful and simpler than herself: in her case an Apocalypse, which would nullify forever her compulsive quarrel with the Word.

Young's reference to the Apocalypse might have been provoked by Sontag's appearance on television during the seventh annual New York Film Festival. She told interviewer Jack Kroll that the world was in a bad way and that young people did not expect it to last long enough for them to enjoy their maturity.

Sontag's revolutionary attributes were secondary, Young observed, because she lacked the revolutionary's primary one: passion. She felt only resentment, he argued. She rarely entertained alternative points of view; her method was "*exclusive*; her strategy is that of the post-graduate seminar: from the matter at hand eliminate all normative, 'moral' considerations and concentrate on its linguistic and structural components." For certain types of films—such as *Persona*—her method was effective, he conceded. But her advocacy of pornography as a species of literature only proved, Young contended, how reductive and simplistic her political and aesthetic positions were. Was her kind of avant-garde art really necessary to break down sexual mores? Wasn't capitalism doing just as effective a job? he asked.

Young was skeptical of Sontag's revolutionary credentials, which looked to him like a form of sixties careerism: for example, she called a Leslie Fiedler essay "remarkably wrong-headed and interesting" for diverging from her touting of a new sensibility. "She always leaves a tip; she might need to be back in that town some day," Young commented.

Young was so angry that he had no room to acknowledge that the essays of *Styles of Radical Will* were more probing and less programmatic than *Against Interpretation*. As with her best essays in every period of her career, writers on the subjects she chooses (especially film, pornography, and art) cannot avoid tangling with her. There is scarcely a book that the eminent critic John Simon has written that does not take issue with Sontag on camp, on Godard, on virtually any subject he deems important. Art historian Arthur Danto makes similar bows in her direction—as do countless other critics of popular culture, photography, and disease.

What disturbed Young and other reviewers was the sheer solipsism of Sontag's work, the lack of any "milieu" or social context in her novels and in her criticism. Sontag herself would admit as much later in her career, when in interviews she lamented her earlier lack of historical vision. And her later novels are deliberate—often too deliberate—exercises in historical thinking.

Young noted that in Sontag's encomium to the North Vietnamese in "Trip to Hanoi" there is "never a hint of the 50,000 village headmen murdered in the Collective preparation of 1954; of prostitutes who had their breasts cut off for fraternizing with the French; of 1200 Laotian tribesmen, women and children among them, battered to death with clubs and guns (this is a mere incident in the history of Viet Cong atrocities)."

Even a critic as sympathetic to Sontag as John Leonard pointed out in *Life* how facile, how unproven Sontag's premises about "modern capitalist society" were. Even granting her argument that America was founded on genocide, it was hardly the first empire to act so violently. Why did she repeat Marxist simplicities? What about what the North Vietnamese had done to Thai, Meo, and Mung ethnic minorities? "She may have gone to Vietnam, but she never really left the solipsistic thicket of her questions, nor stopped singing the same song," Leonard concluded.

In *Partisan Review*, William Phillips provided one of the most thoughtful evaluations of Sontag's essays. She had bypassed American criticism, he argued, by seeking to look at art that was both popular and unconventional. Her best example of such an art was film, he thought. He praised the self-examination in "Trip to Hanoi," but he also regretted its lack of a "new or larger political perspective." Similarly Richard Gilman, in the *New Republic*, defended Sontag's kind of speculative criticism in the French tradition. He found her efforts to evoke a vision of art as sensual and spontaneous both fruitful and faulty. For example, had she really distinguished clearly between pornography and literature that had a sexual theme?

Sontag's search for new kinds of art segued into her quest for a new politics. She hoped that societies like Cuba, North Vietnam, and later Nicaragua would be able to combine socialist/Communist ideas with democratic principles. Initially, she thought that Castro's government was hospitable to artists, but by the early 1980s she concluded that Cuba and the other new Communist states had turned into repressive regimes and that communism itself had turned into "fascism with a human face"—as she put it in a controversial speech in 1982 at Manhattan's Town Hall.

But Sontag was never able to write the essay or the book that would lead her beyond the politics of *Styles of Radical Will*. Nor has she ever revised this book to reflect her changes of mind. Instead she has used interviews to repudiate certain statements—such as her notorious characterization of the white race as the cancer of history.

Not that Sontag did not try to formulate a new thesis—a paradigm that would explain her journey from fellow traveler to . . . what? This was her dilemma. As she admitted to Eileen Manion and Sherry Simon: "I'm not interested in giving aid and comfort to the neo-Conservatives. It's a crucifying dilemma. I was finally defeated by it. I spent a year and a half writing hundreds of pages and gave up." It is a stunning admission, because Sontag had recognized the need to reply to Paul Hollander's book, *Political Pilgrims: Travels of Western Intellectuals to the Soviet Union, China, and*

Cuba, 1928–1978, which had attacked her politics and put her in the camp of duped fellow travelers.

To articulate her dilemma as a concern about neo-conservatives, however, revealed that Sontag still thought in terms of cold war politics, of a left and right, of anti-Communists and anti-anti-Communists. In "Trip to Hanoi" she refers to herself as a "neo-Radical," meaning that she had resumed in a new context (the anti–Vietnam War movement) her old adolescent affinity with communism and its critique of capitalist/imperialist society. Although Sontag expresses her awareness in "Trip to Hanoi" that writers of the 1930s had been duped by stage-managed trips to the Soviet Union, so that they were not exposed to the massive tyranny of Stalinism, and though she concedes that her own trip to North Vietnam has been carefully orchestrated, she is nevertheless determined to endorse North Vietnam as a democracy. It is as if she felt compelled to make the same mistakes as an earlier generation of intellectuals. Like André Gide, her literary hero, who went to the Soviet Union and celebrated its accomplishment only to reverse himself later and admit communism was a fraud, so Sontag had to go to North Vietnam, support its ideology, and then announce years later that she had been misled.

This determination to transform the world into the projection of one's will inevitably leads back to Sontag's writing on Cioran and to the desire to think against oneself. In both aesthetics and politics, Sontag has fought against herself by creating the conditions in her life and in her writing that demand she contradict herself—or as Hippolyte puts it, to acquire and disburden herself of ideas. She has to try out one side of the argument and then adopt its opposite. This oscillation will become evident again when Sontag rethinks in *Under the Sign of Saturn* the comments she made on Leni Riefenstahl's work in *Against Interpretation*.

On Photography

(1977)

Between 1973 and 1977, Susan Sontag published six articles on photography in the *New York Review of Books*, then revised them for book publication. In book form the essays became less like book reviews and more aphoristic. Only in book form would readers find the provocative claim: "To collect photographs is to collect the world." Walter Benjamin, the subject of an essay in *Under the Sign of Saturn*, is a much bigger presence in *On Photography* than in the initial articles. The essays had evolved over nearly five years, and toward the end of this period Sontag's grasp of the relationship among words, meanings, and photographs had expanded. In fact, the development of *On Photography* exemplified the way Sontag preferred to work—revising and revising and revising until she had climbed, so to speak, to a height of observation.

SYNOPSIS

In the first essay, "In Plato's Cave," Sontag plays with the philosopher's fable of knowledge: the setting of a cave in which the only knowledge possible is what is seen in the reflections on a wall. That is to say, human knowledge of the world is secondhand, a reflection of the truth, not truth itself—a copy, not the original. St. Paul's statement that we see as through a glass darkly constitutes a similar comment on the human inability to see clearly, to grasp the whole of existence, let alone the divinity of God (St. Paul) or the ideal (perfect world of ideas) posited by Plato. Thus Sontag's first sentence carries moral, aesthetic, and almost religious connotations: "Humankind lingers unregenerately in Plato's cave, still reveling, its age-old habit, in mere images of the truth."

Photographs are seductive, Sontag implies, because they seem to offer genuine pieces of the world. Unlike literature, which is about the world, photographs seem to be the world itself. Photographs are taken to be miniatures of the world presented without interpretation. They seem to provide, in other words, instant access to the real and to the true.

The camera establishes a record. Photographs seem less biased than other media of communication and art. Yet photographs are an example of aggressiveness, of an invasiveness that reduces the substance of the world to a collection of images. Although the whole world suddenly seems available to anyone—the world is democratized—photography begins to develop as an art, emphasizing the techniques of the photographer.

While photography becomes a mass art, allowing families to collect images of themselves—in effect, to certify their experience—it also reduces reality to the "search for the photogenic." What is real is what can be photographed. A photograph gives a shape to experience, thus thwarting other efforts to interpret and respond to the world. The vocabulary of photography is predatory, for it emphasizes the idea of "shooting" and "aiming" a camera at things and people. The photographer takes possession of people, turns them into objects, and thus violates them. In this context the photograph's connection with death is apparent, for it freezes the moment and testifies to "time's relentless melt."

Photographs bring home the world in shocking, unforgettable ways because they fix an image and do not move on. Thus Sontag remembers her own sharp, deep, and instantaneous reaction to the first photographs she saw of Nazi concentration camps. But a part of Sontag also went "numb" as she absorbed what she saw, provoking her to contend: "images anesthetize"—especially repeated exposure to images which can make what is photographed seem less real and presumably less powerful.

Thus Sontag returns to the concern that photography is reductive. It only seems to expand the viewer's sense of the world. Photography fragments the world into a series of shots—images having no narrative thread. Instead of integrating a sense of the world, photographs atomize it. Photographs cannot explain, and they often become the focus of fantasy. While photographs can "goad conscience," they do not in themselves constitute knowledge. In sum, the world is not as accessible through photographs as has been thought. Photographs celebrate surfaces; they cannot probe the depths. "Today everything exists to end in a photograph."

In "America, Seen Through Photographs, Darkly," Sontag discusses how photographers have taken on Walt Whitman's program of absorbing the whole country through his art. As the essays's title implies, however, neither Whitman nor his latter-day followers can encompass a nation. No art, no medium, is that comprehensive, though photography can present remarkable facsimiles of the world. Photographs are a dim representation of the truth, the dark glass, as it were, of St. Paul's metaphor.

Sontag contrasts Edward Steichen's "Family of Man," a Whitmanesque exhibition at the Museum of Modern Art in 1955, with the Diane Arbus retrospective in 1972 at the same institution. Arbus's portraits of freaks lack Steichen's sympathy for the unfortunate. Her rejection of sentimentality and of a universalizing vision à la Whitman, bespeaks a cultural shift, Sontag suggests. In the 1960s, artists like Arbus felt freer to explore the freakish side of life, to move away from the consensus world of "The Family of Man." She calls Arbus's subject the "unhappy consciousness"—a term that brings these photographs into Sontag's own universe, in which explorations of the troubled minds of her characters and subjects predominates. Shooting her subjects head-on, Arbus does not concern herself with their moral implications. She is not teaching a lesson about humanity—as did Steichen's show. These are hard photographs without a redeeming social purpose. At the same time, Arbus is still within the Whitmanesque tradition in so far as she follows his injunction to treat all subjects democratically—as having equal value.

Sontag aligns Arbus with the surrealists, especially with their interest in the grotesque and their search for found art that is not contaminated by the artist's vision. Arbus was an innocent in the sense that she did not claim an agenda for her photography. Yet by severing herself from the Whitmanesque affirmation of America—his celebration of every American type—Arbus contributes to the surrealistic agenda that emphasizes the deformities of the country. Through Arbus and other photographers of her generation, America is indeed seen "darkly"—as the "quintessential Surrealist country," as a "freak show, a wasteland."

Sontag expands her argument in "Melancholy Objects," contending that photographs—often thought of as the most realistic art—are actually surrealistic. Even though it is surrealistic, photography itself has had a negligible influence on the medium, and even though most photographers would not describe themselves as surrealists, she maintains that in its blurring of the lines between art and real life, between what is made and what is found, photography is the true representative of surrealism: the "creation of a duplicate world, a reality in the second degree, narrower but more dramatic than the one perceived by natural vision." Photographs record the accidental—one of the prized goals of the surrealists. The sudden switches from one environment to another, which photographs can achieve so effortlessly, make it an art of radical juxtaposition, which is also the program of surrealism. Photographs can bridge time, cultures, classes, making "everyone a tourist in other people's reality, and eventually in one's own."

Photography becomes a melancholy object in the twentieth century because so much of it documents the fleeting beauty of nature, the loss of unspoiled environment, and a resulting romanticization of vanished worlds. In the hands of the consumer, the photograph becomes an instant item of nostalgia. As soon as a photograph is taken, it becomes a memento of the past. Americans may not have family heirlooms, but they can treasure old photographs. As in surrealism, the past becomes a collection of objects which can be manipulated. In effect, the past itself becomes surreal; it is separated from any context except the one supplied by the photograph. Photography patronizes reality and reduces it to a set of manipulable objects. "Photographers, operating within the terms of the Surrealist sensibility, suggest the vanity of even trying to understand the world and instead propose that we collect it," Sontag concludes.

In "The Heroism of Vision," Sontag claims that the influence of photographs is now so pervasive that they have become the "norm for the way things appear to us, thereby changing the very idea of reality, and of realism." While pictorial artists presented an interpretation or construction of reality, photography seems merely to "disclose" what is already there. This troubling equation of photography with reality means that photography can never show anything but the visible, making what is visible, on the surface, all that is available to the viewer—making history itself a mere spectacle. Photography isolates images, and the meaning of photographs can change by simply putting them in a new context. Thus photographs become "articles of consumption" and discrete items of "aesthetic appreciation." They stimulate and feed a greedy impulse—to acquire the world. The enormous visual impact of photographs apparently offers an insight into the world, yet beyond that impact there is little to be learned. Sontag quotes Arbus on photography: "The more it tells you the less you know."

In "Photographic Evangels," Sontag examines the extravagant and conflicting claims photographers have made for photography. Strikingly defensive in the apologias for their art, photographers have at once claimed that photography is intuitive or it is lucid, precise, and logical. Some argue, for example, that the photograph is a projection of the photographer's conception. Others have extolled it as a recorder of reality, of phenomena captured accurately by a camera. Photography is, in this perspective, a "promiscuous" way of seeing.

To Sontag, photography remains caught between its pretensions to being an art and an objective measuring instrument of reality. If it is an art, it has not yet developed a very extensive critical vocabulary and instead has borrowed largely from painting for terms like composition, lighting, and so on. Sontag doubts that photography is an art and calls it a kind of language or medium which has the "peculiar capacity to turn all its subjects into works of art."

In "The Image-World," Sontag invokes Plato again, pointing out that many thinkers have tried to dissociate truth or knowledge from the visible or from the image. Photography represents the tyranny of the visible in a particularly virulent form because the photograph seems to be a trace, a material representation of the very thing it represents. A photograph, not a painting, may be considered the "vestige" of a thing. A photograph seems an extension of its subject, so that the taker or possessor of a photograph feels he has some control over the world the photograph exhibits. Photography is a way of robbing the world of its substance, Sontag implies, citing the fears of primitive people who believe the camera will deprive them of their identities. Similarly Balzac had a theory that the body had a number of ghostly images, an aggregate of appearances so to speak. She links this idea to the need people have to secure their identities by having their pictures taken. Paradoxically, the more images there are in circulation, the less knowable the world is, for it can seem remote or elusive precisely because the images cannot be penetrated; they distance the viewer from reality even as reality seems to be brought closer to the viewer.

What photographs lack is a sense of process. Sontag contrasts her witnessing of an operation in China with what that same operation would look like viewed through a camera, which does the looking for the viewer. Reality is condensed and dramatized and foreshortened in ways that the participant/observer in the operating room does not experience.

The production of images is particularly useful to a capitalist society, Sontag argues, because images are such an aid to consumption. Watching and taking photographs stimulates the appetite for more images. In this sense, images consume reality, or make reality merely a matter of consumption. What is a copy, what is an original, no longer matters very much. The only antidote or therapy for this overdose of images is an "ecology not only of real things but of images as well."

Sontag reprises a good deal of her argument in "A Brief Anthology of Quotations [Homage to W.B.]." In this section she has collected quotations about photography to form some sense of the contradictory, back-and-forth argument that photographers and critics have engaged in for the last 150 years. Her homage is to Walter Benjamin, for he once expressed the desire to compose an entire book made up of quotations that fit seamlessly together.

SONTAG READING SONTAG

Sontag was surprised to learn that many readers of her book saw only negative implications in her use of the word "aggressive" as applied to photography. To say that something is aggressive is not, in itself, a "good or bad thing," Sontag told Jonathan Cott. Any form of life, she pointed out, constituted some form of aggression. And photography took place in a very aggressive world and in a human society based on aggression against nature. Just to use a camera, to ask someone to "stand still" was exercising a kind of control or aggression. The point of Sontag's book was not to attack photography—Sontag herself loved photographs, she insisted—but rather to call attention to a major form of activity and its consequences. It was also a way of exploring society and its contradictions. To Roger Copeland Sontag situated *On Photography* as part of her quest to "ask what it means to be modern." Speaking of photography and its surrealistic aspects was just another angle on modernism.

CRITICAL COMMENTARY

On Photography has proven to be one of Sontag's most successful and controversial books. Even the positive reviews tended to take issue with some of her judgments and perceptions. In the *Journal of Aesthetics and Art Criticism*, the distinguished critic Rudolf Arnheim praised Sontag's "rhapsodic" style and her ability to evoke the power of photography. Similarly, James Guimond, in the *Georgia Review*, saw the book as evidence of Sontag's "personal mythology," a kind of romanticism that invested her arguments about photography with intense feeling. In the *New Leader*, John Simon liked her dwelling on "unanswered questions in the place of false security and dangerous misconceptions." Michael Starenko, in the *New Art Examiner*, saw *On Photography* as an extended meditation, with thinking itself as the subject. Sontag's dialectical approach to her subject presented a portrait of Susan Sontag.

Robert Hughes, in *Time*, thought Sontag exaggerated photography's inability to narrate or to provide a social context. Similarly, Laurie Stone, in *Viva*, questioned Sontag's analogies: "If comparing cancer to an imperialist army distorts our conception of cancer, doesn't comparing a camera to a gun distort the reality of a camera?" Paul Lewis saw Sontag's constant juxtaposition of quotations and contradictory arguments about photography as exemplifying her definition of surrealism. In other words, how was her book any more satisfactory than the surrealism of photography?

In the *Times Literary Supplement*, George Elliott mounted one of the fiercest attacks on Sontag and on her book. He criticized her for observing that the "fact of her [Arbus's] suicide seems to guarantee that her work is sincere, not voyeuristic, that it is compassionate, not cold." Elliott wondered:

> Seems to whom—to the world at large, to Arbus's admirers, to all or some of those alert to current attitudes towards art and/or photography? More important does it seem that way to Sontag herself? She is usually very slippery in this respect, as she is here, being able to claim, or disavow ideas at her convenience so that, quite often, to pin her down is to appear ridiculous in the eyes of her camp.

Elliott's allusion to Sontag's camp conveyed the perception that Sontag brought to publication day her own troops; her books were generaled through the literary/intellectual world. In the war of ideas, Sontag armed her prose so as to ward off defeat, if not attack. Elliott fumed because he could not strip away her argument. There were too many layers of self-protection.

In *Esquire*, Alfred Kazin wondered about photography's influence on Susan Sontag. After all, she was a filmmaker, and yet her book did not deal with the impact of the genre on her own sensibility. He was looking for an extraliterary, autobiographical dimension that was absent from the book.

To Cary Nelson, one of Sontag's most astute critics, her self-protective language and ambivalent disclaimers were her way of dealing with her own critical consciousness, her argument with herself. She made a drama out of criticism, transforming it into a dialogue with herself. To Elizabeth Bruss, Sontag's adversarial stance toward photography was a way of defining her own sensibility. She expected her generalizations to inspire counterarguments. Thus Sontag's switches of position were not in response to fashion but to the inevitable inaccuracies of any generalization. As Nelson argued in a later essay, Sontag's aim was usually to upset or challenge received opinion.

In *On Photography*, however much one agrees or disagrees with her specific arguments, Sontag succeeds in thoroughly venting both the notion that photography is a realistic, documentary mode of perception, and the case for it as conscious art. Both views of photography cannot be true, Sontag points out, yet each view has its plausible proofs. By exposing the weaknesses of these contradictory claims, it is inevitable that Sontag would find herself attacked from all sides. Indeed, the book is written in such a way as to provoke objections, at some point, from almost every reader. This is surely the book's strength, even if it proves an irritant. Few books of analytical criticism are as tenacious as *On Photography* or as willing to invite the reader's disapproval. It is, in the final analysis, a book that keeps its subject in a state of perpetual discussion. It is one of the great books of American criticism because it exemplifies so vividly the life of the mind.

SEVEN

Illness as Metaphor

(1978)

SYNOPSIS

Sontag's short book argues that illness should not be perceived as a metaphor. Metaphors are interpretations attached to diseases, and as such sickness is judged in terms of morality and psychology. But people do not cause their diseases, Sontag insists, and they should not be blamed for them. Illness has physical and material causes; treating it as a manifestation of something else only obscures or retards medical treatment.

Tuberculosis and cancer are Sontag's main concerns. She points out that until a cure for tuberculosis was found, the disease was associated with certain types of personality, and a romantic mythology developed to explain why certain people contracted the illness. This line of explanation simply vanished as soon as the tubercle bacillus was discovered. The same will be the case with cancer and other diseases as soon as their physical causes are found.

The air of mystery inspired by certain diseases means that even doctors have contributed to serving patients badly by not telling them they have the disease and thus making it difficult for patients to secure the full range of medical interventions that might check, if not cure, their illness. As long as diseases such as tuberculosis and cancer are thought to stem from emotional or passionate natures, it will be harder for people to think they can overcome or at least treat their illnesses effectively. A patient's disease can be shrouded in such mystery that he or she can feel ashamed and to blame for his or her plight.

Tuberculosis was even thought to be a sign of superior intelligence or sensitivity. It was a disease often associated with poets and other literary figures. The wasting away of the body made the afflicted person seem otherworldly, dematerialized, and seemingly spiritualized. The dying person can seem ennobled and soulful. Cancer, on the other hand, does not have this mystique. It is associated with terrible pain and suffering, and with attacking parts of the body like the rectum or breast or bladder that are concealed and regarded as shameful. Cancer, moreover, is often presumed to be the result of an emotional maladjustment. The fever of TB is a sign of passion; the suffering of cancer, on the other hand, is viewed as the outcome of repressed emotion. Holding in feelings has damaged the body. Sontag traces this school of interpretation to Wilhelm Reich, who called cancer a "disease following emotional resignation." In so far as resignation itself is considered, tuberculosis and cancer have been viewed similarly: characters in literature give in to the disease and are defined, like Camille or Milly Theale in *Wings of the Dove*, by their passivity.

A culture of the TB sufferer developed in the nineteenth century into bohemianism, with the afflicted artist becoming a type of wanderer and dropout from society. Sontag cites the case of Robert Louis Stevenson's travels and exile in the Pacific and D. H. Lawrence's restless journeys. The disease seemed to fit the sufferer's character. If TB is the disease of the misfit or outlaw, cancer is the disease of the loser and the defeated. John Keats, Emily Brontë, and Edgar Allan Poe's characters succumb to tuberculosis as to an apotheosis; Ulysses S. Grant, Hubert Humphrey, and Robert A. Taft have had their cancers attributed to political reverses.

Thus cancer is not romanticized, and various studies have attributed certain personality traits as prone to cause or to be associated with cancer. Disease becomes psychologized as people are identified as cancer types. Such psychologizing is a pseudoscience in itself, offering the comfort of at least understanding why certain people contract the disease and others do not. In that sense the disease itself comes under a kind of control.

Whereas tuberculosis seemed a disease of the "sick self," cancer is treated like a science fiction scenario. The body is invaded by alien or mutant cells that outgrow the body's capacity to contain them. Images of disaster and annihilation ensue, especially when consciousness of ecological disaster pervades the culture, making the idea of a spreading plague or epidemic imaginable. Military metaphors abound as the disease is treated as a warlike threat that must be repelled.

Citing a range of authors from Machiavelli to Hobbes to Shaftesbury, Sontag acknowledges that disease as metaphor is endemic to human culture. Cancer, in particular, has become a staple of political discourse. Often the metaphor is no more than an expression of feeling. In other words, it does not describe fact or reality. As Sontag admits, "I once wrote, in the heat of despair over America's war on Vietnam, 'the white race is the cancer of human history.'" Now she considers modern disease metaphors "all cheap shots." She can understand the stress that provokes such use of metaphor, but she cannot condone it. Like all diseases that find their cures, cancer will no longer provide metaphors when its etiology is understood.

SONTAG READING SONTAG

Although Sontag did not acknowledge her own breast cancer in *Illness as Metaphor*, she admitted in several interviews that becoming ill had stimulated a series of questions: "What really goes on in the world of the sick? What are the ideas that people have?" Going to the hospital three times a week for treatment, Sontag heard people who were victims of "stupid ideas," she told Jonathan

Cott. She wanted to write a book that would help people in a practical way. She wanted to save lives.

Sontag's doctors had given her only a 10 percent chance to live more than two years after her mastectomy. But she embarked on a radical and experimental course of chemotherapy that lasted more than two years. To interviewers she admitted that her first reaction to the disease had been terror. She thought of it as a death sentence, a curse, and wondered, "What did I do in my life that brought this on?" When a benign tumor had first been discovered in her breast several years earlier, she wrote a letter in December 1969 to actor/director Joseph Chaikin: "I never can tell when I'm feeling bad if it's physical as well as psychological, and my tendency is to think that it's always psychological, and therefore, ultimately, my fault." In the early weeks of her recovery from the mastectomy, Sontag tortured herself with the idea that one could get cancer from holding in one's grief.

It took Sontag a good month to work through these negative feelings, to realize how much she wanted to fight for her life. She became angry about the way ill people felt ashamed and humiliated, the way they blamed themselves for their disease. They were frightened and acted as if what they had was obscene. Paralyzed with worry, they became incapable of coping with their disease. Cancer had a special stigma. It was not like having heart disease. Cancer patients were treated to a conspiracy of silence. Sontag became outraged when she noticed that the hospital sent her mail in unmarked envelopes as though the contents were pornographic.

To Jean-Louis Servan-Schreiber, Sontag suggested her book was a "study of language . . . a certain way of talking." The language surrounding cancer, for example, mystified the disease, and metaphors for cancer promulgated a passive attitude. Such diseases became myths that played havoc with people's lives. Her attack on the myths was a kind of political act, she implied, when she compared *Illness as Metaphor* to "Trip to Hanoi." Both works were passionate efforts to make a difference in contemporary consciousness.

Sontag said she was also attacking the idea of illness as "interesting," as a distinguishing mark. There was nothing inherently interesting about illness, and she thought it dangerous to create separate categories or privilege certain kinds of experiences and phenomena. As she emphasized to Roger Copeland, she had written *On Photography* to show that "one of the ways in which photographs are untrue is that they make *everything* interesting."

Sontag was perplexed by those who thought her book detached because she did not include her personal experience with cancer, pointing out to Wendy Lesser: "It was a book written in the heat of rage, fear, anguish, terror, indignation—at a time when I was very ill and my prognosis was poor." Sontag made a distinction between being personal and being passionate: "I often feel that the best way to convey the passions I feel is not by speaking about myself."

CRITICAL COMMENTARY

Like *On Photography*, *Illness as Metaphor* proved quite controversial, though most reviewers respected Sontag's effort as an honorable and courageous study of a complex subject. John Leonard, in the *New York Times*, thought the book one of Sontag's best, without distracting mannerisms or glibness. Walter Clemons, in *Newsweek*, called it an "exhilarating literary performance" and an advance over Sontag's previous work. Edwin Kenney, in the *New Republic*, liked her "combative" approach to ideas and her searching exploration of metaphors. In the *Atlantic*, Benjamin DeMott declared that with *Illness as Metaphor* Sontag had redeemed herself. Her earlier work had seemed thin to him, as if she had removed herself from common experience and existed only in her self-involved, intellectual arguments. Now she was beginning to write books that challenged the "dogmas about the human condition that have shaped the work of the artists she has most admired and imitated."

William Logan, in the *Chicago Tribune*, spoke for many reviewers who thought Sontag was too literary; that is, all her examples of attitudes toward illness were taken from literature. She seemed to have little historical grounding in the subject. In *Psychology Today*, Maggie Scarf criticized Sontag's exaggeration of her literary evidence. She also speculated that cancer sufferers were reacting to their mortality at least as much as to cancer itself. Denis Donoghue, in the *New York Times Book Review*, saw more rhetoric than evidence in Sontag's arguments. Nigel Dennis, in the *New York Review of Books*, chided her for an extravagant use of her own metaphors while condemning those of others. Similarly Dan Jacobson, in *Commentary*, noted that Sontag rejected the psychologizing of cancer even as she engaged in her own psychologizing of society. In the *Listener*, Anthony Clare suggested that just because the physical cause of an illness such as tuberculosis had been discovered, it did not mean other factors did not contribute to contracting a disease.

The question these conflicting reviews raise is the degree to which Sontag was obligated to consider arguments counter to her own. She intended, as she made clear in interviews, to rouse people, to get them to take charge of their medical cases by seeking the best advice and by remaining active in the search for a cure. In other words, she rejected any view of illness that might depress a person and prevent the best treatments. Even if psychology were a factor in contracting illness, her mission was to downplay it. Sontag was not canvasing every conceivable way of looking at illness. She was trying to strike out the most harmful responses to disease and to emphasize the most helpful. She was writing not a history, or even a literary study as such, but a polemic—a sharply worded piece of writing meant to persuade readers and provoke them to action.

Arguments that are constantly qualified and questioned, rebutted and rephrased, cannot incite readers to action. *Illness as Metaphor* is for readers who want to act on their feelings and who want a clear path to a solution. Some reviewers and critics chastised Sontag for not being more thoughtful, which is to say more cautious. But that was not her purpose. She wanted clean lines and contours for her argument.

To appreciate the uniqueness of *Illness as Metaphor*, compare it to *On Photography*, which is constantly circling and doubling back on itself. Sontag's arguments multiply in that book, and she repeats the same arguments, in different form, from one chapter to another. She is creating an argument with herself; she wants to keep alive the ambiguity of photography as a subject.

That there may be historical, sociological, psychological, and philosophical arguments that Sontag does not entertain in *Illness as Metaphor* is important to realize yet almost beside the point. More than any other book Sontag has written, *Illness as Metaphor* moves ahead. It has the progressive feel of someone recovering from an illness, as Sontag herself recovered from her cancer.

There is always some sleight-of-hand at work in a polemic, however. If Sontag argues against metaphor, against comparing illness to something that it is not, she also (as critics observed) employs metaphors to her advantage. She cannot really be against metaphor any more than she can really be against interpretation. But she exaggerates her argument to point out a danger—the danger of taking metaphors and interpretations too seriously. Neither metaphor nor interpretation is the thing itself. Having had cancer—the real thing—Sontag became wary of using the word cancer to describe other phenomena.

Like all of Sontag's books, *Illness as Metaphor* was written to start an argument. As Maggie Scarf put it: "I have obviously stopped to take exception, to argue, to quarrel with some of her points. But I found her book unfailingly exciting, like nothing else on the subject I have ever read." With her book, Susan Sontag saved lives.

EIGHT

I, etcetera

(1978)

After the publication of *Death Kit* in 1967, Sontag continued to write fiction but found herself unable to complete a new novel. But in the intense period of creativity that brought forth *On Photography* and *Illness as Metaphor*, she returned to various stories and parts of unfinished novels and put together a collection of short fiction that exemplified her desire to write innovative and experimental creative prose. As the collection's title implies, this was Sontag's most autobiographical book; her fiction seemed closer to the memoir form than to the conventional short story. The book is dedicated to "M," Sontag's mother. The use of only an initial suggests the half-disguised autobiographical origins of the "I" in these stories.

SYNOPSIS

"Project for a Trip to China" is the China of the narrator's imagination. She has never been there, but she begins to plan her itinerary, the sites she will visit, the bridges she will cross. She says she has always wanted to go to China. She thinks the desire dates back to before her birth, for she thinks she was conceived in China. She wonders whether she should write or telephone M—presumably to ask her about her birth. She mentions that her father was a fur trader in China (so was Sontag's father). Her parents (the narrator's and Sontag's) brought back trophies and souvenirs from China, which the narrator (I/Sontag) saw as a child. She told her first-grade classmates that she was born in China, though she knows she was not.

M is presented as an aloof figure who tells I/Sontag that in China "children don't talk." Such comments suggest that the narrator's "project" is to recover the family history that her mother will not discuss. At any rate, I/Sontag announces at school that she is a "half-orphan." Her mother had come home from China in 1939 without her father, and the narrator later learned that her father died there. China comes to represent the outside world, a destination that I/Sontag craves in her Southwest (Arizona) "desert childhood, off-balance, dry, hot."

To go to China is to recover a part of her father. "I still weep in any movie with a scene in which a father returns home after a long desperate absence, at the moment when he hugs his child." The narrator mentions her trip to Hanoi in 1968 when she acquired her first Chinese object, sneakers, and she thinks of the photograph of her father in a rickshaw. Thus the story is, in the narrator's words, "a trip into the history of my family." She remembers her father's partner, Mr. Chen, who taught her at four how to eat with chopsticks. She mentions David (Sontag's son) who wears her father's ring.

Throughout these personal memories, the narrator meditates on the meaning of journeys, of colonial governments, and of revolutions, and she intersperses quotations from Chairman Mao. China was a land of oppression in her parents' day, but the country has disburdened itself of foreign domination. The narrator hopes to disburden herself of a lifelong grief, to go to China, and then to Honolulu (where Sontag's mother lived) for another meeting with M, though I/Sontag does not sound very hopeful, for she has been "exhausted by the nonexistent literature of unwritten letters and unmade telephone calls that passes between me and M."

In effect the narrator, the I of the story, and Sontag have made a literature out of frustrated longings. As the story's concluding sentence has it: "Perhaps I will write the book about my trip to China before I go." Sontag did go to China, and she never wrote about her trip.

"Debriefing," with its allusions to the narrator's meeting at Harvard's Widener Library with Julia (when the narrator was nineteen and Julia twenty-three), to Simone Weil, and to the Manhattan setting, is another thinly disguised autobiographical sketch, with the suicidal Julia standing in for the suicidal Susan Taubes (see Chapter 3), who took her life by walking into the Hudson River. Julia wonders about the connections and relations of things. Does one leaf lying next to another exemplify some kind of order in the world, or are they randomly juxtaposed? The bigger question is whether the world itself has a meaning, a connectedness. The narrator tries to stop her friend from so much speculation, as if it leads to the cliché "That way lies madness." But that is precisely Julia's problem: she wants to know whether reality is determined or purely accidental. Julia's wondering infects the narrator, who asks whether one character she names Doris is related to two other Dorises who appear in the "story." Is there a story? Can we be debriefed about reality? seems to be the question in this exploration of the seeming anarchy of contemporary life. The Dorises are like so many leaves scattered about the landscape.

Julia's response to the apparent chaos is to withdraw into her apartment. While other people make an effort or are content with the surface meanings of life, Julia shuts down, not even washing herself. The narrator tries to get Julia to "come out and play with me." While other people tap each other's phone calls and perform "bedroom feats" for video cameras, Julia is "throwing away her children." The narrator reads graffiti that seems to echo Simone Weil's message that "there is no end to suffering." Julia won't talk to her father who is (like Susan Taubes's father) a renowned psychiatrist.

Sounding very much like the Susan Sontag who extols E. M. Cioran in *Against Interpretation*, the narrator swoops into Julia's life, acknowledging the "pessimism of the intellect, optimism of the will!" But Julia jumps in the river while the narrator clings to a rock, like Sisyphus, doomed to repeat her futile efforts and unwilling to let anything "tear me away from this rock."

"American Spirits," like many of the other stories in *I, etcetera*, has an allegorical, generic feel. The characters seem merely tokens of ideas. Thus Miss Flatface, inspired by Ben Franklin and Tom Paine, leaves her husband and family for the lure of Mr. Obscenity. She has left the flatness of her middle-class, conventional life for the more pungent world of "swarthy" people who talk communism and mix races. Inspired by James Fenimore Cooper and Betsy Ross, Miss Flatface continues patriotically and dutifully (presumably in her quest to find an American identity). But this immersion in self-gratification apparently prompts Mr. Obscenity's ultimatum: Miss Flatface can engage in an orgy or be expelled from his company. Choosing the latter, she finds herself alone for the first time, contemplating whether or not she has become a feminist. Now her inspirations are Edith Wharton and Ethel Rosenberg. Trying to make her escape (from where, to what, is not clear), Miss Flatface is confronted by Inspector Jug, who announces that he has "gotten wind of what yer up to and it won't wash." Mr. Obscenity reappears to claim her, but she escapes, having found her vocation as a prostitute—chided by the spirits of William Jennings Bryan and Leland Stanford when she does not get a good price for her services. Although both Mr. Obscenity and Inspector Jug reappear, Miss Flatface now eludes their pursuit, declaring she is a free woman. Then she falls in love again—this time with Arthur, who looks like Jim (her first husband) but is not. "Nor am I I," Miss Flatface concludes. Yet she is afraid to go out much, rightly fearing the reappearance of Mr. Obscenity and Inspector Jug, who do show up again at the Blue Star bar and accost Arthur. After Miss Flatface laughs off this incident, she falls mortally ill after eating a taco. She leaves a will addressed to Jim, Inspector Jug, and Mr. Obscenity. At the funeral home, Jim and Arthur share confidences, and Miss Flatface in heaven "watched approvingly."

In "The Dummy," the narrator mentions that his life has been "intolerable" and his solution is to make out of Japanese plastics a dummy to take his place at work and at home, leaving the narrator free to observe life without any responsibility. The narrator has escaped all confinements and obligations of domestic and public life. Then the dummy falls in love with Miss Love at work. The dummy threatens suicide unless the narrator builds a dummy of a dummy so that dummy 1 can go off with Miss Love while dummy 2 will stay with the narrator's wife and go to work. The narrator reports that nine years later both dummies are happily married with families. The narrator visits both dummies who welcome their "shabby" looking creator who congratulates himself for having "solved in so equitable and responsible a manner the problems of this one poor short life that was allotted me."

"Old Complaints Revisited" is an ambiguous narrative about the entanglements of group identity. What group is never specified. The point is that the narrator is both attracted to and repelled by group-think: "I want to leave but I can't." The "I" is not identified as male or female. Sounding at times like a Communist or cultist, the narrator admits: "it's a privilege to be a party to their error." In other words, to be excluded from the group is to feel bereft and without privilege.

The organization has, of course, an organizer, the charismatic figure who promotes a sense of exclusivity: "what unites us is rather what we reject," the narrator notes. Like the Communist party, the organization attracts distinguished writers, and it appeals to those seeking to be different. Yet membership in the group is isolating, and it narrows an individual's choices. Complicating the narrator's indecision is the fact that it is not exactly clear how to leave the organization, since it seems merely to divide itself into sects, which perpetuate in new ways the life of the organization. Then, too, it has stimulated the narrator's mind. Exile might prove too high a price to pay for independence.

The narrator who has served as a translator for the organization is now caught in several layers of translation problems, that is, how to translate to the reader and to the organization's members exactly what the organization is. How to translate the narrator into language since "I'm more than my voice"? The last section of the story seems to pose the problem of the individual and the group, which defies translation (explanation). It is an old complaint (an old philosophical problem) revisited.

Next to "Project for a Trip to China," "Baby" is the most autobiographical story in *I, etcetera* (see critical commentary). A husband and wife consult a psychiatrist about their disturbed child, "Baby," who seems to range in age from infancy to the teens. They regard him as their creation in every sense of the word. Although the parents talk to the psychiatrist, only their voices are heard responding to questions that must be inferred from their answers. They become increasingly hysterical at their failed efforts to control Baby. The more they try to guide him, the more rebellious he becomes until they reveal that he has plotted to poison them. They, in turn, begin to dismember him as the surest way to keep him from leaving home and disobeying them. Metaphorically speaking, their dissection of his personality has led to this dismemberment of his person. The destruction of family life completes itself at the end of the story when the parents tell Baby he is not going to live forever. Then they exclaim to the doctor, "Why did our Baby have to die?"

"Dr. Jekyll" is only in the loosest sense a rewriting of Robert Louis Stevenson's classic tale *Dr. Jekyll and Mr. Hyde*. The story is, however, another exercise in doubling that is the subject of "The Dummy," and it raises questions about identity, about what an "I," a single self, can mean given the divergent impulses of individuals.

The main character is Dr. Utterson, the director of the "Institute for Deprogramming Potential Human Beings." He seems to derive from Sontag's interest in the Nietzschean hero (Utterson is the "master magician, the one beyond good and bad"), and he is the Gnostic sage whose esoteric knowledge attracts and subdues his patients, acolytes, and enemies. Utterson is Jekyll's nemesis, for Utterson remains in control even as Jekyll seems to have exhausted his identity and considers trading his body for Hyde's, his ex-patient. But then Jekyll turns on Hyde, trying to murder him with a bicycle chain (Hyde had advised Jekyll to commit a crime as a way to secure his freedom). Jekyll is sent to prison and then hears that Hyde has committed suicide. Utterson's concluding comment is, "Everybody is free to do as he or she likes."

"Unguided Tour" is about the traveling self, the search for identity. An unnamed voice (not even clearly the narrator of the story) seeks beauty, transcendence, the eternal, but is beset with thoughts of the temporary and the transient. More poem than story, "Unguided Tour" evokes an anxious state of consciousness, which is constantly challenged by another questioning voice, though both voices may be the dialogue of one self expressing the divergences of the self. Whereas "Project for a Trip to China" is about a trip before it is taken, "Unguided Tour" includes excerpts from guidebooks that are presented after the trip. (Sontag's film of this story makes clear that much of it takes place in Venice, but in the story the location is obviously mental, not geographical.) The voice or voices seem, at the end, to have come to the end of their journey, since he/she/they (it is not clear) have been "everywhere." And then there is a correction: "I haven't been everywhere, but it's on my list." Having reached this point, it is announced (in italics) "*The end of the world*," which is followed by the negation: "This is not the end of the world," the final words in *I, etcetera.*

SONTAG READING SONTAG

"As a *reader*," Sontag told Jonathan Cott, she thought the stories of *I, etcetera* had a "theme in common—which is the search for self-transcendence, the enterprise of trying to become a different or a better or a nobler or a more moral person." Travel was one way of expressing this search for an elsewhere that might better define the self. It is why she concluded *I, etcetera* with a story that evokes the "great longing for another place. To make this place another." It is why she says the location of "Unguided Tour" is "as it were, everywhere." It is why *I, etcetera* begins and ends with stories about travel, Sontag pointed out. But the search has contradictory consequences, especially for Miss Flatface, the narrator in "The Dummy," and the characters in "Dr. Jekyll." As Sontag observed to Amy Lippman, the fiction often presents the theme "ironically."

She suggested her characters were trying to "wake up" and to change their lives. This involves an assertion of the will, a "theme in most of the stories," Sontag pointed out to Wendy Lesser while also acknowledging something

> desperate in all that talk about the will.
>
> Again, it's something personal—I feel in many ways self-created, self-educated. There's some truth in that, but it's also part of that national cultural equipment. Americans have a tendency to overestimate the will—hence all those therapy groups, and endlessly renewable projects of self-reclamation, transformation, detoxification, rebirth, that Americans are so fond of.

Certainly stories such as "American Spirits," with its constant evocation of American prototypes of the will and self-improvement (such as Ben Franklin and Tom Paine), evoke and satirize the American penchant for believing in a perfectible self. Sontag went on to say that the will was no longer so important for her in the "same raw way" since her cancer and her resulting proximity to death. (In fact she underestimated how important the will and the idea of self-renewal would be later in her career.)

Sontag also asserted to Cott that she did not "identify completely with the voices" even of her most autobiographical story, "Project for a Trip to China." She also told Amy Lippman that her "impulse" was "mostly anti-autobiographical." She very rarely drew directly on herself or on people she had known. She wanted to divorce her first two novels from herself by making the narrators male. Yet she has readily admitted the autobiographical elements of *I, etcetera* and that they had given her "access" to her life. About "Baby" she remarked that she had used experiences from both her own childhood and her son David's. She also commented to Cott on her connection to the theme of the story:

> I know that parents are also monsters and are experienced correctly by their children that way. They're so much bigger; when you're a small child, your parents are giants! So I had to face up to all those complicated feelings in a nonsimplified way: my feeling of victimization as a child, which every child understands, and my also having been a parent.

Quite aside from the themes of her story, however, Sontag emphasized the unity of form and technique: "a series of adventures with the first person." To have an "adventure," suggests the multiple I's or the etcetera of Sontag's title, which she alludes to in her comment that the theme of "duplication" or "replication" suffuses much of her essay writing and her fiction. In this context "The Dummy" is simply an explicit restatement of Sontag's pervasive theme. There can be two or more selves in one person, just as two people (the parents of "Baby") can talk as one. The form of the stories, in other words, is meant to mimic the process of acquiring and jettisoning selves, what Sontag calls "accumulation" and "disburdenment."

CRITICAL COMMENTARY

I, etcetera received mixed but sympathetic reviews. Reviewers were impressed with Sontag's virtuoso use of language and her surprising identification with her American roots. Anatole Broyard, in the *New York Times*, for example, praised her lyricism in "Project for a Trip to China" and the Americanness exhibited in "Unguided Tour." John Breslin, in the *Washington Post*, linked her argument in "The Pornographic Imagination"—that pornography depicts extreme states of mind—to her own style in stories such as "American Spirits." In the *New Leader*, Daphne Merkin recognized Sontag's daring fictional experiments, some of which flopped while others were quite moving and perceptive. Frances Taliaferro, in *Harper's*, found the stories too cerebral and "gimmicky." Pearl K. Bell, in *Commentary*, thought the book's struggle with language reminiscent of "The Aesthetics of Silence," which argued that certain artists found that language could as easily betray meaning as convey it. Todd Gitlin's review in the *Progressive* called the stories "scraps" that did not cohere, since they lacked a historical context. Novelist Anne Tyler, in the *New Republic*, admired Sontag's verve and boldness but also judged the fiction incomplete because its author was too self-involved, too enamored of her own fiction to see the reader's objective requirements.

I, etcetera is Sontag's most personal book, her effort to fathom and to repair, through literature, the devastating losses of her childhood: the death of her father and the estrangement of her mother. Sontag lacked what every child psychologist insists is necessary: a mother to mirror her moods. Mothering involves some degree of sacrifice and selflessness, though who can be sure about the right proportions? That is the dilemma Sontag explores in "Baby." The story grew out of her earliest period with David, when she was only twenty, when she and her husband would say, "The baby, how's the baby?" The story is set in Southern California. The baby reads comics, Poe, and Jack London—the very reading Sontag herself enjoyed as a child. He is precocious, speaking in complete sentences "right off the bat." Like the child Susan Sontag, he has a chemistry lab. He keeps a journal, and his parents want him to have the piano lessons that Sontag pestered her mother for but never got. Baby rejects his parents, saying he comes from Krypton, and he dreams of winning the Nobel Prize. (Sontag had similar dreams after reading a biography of Marie Curie.) His parents complain that he is "so withdrawn" and such a puritan. He edits his high school newspaper (so did Sontag). He is stoical. He even goes to the Wilshire Ebell Theater mentioned in "Pilgrimage" (Sontag's memoir of her adolescence) and has a classmate just like Sontag's who is sent to San Quentin. Baby, in other words, is Sontag imagining herself as Baby and as her son David. As Baby grows up, however, his behavior becomes un-Sontag—that is, he becomes his own person and his characteristics take on those of David Rieff. He has trouble in school, he takes drugs, and his parents want him in therapy. They begin the story "very sure" of themselves and end in a cry of pain, completely at a loss as to what to do with their son. They dote on him, but his separateness destroys them.

The story is as much about the breakup of a marriage as it is about bringing up a child. As the parents focus on their child, their separate selves emerge. They begin talking about taking separate vacations. They have affairs. They decide to get a divorce, then put it off, worrying about its impact on their child. Eventually, in this surrealistic treatment of childhood and marriage, Baby becomes the parents' exclusive focus, and they cut off an arm and a leg so that he cannot get away from them.

The story dramatizes how parents try to enforce infancy and never really see their offspring as adults, and how children reject home and family in favor of self-absorption. But the story also derives from the experience of a "complicated marriage" in which a couple who thought of themselves as so close came to see that in fact the very idea of home and family was driving them apart. At least Sontag saw it that way; Rieff would take years to come around to an assessment that could serve well as a gloss on "Baby," telling Michael D'Antonio:

> I was a traditional man. I thought marriage was for having children, a traditional family. I just couldn't adjust to the kind of family life she wanted. You see, there are families and anti-families. Ours was the latter, I suppose.

In "Baby," a traditional set of expectations is systematically deconstructed, and what the parents think they want is not what they get. Their "Baby" is a projection of their fantasies about traditional family life. He is there, so to speak, to thwart them—and to express Sontag's lamentation, her sad but also astringent recognition that traditional family life was not for her.

Sontag's young adulthood is also canvased in *I, etcetera*, with a veiled portrait of herself entering intellectual life in "Old Complaints Revisited." There the narrator, who has a mother who is "a heavy drinker," turns to a professor at the university she attends. He bears a striking resemblance to Philip Rieff, dressing nattily in three-piece suits and affecting an "arrogant manner." The narrator responds to him with the "pathos of youth." Like Rieff, he is an "internationally acclaimed expert in his abstruse field." She is attracted to his asceticism, his austerity and dedication. Metaphorically speaking, the self-contained unit of man and wife and his esoteric expertise constitute a kind of group-think probed in "Old Complaints Revisited." That Sontag is thinking quite specifically of Rieff is clear from details that do not have to be in the story but do form part of Rieff's biography—such as references to his "poor and uneducated family." The narrator of "Old Complaints Revisited" shares with Sontag the sense of self-creation and a separation from one's background. Rieff will return to Sontag's fiction in the preface of *In America*, which contains her harshest portrait of the "organizer"whom it took her ten years to separate from.

The overarching theme of *I, etcetera*, then, is Sontag's argument with tradition and convention. Characters such as Miss Flatface rebel against their commonplace lives. Julia in "Debriefing" cannot cope with a world that muddles on in spite of its absurdity, its inability to connect one person with another, one idea with another. The narrator in "The Dummy" just withdraws from society, a society so routinized that no one can tell the difference between him and his substitute. The narrator in "Old Complaints Revisited" is torn between finding an identity inside and outside the group. The consciousness on an "unguided tour" or the I of "Project for a Trip to China" seeks to be somewhere else, with travel itself as the metaphor for their inability to settle anywhere. The project of becoming or maintaining or transforming the self is so all-consuming in *I, etcetera* that the reader is left suspended—that is, ungrounded. This may be Sontag's intent, since she finds this anxiety about the self so prevalently American, and American spirits are clearly her subject in this book. The idea of the quest for a new self energizes her, but with no end in sight the stories do seem to dissipate their own considerable power.

NINE

Under the Sign of Saturn

(1980)

This collection is a series of portraits and, to some extent, narratives of the intellectual figures who have influenced Susan Sontag. As she would later remark, the storylike elements of this volume presage her full-time return to fiction. Each essay, as in *I, etcetera*, is also a disguised autobiography, for again Sontag has not hesitated to say that the essays are a projection of her own saturnine sensibility.

SYNOPSIS

"On Paul Goodman" is an obituary which expresses Sontag's admiration for a writer who wrote in many different genres: poetry, fiction, drama, and various kinds of nonfiction. Such writers are resented, Sontag claims, because they do not settle on one type of writing but claim a mastery of many. She extols Goodman's "breadth of moral vision." She likes his honesty about his homosexuality, which came many years before "coming out of the closet" was "chic."

Sontag admits that on her many encounters with Goodman he always "rebuffed" her. Indeed, she makes a point of the disjunction between his cool treatment of her and her passionate attachment to his work. He was her "hero," she declares—even though they never were able to make conversation. The essay is framed by references to her "tiny room in Paris," a kind of Spartan cell where she has been living and working for the past year. Goodman—or perhaps the idea of Goodman—inspires her to continue writing.

In "Approaching Artaud," Sontag argues that he is one of those authors who question the conventional idea of authorship. He is like other modernist writers who are aiming at conveying the "total book," that is, the complete contents of consciousness. And no single work of literature can contain consciousness in this way. Artaud's work, in other words, points beyond itself; it is literature that simultaneously points out the limitations of literature.

Since Artaud's goal is to convey consciousness, and consciousness is a process, no piece of writing can entirely satisfy him. On the contrary, he feels his ideas shifting within him, and in that sense he is what Sontag calls a "victim of consciousness." Ideas are not things he can possess; at best he can only assess the quality of his consciousness.

Art then is a "trope for the functioning of all consciousness— of life itself." Although he rejected the surrealists' faith in art itself as a counter to conventional reality, the pessimistic Artaud nevertheless shared with the surrealists a disdain for the status quo and identified with the mad and the alienated in a quest for art as a "revolutionary mission." Sontag acknowledges the contradictory quality of his writing (just as she admires Cioran's concept of "Thinking Against Oneself").

The theatre is Artaud's natural medium since he conceives of art as a dramatic performance. Theatre can approach the idea of total art since it uses the human body and draws on the other arts. At the same time, in order to embody human consciousness the theatre must become more spontaneous without the "mediation of an already written script." In this sense, Artaud's writing is an attack on conventional theatre. His theatre is one that is coming out of confinement. It becomes adversarial, a means of opposing and even alienating his own audience. The irony is that for his theory to succeed, his theatre must fail.

Artaud's theatre is the remedy for a failing culture. It is a means to renew the sense of life. This new theatre draws on non-Western cultures, on subversive trends within Western history—such as Gnosticism—and on a "pure playfulness" that allies him to the surrealists and other modernist writers like Nietzsche, D. H. Lawrence, and Ezra Pound, who call for a cultural revolution. But the pursuit of a knowledge beyond society, or suppressed by society—which is one definition of Gnosticism as Sontag uses the term—can lead to paranoia and the madness that eventually overtook Artaud. The artist becomes the deviant who makes claims to a knowledge that is beyond good and evil. This knowledge or "gnosis" isolates Artaud as artist, but it also makes him an inspiring, undaunted figure, a hero and "martyr of thought," willing to explore his consciousness no matter what the cost to himself. His greatness is his very inability to be assimilated. He remains, Sontag concludes, "fiercely out of reach."

"Fascinating Fascism" is Sontag's reevaluation of filmmaker Leni Riefenstahl. Whereas in *Against Interpretation* Sontag emphasized the artistic form of Riefenstahl's films, in *Under the Sign of Saturn* she is at pains to attack the director's content and her effort to minimize her involvement with the Nazis. Sontag offers a corrective to the tributes Riefenstahl has received in American and Western European film magazines. Even more disturbing to Sontag is the fact that because Riefenstahl is a woman, she has been touted by feminists. Riefenstahl has emphasized that her main concern is form and beauty, not the recording of the "average" or "quotidian." In other words, Riefenstahl rejects realism, and thus she treats the Nuba in her book of photographs as a group of beautiful primitives, a "tribe of aesthetes," Sontag asserts. This view of a "Noble Savage" is, in fact, a throwback to a proto-fascist view that rejects "all that is reflective, critical, and pluralistic." Riefenstahl's ideology remains fascist, Sontag insists, since it revels in the "victory of the stronger man over the weaker." This "virile" aesthetic actually denigrates women, extols submission to the all-powerful male, and turns people into things.

Yet Sontag cannot quite relinquish her earlier judgment of Riefenstahl even as she tries to modify it: "*Triumph of the Will* and *Olympia* are undoubtedly superb films (they may be the two greatest documentaries ever made), but they are not really important in the history of cinema as an art form." Instead she relegates the director to a prized place in the history of propaganda. In other words, Sontag attempts to limit the extent of Riefenstahl's greatness, implying that Sontag's own earlier praise occurred in a different context: "Art that seemed eminently worth defending ten years ago, as a minority or adversary taste, no longer seems defensible today, because the ethical and cultural issues it raises have become serious, even dangerous, in a way they were not then." In other words, the growth in Riefenstahl's reputation requires Sontag to reverse her own earlier critical judgment, because what seemed daring in 1964 has become a commonplace in 1974.

Although Sontag's title essay, "Under the Sign of Saturn," contains a good deal of biographical information about Walter Benjamin and begins with a description of his appearance in photographs, Sontag argues: "One cannot use the life to interpret the work. But one can use the work to interpret the life." Sontag's Benjamin is a sad man, a melancholiac—born under the sign of Saturn. Her use of the astrological sign signals her characteristic rejection of psychological analysis. Benjamin is portrayed as a type and as having a predominant sensibility or temper rather than as the product of a specific era or family life. His longing to be superior isolates him, makes him self-conscious, so that the self becomes a "text." A propos of Benjamin's life, Sontag observes: "The self is a project, something to be built." But the process takes so long that it invites a mood of regret: "One is always in arrears to oneself." Ultimately such a person with such a conception of self can be only faithful to himself; thus Benjamin is capable of brutally dropping friends. His craving to collect is a sign of his indomitable will. Book hunting, book reading, become a form of exerting his will, and Benjamin is

Sontag's "hero of will." For him writing books is a tactic, a strategy, as much as books are entities in themselves. His essays end just before they self-destruct, which is to say that they are exquisitely balanced between argument and counterargument, much as Sontag earlier extolled Cioran for "thinking against oneself." Or as Sontag puts it, "one position corrects another." She implies her affiliation with Benjamin when she notes that he is "against interpretation wherever it is obvious."

In "Syberberg's Hitler," Sontag lauds the German filmmaker for creating a "theater of the mind" in *Hitler, A Film from Germany*. The work is not a documentary, not a spectacle, not a realistic presentation of Hitler, but a film that exploits the possibilities of moviemaking, likening cinema's effects to the "world of our inner projections." Thus radically opposed images can be juxtaposed against each other in a surrealistic fashion. Multiple images and sounds evoke Hitler, Goebbels, Goering, Himmler, and other Nazi notables as figments of the imagination. They are known to later generations as emblematic images. The film is filled with allusions to Wagner, to Freud, to German history, to German writers such as Heinrich Heine, Thomas Mann, and Bertolt Brecht, presenting both idealized and critical images of Hitler. It is a grandiose film influenced by Wagnerian opera, but it is also Brechtian in its exposure of Romanticism and the cult of the hero. Syberberg's use of puppets, of mannequins, a canvas director's chair, and masks is also part of an effort to expose the manipulative and artificial aspects of Nazism. His film's range of allusions to history and to art are so manifold that Sontag suggests that it "tries to be everything." It is a "noble masterpiece" that demands a "special kind of attention and partisanship; and invites being reflected upon, reseen."

Like her essay on Walter Benjamin, "Remembering Barthes" is one of Sontag's most personal, biographical essays. Indeed, Benjamin and Barthes are alike in their view of ideas competing with one another. And like Benjamin, Barthes excels in collections of essays. Although Barthes is more celebratory than Benjamin, he is just as polemical. Toward the end of his career Barthes had moved toward a style that was part essay, part fiction, part autobiography, Sontag notes. But her essay is remarkable for evoking the living person, not his work, the "childlike" man with the "plump body and soft voice and beautiful skin." She concludes by putting Barthes and his work under the same sign as Benjamin: "He had beautiful eyes, which are always sad eyes. There was something sad in all this talk about pleasure. *A Lover's Discourse* is a very sad book."

"Mind as Passion" is a fitting conclusion to *Under the Sign of Saturn*, since Sontag shows how Elias Canetti strove to place himself in a certain tradition of writers—just as Sontag is surely doing in her book. Canetti sees himself as part of a "succession" of writers and yearns for "strong, even overpowering models," so that Canetti represents for Sontag the writer as "noble admirer." Devoting himself exclusively to the idea of writing, Canetti seems "extremely self-involved" and "impersonal." He is a "tongue 'set free' to roam the world."

Sontag then explores Canetti's biography—his childhood "rich with displacements." Again, his only roots are in writing itself, and he lives, like Cioran, as an exile. She exemplifies Canetti's approach by concentrating on his only novel, *Auto-da-Fe*, whose main character, Kien, is a book collector who tries to confine himself to the "world in his head"—a phrase that recurs often in Sontag's writing and interviews. Similarly, when describing Kien's urge to collect and Canetti's later books that try to jettison the baggage of knowledge—when what has been appropriated has become an encumbrance—Sontag employs the vocabulary of acquisition and disburdenment which she used to define Hippolyte's guest in *The Benefactor*.

In Sontag's view, Canetti is one of those writers who demands "fealty" to writing itself, just as she argued that the all-encompassing quality of Syberberg's film on Hitler demanded its viewers' "fealty." It is the mind itself, its passions, which makes Canetti another Sontag "hero of the will." Like Artaud, Canetti is a celebrant of consciousness.

SONTAG READING SONTAG

Sontag has been particularly open about the feelings that inform *Under the Sign of Saturn*. Her tribute to Paul Goodman, she told Charles Ruas, was written in an afternoon and it was a "breakthrough for me," she thought, because it had the fluency of journalism, for which she does not believe she has any talent. Similarly, "Fascinating Fascism" was "written most quickly . . . because it's much easier to write when you feel angry, self-righteous and you know you're right."

Maxine Bernstein and Robert Boyers questioned Sontag closely about her apparent reversal of argument in the case of Riefenstahl. They pointed out what seemed like contradictory statements:

> A work of art, so far as it is a work of art, cannot—whatever the artist's personal intention—advocate anything at all. ("On Style," 1965)

> . . . the most successfully, most purely propagandistic film ever made, whose very conception negates the possibility of the filmmaker's having an aesthetic or visual conception independent of propaganda. ("Fascinating Fascism," 1975)

Sontag argued for a continuity between the two statements: they "illustrate the richness of the form-content distinction, as long as one is careful always to use it against itself." While the earlier argument in "On Style" was "correct—as far as it goes. It just doesn't go very far." It did not take into account the history of totalitarianism that Sontag felt she had absorbed from 1965 to 1975.

In other words, she had come to see that she could not divorce her idea of aesthetics from historical context. She gave Bernstein and Boyers a concrete example:

> In the 19th century, ideologues of provocation and transvaluation like Nietzsche and Wilde expounded on "the aesthetic view of the world," one of whose superiorities was that it was supposed to be the most generous and large-spirited view, a form of civility, beyond politics. The evolution of fascism in the 20th century has taught us that they were wrong. As it turns out, "the aesthetic view of the world" is extremely hospitable to many of the uncivilized ideas and dissociated yearning that were made explicitly in fascism, and which also have great currency in our consumer culture.

Thus a work of art in itself may not advocate anything, but the fact remains that a work of art can be used as propaganda and even, in Riefenstahl's case, become the dominating feature of the art. It was a "denser notion of historical context" that led Sontag to this conclusion. As she admitted to Roger Copeland, she had "indulged myself from time to time in neo-Wildean sallies as one does sometimes when one gets impatient with other people's insensitivity to beauty."

When Bernstein and Boyers asked Sontag about poet Adrienne Rich's complaint that Sontag had overlooked the fact that Nazi Germany was, in Sontag's words, the "culmination of a sexist and patriarchal society," Sontag did not take issue with Rich's analysis as such but rather with the phenomenon of feminist criticism that it represented. Sontag did not believe she was obligated to subject every work of art to a feminist analysis since such an approach reduced the level of criticism itself and required of the critic an "intellectual simplicity" and "ethical solidarity" that Sontag regarded as philistine and repressive. In other words, Sontag implied she was being pressured to follow a party line.

In the main, however, Sontag wanted *Under the Sign of Saturn* to be viewed as stories about thinkers. The "individual portraits are less idea-ridden, less expository" than her earlier work, she told Amy Lippman. She had "discharged my debts to my own obsessions. A tremendous liberation." She recognized a part of herself in every figure she had written about. Consequently her portraits were highly selective, and she did not pretend to be presenting anything like a complete picture of her subjects. Her intense feeling about books was like Benjamin's, she felt, and it is why she was drawn to Canetti and his portrait of a "bookman."

The personal quality of the essays also incorporated Sontag's stretching of terms to suit herself. Thus surrealism was conceived in a very "personal way," she confided to Copeland, which meant that she felt free to ignore any elements—such as the surrealist's conception of love—that did not appeal to her. This approach seemed appropriate for a book that featured essays in story form just as the stories in *I, etcetera* had "essay elements."

CRITICAL COMMENTARY

Reviewers such as John Leonard in the *New York Times* welcomed what he deemed Sontag's more personal voice—"ironic, humorous, playful, thought-provoking." On the other hand, others expressed Seymour Krim's view in the *Chicago Tribune* that she was continuing her "missionary" program of pointing out those contemporary European hero-writers whom she thought ought to be read and celebrated. John Lahr, in the *Washington Post*, emphasized that she was writing her "spiritual autobiography," and he took issue with the way she skewed her view of certain writers so as to express her own sensibility. But Frank Kermode, in the *New York Review of Books*, liked the way she took these "alien sages" and made them more accessible to a broader audience. He did not seem troubled—as was David Bromwich in the *New York Times Book Review*—that in the process of "translating" cultic figures such as Artaud she was simultaneously making them seem more accessible than their own writing merited. Jonathan Rosenbaum, in the *Soho News*, criticized Sontag for her Olympian attitude that deprived her chosen writers of their "social context."

Writing in *Salmagundi*, Regina Janes reflected on how parts of Sontag's book contradicted each other, especially in so far as "Fascinating Fascism" attacks forms of hero worship even as her other essays extol heroes. Similarly Leo Braudy, in the *New Republic*, wondered at Sontag's embrace of Romanticism in her Syberberg essay and her renunciation of it in her attack on Riefenstahl. To Walter Kendrick, in the *Village Voice*, Sontag was not so much a Romantic as a Victorian, writing a version of the literary portrait favored by nineteenth-century writers such as Henry James and Matthew Arnold.

Sontag's apparent inconsistencies trouble some readers more than others. Given her absorption in Cioran's view that writers must "think against" themselves, she seems remarkably untroubled by reversals in her arguments. Even in retrospect, she professes to see no problem except in so far as she has not stated her terms clearly or not shown how one position can lead to its opposite in the Hegelian mode of thesis/antithesis. For Sontag, writing is always a process, a revelation of consciousness, not merely a record of opinion or an analysis that can be fixed. Given her dedication to the act of writing and of following the writing process to wherever it takes her, it is not surprising that she does not view the body of her writing as some kind of arsenal of ideas to be defended. As we shall see in this book's last chapter, over time Sontag has put considerable distance between her earlier writing and her current devotion to fiction. Since the self is not an established fact but rather a relentless product of cerebration and imagination, she is not unduly concerned with defending her previous ideas. And even within a book like *Under the Sign of Saturn*, the fact that the premises of one essay may subvert the premises of another is not a sign of weakness but of strength.

Critic Elizabeth Bruss identifies the highly polemical nature of Sontag's writing and its tendency to produce "lawlike" statements that are nevertheless only "temporary universals." Thus Sontag is able to make strong arguments that are nevertheless open to refutation and qualification. Sontag can be accused of rationalizing the inadequacies of her own arguments, but that would hardly dent her defense of her method, because it is clear that she regards all arguments as provisional and vying against one another for superiority. She has almost no interest in foreclosing argument or in making a definitive choice between arguments, though in any particular essay or book she is taking a position that at the time seems to her to be the best choice.

What matters, then, is the joy of argument itself, not its conclusion, even though some kind of conclusion is always demanded from the essay form. What turns Sontag away from essay writing in the latter stages of her career is precisely her unease with the demand that she take her ideas out of suspension and codify them. In fiction she has sought greater freedom, finding in the novel the perfect form for a writer who wishes to explore issues, not to settle them.

TEN

AIDS

Stirred by the deaths of friends who had succumbed to a new, terrifying, and bewildering disease, Susan Sontag responded by writing two very different treatments of how AIDS attacked the health of individuals and society. Her story "The Way We Live Now" (1986) and book-length essay *AIDS and Its Metaphors* (1989) epitomize the way she has tried to bridge the gap between the dramatic and expository modes of her imagination. The story became an instant classic, reprinted at the beginning of *The Best American Short Stories, 1987,* dramatized in performances across the country, and widely discussed in books and articles surveying the literary treatments of AIDS. Why the story much more than her essay has won critical acclaim will be explored in the critical commentary section of this chapter.

"The Way We Live Now"

SYNOPSIS

The word "AIDS" is never used in the story, which is, like so much of Sontag's fiction, generic and allegorical, a moving away from the specifics of culture to the platonic universals or first principles she has pursued so persistently. What makes "The Way We Live Now" compelling, however, is her grounding in the human voice, in the twenty-six narrators (one for each letter of the alphabet) who comprise the society that reacts to the AIDS phenomenon. The story's title is taken from Anthony Trollope's monumental novel, a classic study of mid-Victorian society, especially of its social manners and political life.

The plight of Max, who has AIDS, is told entirely through the voices of his friends. They observe his first reactions to his illness—denying that he has it and delaying a trip to the doctor for the blood test that will establish his condition definitively. Each friend has a different reaction to Max's dilemma. Some sympathize with his state of denial; others worry that he is not seeking medical attention early enough. Aileen thinks of herself. Is she at risk? She doubts it, but her friend Frank reminds her that this is an unprecedented illness; no one can be sure he or she is not vulnerable. Stephen hopes that Max realizes he has options; he should not consider himself helpless at the onset of the disease.

The next stage is Max's hospitalization. Ursula says that Max has received the AIDS diagnosis almost as a relief after his months of anxiety. Friends wonder how to treat him. They decide to indulge him with the things he likes—chocolate, for example. They visit him frequently, and his mood seems to lighten.

But does Max really want to see so many people? Are they doing the right thing by visiting him so frequently? Aileen asks. Sure they are, Ursula answers, who is certain Max values the company and is not judging people's motives. Friends such as Stephen question Max's doctor, trying to assess the gravity of this stage of Max's illness. The doctor is willing to treat him with experimental drugs, but she disconcerts Stephen by saying the chocolate might bolster Max's spirit and do as much good as anything else. Stephen, who has followed all the recent efforts to treat the disease, is dismayed by this old-fashioned advice.

Kate shudders when she realizes that Max's friends have started talking about him in the past tense, as if he has already died. Several friends suspect their visits have begun to pall on him. Other friends argue that he has come to expect their daily presence. There is a brief respite from anxiety as Max's friends welcome him home and observe him put on weight. Xavier thinks they should stop worrying about how their visits affect Max; they are getting as much out of trying to help him as he is. They realize that they are dreading the possibility that they might also get the disease, that it is just a matter of time before they or their friends succumb to it. Betsy says "everybody is worried about everybody now . . . that seems to be the way we live, the way we live now."

Max's friends think about how he has managed his life. He practiced unsafe sex, saying it was so important to him that he would risk getting the disease. But Betsy thinks he must feel foolish now—like someone who kept on smoking cigarettes until he contracted a fatal disease. When it happens to you, Betsy believes, you no longer feel fatalistic; you feel instead that you have been reckless with your life. Lewis angrily rejects her thinking, pointing out that AIDS infected people long before they took any precautions. Max might have been more prudent and still have caught AIDS. Unlike cigarettes, all that is needed is one exposure to the disease.

Friends report the various phases of Max's reaction to the disease. He is afraid to sleep because it is too much like dying. Some days he feels so good that he thinks he can beat it. Other days he looks upon the disease as giving him a remarkable experience. He likes all the attention he is getting. It gives him a sort of distinction and a following. Some friends find his temperament softened and sweetened; others reject this attitudinizing about Max as sentimental. Each friend clings stubbornly to a vision of Max, the story ending with Stephen's insistent statement that "He's still alive."

As the narrators speculate about what Max is going through, it is as though they are suffering from the disease themselves, trying to keep him alive in their thoughts and wishes. How they react to his disease depends very much on the kind of people they are.

They argue with each other and sometimes support each other, desperately seeking ways to cope with the imminence of death. Max's approaching fate forces them to confront their own mortality, though they rarely acknowledge that they are indeed thinking of themselves as much as they are of him.

Death has many faces, many manifestations, Sontag seems to be implying. For some, it is to be evaded. Some of Max's friends visit him rarely—one supposing that they have never been close friends anyway. Other friends—such as Stephen—almost seem to want to take over the fight against death, quizzing the doctors, boning up on the latest medical research, and conducting a kind of campaign against any capitulation to the disease. Very few friends are fatalistic; almost all of them hope for a medical breakthrough that will rescue Max.

They live in fear. One friend finds out that his seventy-five-year-old mother has contracted AIDS through a blood transfusion she received five years ago. No one is immune to the disease; even if everyone does not get it, someone close to them probably will. It is the extraordinary vulnerability of these people that makes them argue with or reassure each other, to question what is the best behavior. Everyone encounters an ethical dilemma about how to lead his or her life and how to respond to those who are afflicted with the disease.

The blending and clash of voices reveals a society in argument with itself, testing ways of responding to AIDS, advancing, then rejecting, certain attitudes. Voices overlap each other, as they do in real conversation:

> He seemed optimistic, Kate thought, his appetite was good, and what he said, Orson reported, was that he agreed when Stephen advised him that the main thing was to keep in shape, he was a fighter, right, he wouldn't be who he was if he weren't, and was he ready for the big fight, Stephen asked rhetorically (as Max told it to Donny), and he said you bet. . . .

A complex layering of speeches within speeches, and of social and psychological observation, are emphasized by long sentences that continually switch speakers, so that a community of friends and points of view get expressed sentence by sentence. The story is like compressing the one hundred chapters of Trollope's novel into one hundred sentences.

It is the rhythm of these voices, of the ups and downs in their moods, of the phases people go through in responding to the disease, that is one of the most impressive accomplishments of Sontag's techniques. She presents the tragedy of one man, yet from the first to the last sentence the story is also a society's tragedy as well. It is the society that is ill. The speakers retain their individuality, yet they also become a chorus—almost like one in a Greek tragedy. They do not speak the same thoughts at once, but the syntax of the sentences make them seem bound to one another— as enclosed by their community of feeling as are the clauses in Sontag's sentences enclosed by commas. The speaker's thought at the beginning of a sentence is carried on, refuted, modified, or added to by speakers in later parts of the sentence. The sentence as a grammatical unit links speakers to each other. Whatever their attitudes toward the disease, they cannot escape the thought of it. Thinking of it is, as one of them says, the way they live now.

SONTAG READING SONTAG

Sontag told interviewer Kenny Fries that she wrote her story after receiving a phone call from a friend who told her he had AIDS. Later that night, crying and unable to sleep, she took a bath and the story began to take shape: "It was given to me, ready to be born. I got out of the bathtub and starting writing standing up," she told Fries. "I wrote the story very quickly, in two days, drawing on experiences of my own cancer and a friend's stroke. Radical experiences are similar." The urgency of creation and the frankness of fiction appealed to her: "Fiction is closer to my private life, more immediate, direct, less constrained—more reckless. Essays involve more effort in layering and condensation, more revisions." Fries noted that Sontag was "very proud" of her story.

In a radio interview, Sontag called the story a "stunt" but also one of her best pieces of writing, because it captured both the "velocity" and the "static quality" of enduring a mortal illness. She thought the story explored the human issues of illness more deeply than an essay could, for the former reveals deep emotions and feelings whereas the latter has a tendency to encourage "superficial" moral judgments.

CRITICAL COMMENTARY

Novelist David Leavitt thought the story therapeutic, making him feel "less alone in my dread, and therefore brave enough to read more." The story "transcended horror and grief, and . . . was therefore redemptive, if not of AIDS itself, then at least of the processes by which people cope with it. . . . It offered a possibility of catharsis, and at that point catharsis was something we all badly needed." Leavitt is referring to a time when contracting AIDS seemed an immediate death sentence, when artists such as Robert Mapplethorpe, suspecting they had AIDS, refused to be tested for the disease. Sontag saw that the stigma attached to AIDS made patients feel isolated and fearful, much as cancer had earlier made society shun the ill and the ill shun society. (Mapplethorpe was finally diagnosed with AIDS in the fall of 1986, about two months before Sontag published her story.)

But as Sontag would say about *AIDS and Its Metaphors*, "The Way We Live Now" is not just about AIDS, it is about extreme changes in society. Like the overarching theme of Trollope's great novel, Sontag's story is about "a loss of community and ethical value," to quote Elaine Showalter. Joseph Cady calls "The Way We Live Now" a "counterimmersive" story, one of several that do not involve readers directly with scenes of suffering and physical descriptions of AIDS but rather avoid specific mention of the disease, concentrating instead on the stages of denial among the ill and society at large. Such counterimmersive stories he calls "deferential," since they protect readers from "too jarring a confrontation with the subject through a variety of distancing devices." In "The Way We Live Now," the relay race of narrators provides the distancing, which is perhaps why Sylvie Drake called a dramatization of the story "bloodless." Cady finds it troubling that the disease is not named in counterimmersive stories, thereby playing to society's sense of delicacy and phobia about the illness: "Sontag offers no forceful alternative to the characters' perspective in her text, and denying readers could still finish the story with their defenses largely intact."

On the other hand, critic Emmanuel S. Nelson argues that in Sontag's story "there is no reassuring voice the reader can comfortably connect with; her insistence that AIDS puts all of us at risk disrupts the complacency of those readers who consider themselves quite safe from the epidemic." True, the story does not name the disease, but Nelson notes this sentence: "And it was encouraging he was willing to say the name of the disease, pronounce it often and easily, as if it were just another word, like a boy or gallery . . . because . . . to utter the name is a sign of health."

Annie Dawid, who taught the story to students born after 1972, reports they found its fast pace and multiple narrators confusing and upsetting. It was hard to root for Max because they never got to know him. Of all the AIDS stories Dawid taught, "The Way We Live Now" was the "harshest . . . the least gentle by way of assuring the readers that they can all return to their lives, business as usual."

To some extent, these differences in critical opinion mirror Sontag's own swaying arguments about the import of literature, about art as form and art as content, art that makes a statement and art that is all style and refuses to be pinned to a point. There is a kind of decorum observed in the story, a "none dare speak its name" resonance, a reticence about "coming out" that certain gay and lesbian critics in the late 1980s and early 1990s would scorn. For them, the story's reluctance to be more specific drains it of potential power. For the proponents of reticence (see Rochelle Gurstein's provocative *The Repeal of Reticence*), on the contrary, "The Way We Live Now" is powerful precisely because it is not explicit; it does not strip the person with AIDS of his most intimate moments; it does not provide the gory details; it is not, in short, pornographic in its handling of the disease. "The Way We Live Now" might almost be taken as an illustration of Gurstein's brief for a reticence our society no longer respects, a reticence that once preserved the "inherent fragility of intimate life, the tone of public conversation, standards of taste and morality, and reverence owed to mysteries."

AIDS and Its Metaphors

SYNOPSIS

Sontag begins by examining the compulsion to use metaphor, by which she means Aristotle's definition: "giving the thing a name that belongs to something else." Metaphors are inescapable, Sontag concedes, but that does not mean that some of them should not be "retired" or that, in some instances, it is not correct to be "against interpretation." For inevitably metaphors distort as much as they describe phenomena. Based on her own experience with cancer, Sontag doubts that military metaphors do anything more than victimize the sufferer—and it does not matter whether the victim of the "war" against disease is regarded as innocent or guilty. Either way the ill feel attacked, invaded, and vulnerable.

AIDS shares with earlier illnesses this overwrought use of metaphor. To contract AIDS is tantamount to receiving a death sentence. AIDS stigmatizes individuals. Like cancer, the reputation of the disease isolates the patient. During her own cancer treatment Sontag saw how patients became disgusted with them- selves. The metaphorical atmosphere around such diseases simply increases suffering and is unnecessary, Sontag asserts. By strin- gently abstaining from the use of metaphors, her aim is to deprive illness of its accreted meanings. Illness, in other words, has been interpreted too much. Sontag feels her approach has been vindi- cated in the new attitude evinced by doctors, who now treat ill- nesses such as cancer more frankly and without the secrecy or mystery that once surrounded sickness.

As a sexually transmitted disease, AIDS has been subject to the vehement use of metaphors. It is an invasive virus that must be combated. It is an alien that victims harbor in their bodies, and it is a contaminant—in other words, a spreading evil. In the first phase of awareness of the disease, AIDS patients were thought of as guilty parties punished for their sexual deviancy—especially since the first cases were discovered in homosexuals. Unlike such diseases as tuberculosis or cancer, however, AIDS speaks to a more primitive sense of disease, for the AIDS sufferer is thought to be morally blameworthy. In other words, his illness is not merely a function of his psychology; rather the disease is a condemnation of character. Thus AIDS is a throwback to medieval notions of a plague—in this case a "gay plague."

Conservatives find in AIDS a convenient metaphor for the ravages of a permissive society, in which permitting all abomina- tions leads to certain death. AIDS is a calamity that society has brought upon itself, according to this line of reasoning. AIDS and permissiveness become, through the agency of metaphor, one and the same thing: contagious. Sontag rejects this argument, pointing out that AIDS, which has only recently been identified, cannot be regarded as always leading to death. (In the decade since her book was published, this aspect of her argument has been vindicated.)

Concentrating on AIDS as an inevitable death warrant ob- scures the fact that early deaths from the disease were at least in part the result of ignorance and ineffective therapies. It is the disease that has to treated without the emotional overlay of metaphors—especially since so much about the etiology of the disease has yet to be studied.

Yet Sontag acknowledges that AIDS must also be viewed in terms of a society that has become more sexually permissive and ever more consumer oriented. "How could sexuality *not* come to be, for some, a consumer option: an exercise of liberty, of increased mobility, of the pushing back of limits." This broad change in cultural mores is "hardly an invention of the male homosexual subculture," she points out. And the response to AIDS has been to adopt "programs of self-management and self-discipline (diet, exercise). Watch your appetites. Take care of yourself. Don't let yourself go"—these are the watchwords, Sontag suggests. These calls to "stricter limits in the conduct of personal life" earn her approval— as do a return to the conventions of society that help to regulate individual behavior.

Sontag understands but wants to resist the sense of apocalypse associated with diseases like AIDS. The world is not coming to an end, but each new campaign or "war" on disease makes it seem as though it is. "Apocalypse is now a long-running serial: not 'Apocalypse Now' but 'Apocalypse from Now On,'" she quips. Such constant evocations of catastrophe are, in the end, exhausting and counterproductive. The worst outcome, she concludes, is to treat AIDS or any other disease as a "total" anything. She argues that illness should be regarded as "ordinary" and treatable.

SONTAG READING SONTAG

To Kenny Fries, Sontag characterized her book as a "literary performance. It is an essay, a literary form with a tradition and speculative purpose." Her reiteration of the obvious was in response to a barrage of reviews that took issue with both her facts and her arguments. She was not trying to take a position on AIDS in the way an activist might but rather exploring the mind-set about AIDS and other diseases. "My ideas of AIDS alone, stripped of the associations, are the same as any civilized, compassionate, liberal's." In a similar vein, she pointed out to Margaria Fichtner: "This book . . . isn't really about AIDS. It's what AIDS makes you think about. It's about things that AIDS reveals or points to."

Sontag also acknowledged that her rational view of disease and her resistance to psychologizing it with metaphors was a position she arrived at only during the sixth draft of her book. Until then, she too had succumbed to calling AIDS a plague. Her book was an effort to reject both "hysteria and facile pessimism."

CRITICAL COMMENTARY

AIDS and Its Metaphors appeared in a cultural climate far different from the one that acclaimed *Illness as Metaphor*. Charles Perrow, in the *Chicago Tribune*, spoke for many reviewers when he regretted that Sontag's emphasis on metaphors obscured practical matters— what could be done immediately in terms of education, social conditions, and politics to combat the disease. Simone Watney, in the *Guardian Weekly*, chastised her for writing in a vacuum; she failed to take account of the mounting literature on AIDS. Jan Grover, in the *Women's Review of Books*, criticized Sontag for her apparent ignorance that AIDS was being psychologized in the gay community. Similarly Gregory Kolovakos, in the *Nation*, rejected her praise of monogamy as "shallow revisionism." Her insensitivity to the mood and mores of the gay community was an underlying theme of many responses to the book.

There were many positive responses to Sontag's approach as well, including Patricia W. Dideriksen and John A. Bartlett in the *New England Journal of Medicine* who called the book "noble." Deborah Stone, in the *Journal of Health Politics, Policy and Law*, found the book "brilliant," and Francine Prose, in *Savvy Woman*, admired Sontag's compassion and intensity. While Randy Shilts, one of the country's foremost authorities on AIDS, was severely critical of Sontag, he admired the way she integrated AIDS into her discussion of other diseases. Perhaps the highest compliment paid to *AIDS and Its Metaphors* came from Anatole Broyard in the *New York Times Book Review* who asserted that Sontag's book was to "illness what William Empson's *Seven Types of Ambiguity* is to literature"—that is, she had written a classic text certain to become part of the canon of modern literature.

Surely one of the reasons Sontag's book sparked critical animosity was because of its rather lofty tone. She deliberately divorced herself from the crisis atmosphere that surrounded her subject. Whereas she saw herself as advocating a quieter but just as determined an attitude toward treating the disease as those who were militantly calling for a national campaign or war against AIDS, her critics saw an aloof and even conservative figure apparently out of touch with people's feelings and needs.

Unlike cancer, which for all its threatening associations had become (in part thanks to Sontag) more like an ordinary disease afflicting people, AIDS was put into a special category because it still seemed in 1989 like a plague that modern medicine had not learned how to control, let alone eradicate. Sontag's reflective temper collided with the very hysteria she was attempting to alleviate. Instead of being received as therapeutic, the book was rejected as abrasive.

Sontag herself realized that another kind of book was wanted from her. But it was a book she was not prepared to write, a book that did not appeal to her sensibility, a book that would have looked too much like the other books written about AIDS. Sontag's own notion of herself as a writer destined her to write a book that many readers could not accept. As she pointed out to Kenny Fries, "I have the kind of mind that, whenever I think of something, it makes me think of something else. With this book I do what I do best. This book has more to do with Emerson than with Randy Shilts." Like Emerson, Sontag was using AIDS as another instance of how people use metaphor and how they think about illness. To those readers exercised more about the devastating spread of AIDS and more concerned with the disease itself than with its cultural or historical context, Sontag's approach seemed almost callous. She had not focused specifically enough on the anguish of the dying and on their caretakers. And she seemed to show almost no sympathy at all for gays—the first major community to be affected by the disease.

Perhaps the only way Sontag might have remained true to her sensibility and at the same time satisfied her critics would have been to reveal more of the process by which she came to reject the emotional metaphors used to describe and treat the disease. For example, what happened to her on that sixth draft when she rejected the plague metaphor? Throughout her career, Sontag has tended to use the interview form as a substitute for autobiography, evidently equating autobiography with a more informal, inexact mode of expression that conflicts with the formal elements of her essays—the decorum and rationality she has cultivated as a nonfiction writer. That sense of propriety has contributed significantly to her authority as an essayist, but it has also put off many readers who cannot connect a human voice with the ideas she explores in her essays.

ELEVEN

The Volcano Lover

(1992)

Twenty-five years after the publication of *Death Kit*, Sontag published her third novel. It was a best-seller and received much better reviews than her other fiction. If reviewers did not rank the novel as great literature, they nevertheless saw it as an enormous advance over her previous fiction. That she had produced a historical novel surprised many readers, since her essays of the 1960s argued against the predominance of realism and favored more experimental forms of fiction. But the essayistic quality of *The Volcano Lover* has much in common with works such as *On Photography*.

SYNOPSIS

The novel begins in the spring of 1992 with a prologue set in Manhattan. The narrator describes herself as casually dressed in jeans and a silk blouse. She is at a flea market and is debating whether or not to indulge her penchant for collecting and buying. Her desires and the contemporary setting are juxtaposed against the London of 1772, in which an older and a younger man are discussing a work of art, *Venus Disarming Cupid*. Their debate about art, about what it means to own and sell it, will become a main theme of the book. Not identified yet, the two men are Sir William Hamilton and his nephew, Charles Greville. Indeed these historical figures will never be given their proper names. The narrator will refer to Hamilton as the Cavaliere—a name he acquired in Naples. Already in the prologue his passion for volcanoes is mentioned and the way the volcano's shape and actions are reminiscent of human features and passions.

Part One describes the Cavaliere in London, on home leave from his diplomatic post in Naples, "the kingdom of cinders" which exists in the shadow of the Vesuvius volcano. This English gentleman is selling some of his Etruscan vases but fails to find a purchaser for his *Cupid*. He ponders whether his willingness to sell a work of art diminishes it for him. He is very fond of his wife, Catherine, a fine pianist. She is frail, and the Cavaliere's passion is for art and his volcano. Collecting is his way of uniting the world, of making sense of it. Climbing the volcano, on the other hand, apparently speaks to a romantic, passionate impulse that is not satisfied by his marriage—though he never says as much, and the narrator makes no explicit comment on the marriage.

The Cavaliere is a sophisticated diplomat who gets on well with the vulgar king of Naples and his wife. No indignity seems to phase the Cavaliere—not even when he has to accompany the king to his toilet. The king is a voluptuary, taking great delight in consuming mountains of food. He enjoys animal massacres and huge celebrations—all of which the Cavaliere tolerates without a flicker of disapproval, even though his own tastes are much more refined and rational.

Catherine has asthma, which means she cannot accompany the Cavaliere on his Vesuvian expeditions. But she is entertained by the Cavaliere's second cousin, William Beckford. They become soulmates; they read Goethe's *Sorrow of Young Werther* together, and William confides his most personal feelings to her. She is a kind of mother figure but also a lover (though their love is not consummated sexually). They become like an operatic couple, vibrating together. After William leaves, he sends Catherine letters filled with longing. She becomes more ill but also more passionate just as the Cavalier's devotion to his volcano intensifies. Part One ends with Catherine's death.

Part Two begins with an image of the erupting Vesuvius. The Cavaliere returns to England with Catherine's body and with a Roman vase (the famous Portland Vase now in the British Museum) he must sell as debts are always a problem for him. On his return, he receives Emma, a young woman whom his nephew Charles has sent him. Emma is still in love with Charles, who has no intention of marrying her, and she rejects the Cavaliere's advances. He finds her exquisitely beautiful and her resistance, abetted by her accompanying mother, only fuels his desire.

The Cavaliere makes progress in Emma's affections by tutoring her in the ways of the court and by encouraging her aesthetic side—expressed in a series of performances in which she strikes attitudes and poses in a kind of "living slide show." She becomes adept at reenacting classic stories and scenes, entrancing no less than the visiting poet Goethe.

In this age of the French Revolution, passions erupt like the volcano. Emma becomes the Cavaliere's work of art, his lover, and then his wife. At the same time, this couple receives "the hero"— Admiral Nelson, England's most famous naval hero, though he is never named as such. The hero has turned back the Napoleonic tide and endears himself to both the Cavaliere and Emma when he visits Naples. He has been maimed and blinded in battle but remains gallant and resolute.

In spite of the scandal of an English ambassador marrying a woman with a shady reputation, Emma is a success at court, where she delights the king and especially the queen. But neither the Cavaliere nor Emma can do much about the corrupt Neopolitan regime which crumbles after an assault by Napoleon's forces. As the court party departs, Naples faces a revolution. But the hero returns to crush it and to deal harshly with the revolutionaries. He orders summary executions and reestablishes order. Now smitten with Emma, he deliberately disobeys an order from England to leave Naples. Emma and the hero become lovers, and the Cavaliere remains devoted to both of them in this scandalous love triangle. The narrator notes that the outrage is all the greater because a woman is at the center of the triangle. The Cavaliere is recalled to England in disgrace. The indispensable hero survives the scandal, even though Emma gives birth to his child.

Part Three begins with the Cavaliere's dying monologue. He recalls his life in Naples, his image of himself as the older Pliny who also fell in love with the volcano, and his devotion to art. He dies thinking, "I would like to be remembered for the volcano."

Part Four is a series of monologues—all by women—beginning with Catherine's reflections on her life, on the Cavaliere's devotion to her, on her own melancholy, and on how she cannot think of herself without including her husband. Then Mary Cadogan, Emma's mother, explains her devotion to her daughter. She accepts the way Charles seduced Emma and then abandoned her to the Cavaliere—apparently because in each case the men did offer a good deal in terms of affection, education, and support. A generous woman, she finds the hero, the "little admiral," irresistible. As soon as he entered Emma's life events accelerated without time to consider the consequences. Emma's own monologue develops into a defense of her "magic" that attracted so many men to her. She too is dazzled by how her life could change so rapidly and by the abrupt plummeting of her fortunes as soon as the hero dies. Emma's words are followed in rapid succession by the reminiscences of a Neopolitan upper-class woman who describes the counterrevolution when Nelson restored the monarchy and her own execution, and by the account of Eleonora de Fonseca Pimentel, who furiously denounces the privileged members of Neopolitan society and who condemns the hero, the Cavaliere ("an upper class dilettante"), and his wife (a "nullity"). She closes her indictment with the comment: "They thought they were civilized. They were despicable. Damn them all."

SONTAG READING SONTAG

Sontag told many interviewers that *The Volcano Lover* was the best work she had ever done. "Most of what I've done in the past, I didn't like it so much," she told Paula Span. "I didn't think it was so good; it was just the best I could do. I always felt some dissatisfaction." What seems to have pleased Sontag was the sheer richness of her novel. Reading her earlier work had been "like being hungry after a big meal." But *The Volcano Lover* was a "feast." The novel was particularly pleasing because Sontag finally felt liberated. She had started and abandoned several novels in the 1970s and 1980s. "Somewhere along the line, there was a failure of nerve," she told Span. "A *justified* failure of nerve."

Sontag explained that the genesis of the novel occurred at a rare bookshop in London. There she saw the engravings of Mount Vesuvius that had been commissioned by Sir William Hamilton for a privately printed book. She bought several of the prints and put them on her apartment walls, calling them her "images of disaster" (which calls to mind, of course, her essay on science fiction, "The Imagination of Disaster"). Sontag was attracted to Hamilton's avidity for art and collecting, and only then did she begin to recall and piece together the sensational story of his involvement with Emma and Lord Nelson. Sontag had dim memories of seeing Vivien Leigh and Sir Lawrence Olivier play Hamilton and Emma in the 1941 British film *That Hamilton Woman*. The movie thrilled her as a child, but she thought "Emma and Nelson, they'll be in the story in a minor way," but it "didn't work out that way. Emma kidnapped the book." To Marion Christy, Sontag explained her affinity with Emma: "I have a volcano in my heart. I have such strong enthusiasms that sometimes I don't want to sleep. I feel as if there's a lot going on and there's the possibility of more and I want to be there." Sontag told Sara Mosle that Emma was "enormously talented, enormously energetic. . . . The amazing thing is not that she got as far as she did but that she didn't go further." To Samuel

R. Delany, Sontag ventured: "I love self-made people. I feel rather self-made myself."

But as if to counter her identification with her characters and to make the reader question them as well, Sontag told Edward Hirsch that ending with Eleonora and her "denunciation of the protagonists is as far as you can get from the point of view with which the novel starts." The novel's ending was part of an intricate structure based on Hindemith's *The Four Temperaments*. Like the composer, Sontag determined that she would begin with a "triple prologue followed by four movements that evoked the medieval idea of the humors of predominant characteristics that define human nature: the melancholic, sanguinic, phlegmatic, and choleric." Thus the Cavaliere was the melancholic, Emma the sanguinic (full of blood, passion), the Cavaliere the phlegmatic, and the choleric the ending monologue of the angry women. To Sontag, these monologues were like arias, "unmediated, acutely rueful," with the women describing their own deaths. But she rejected Hirsch's suggestion that she ended with a "woman's point of view." Had she ended the novel with four male voices, "no one would suppose I was giving the male point of view; the differences among the four voices would be too striking. These women are as different from each other as any of four men characters in the novel I might have chosen." What the women did have in common, Sontag admitted, was their awareness that the world is "run by men." She also admitted to Mary Ann Grossman: "Part of this story is about what it's like to be a woman. I'm saying it's complicated. . . . Society gives woman all sorts of contradictory messages, and so do your own standards and temperament; be good, be wild, be safe, be bold, have fun; be serious."

The monologues had the effect of a long shot or fade in a film. "But I can live with their becoming small at the end. I mean, it *is* the end of the novel. I was thinking in cinematic terms," of the French films of the 1960s that "ended with the camera in long shot starting to pull back, and the character moving further and further into the rear of the pictured space, becoming smaller and smaller as the credits start to roll." Eleonora provided an "ethical wide shot." The novel's last word, Sontag explained to Hirsch, represents the victims of the tyranny that her protagonists supported.

Sontag strove for authenticity. She "studied four scholarly treatises on 18th century carriages," she told interviewer Ron Grossman, in order to describe how aristocrats of the day traveled. But it was not her aim to write a "you are there" historical novel. Although she wanted her work to be historically accurate and dense with historical detail, she also wanted the narrator to adopt a contemporary voice as a way of measuring the distance between the past and present.

Finding the right voice for the narrator became tied to Sontag's subtitle "A Romance." She told Leslie Garis that

> in order to find the courage to write this book, it helped me to find a label that allowed me to go over the top. . . . The word "romance" was like a smile. Also, the novel becomes such a self-conscious enterprise for people who read a lot. You want to do something that takes into account all the options you have in fiction. Yet you don't want to be writing *about* fiction, but making fiction. So I sprang myself from fictional self-consciousness by saying, It's a novel—it's more than a novel—it's a romance! . . . And I fell into the book like Alice in Wonderland. For three years I worked 12 hours a day in a delirium of pleasure. This novel is really a turning point for me.

CRITICAL COMMENTARY

Sven Birkets, in *Newsday*, called the novel a "wonderful fusion of the concrete and the conceptual," and he paid Sontag an enormous compliment by claiming that her work reminded him of Marguerite Yourcenar's *Memoirs of Hadrian*, the very standard by which modern historical novels are measured. Kevin Ray, in the *St. Louis Post-Dispatch*, praised a "magnificent and generous novel, recalling Lampedusa's 'The Leopard' in insight as well as in venue." Michiko Kakutani, in the *New York Times*, spoke for many reviewers when she praised Sontag's ability to combine an "intimate and friendly voice" with an historical account. The novelist blended a sense of the contemporary with an evocation of the past—a notoriously difficult accomplishment, since it was difficult not to have the sensibility of the present overwhelm even supposedly historical narratives. The novelist A. S. Byatt, writing in the *Washington Post*, praised the narrator's "detached, energetic curiosity." Sontag created a supple novel composed of many styles and points of view, a "slippery, intelligent, provocative and gripping book." Richard Eder, in the *Los Angeles Times*, called the novel "both great fun and serious fun." He also thought the way Sontag worked her contemporary sensibility into the history gave her work a third dimension.

The novel received very few negative reviews, and the mixed notices tended to question the very aspects of the novel that attracted admirers. In the *Wall Street Journal*, Max Daniel disliked what he termed the historical novel's enslavement to "contemporary social and political concerns." He found the narrative lacking in a passionate commitment to its subjects. Marina Warner, in *Vogue*, praised the female voices in the novel but found that Sontag had become too absorbed in Emma. R. Z. Sheppard, in *Time*, rejected the novel's "jarring" feminist ending. "Sontag, like Vesuvius, simply blew her top." In *Newsweek*, David Gates praised the novel's "small, smart details" and its final monologues while calling the narrative itself "amateurish." Novelist John Banville, writing in the *New York Times Book Review*, on the other hand, found much to praise in this "old fashioned" novel and yet still called it "curiously hollow." John Simon, in the *National Review*, called the novel an "anti-romance" and culled from it many aphorisms that misfired or remained dormant.

Most commentators on the novel did not consider how much Sontag might have owed to her childhood enthusiasm for *That Hamilton Woman*. And yet movies have always been her passion—

not just the foreign films that she wrote about in the 1960s but also popular Hollywood entertainments that she wrote about in her high school newspaper and continued to enjoy in Manhattan and in Paris.

Hamilton, Sontag made clear in several interviews, was to be her main focus, and yet she eventually capitulated to retelling the story of the triangle, risking all the clichés associated with romance. One factor in her deviation from her original plan is precisely the movie she scorned when WGBH television interviewer Christopher Lydon brought it up. In what sense, he wanted to know, had the novel been inspired by the movie. He had to ask because he knew Sontag was a "movie buff." She bristled. She was not a buff; she said she watched only those movies she admired. *That Hamilton Woman* was not a good movie: "I'm not in dialogue with Hollywood movies." (The movie was produced in England.) Yet she conceded that a friend had sent her a copy of the movie about a year after she started the novel, around the time she was having trouble going beyond her melancholy Part One, the part (some reviewers noted) that is the slowest going in the novel.

A scene near the beginning of *That Hamilton Woman* is sure to have caught Sontag's eye. Sir William Hamilton explains to a Neapolitan aristocrat Emma's questionable career. Sir William speaks as a man of the world, not as a censorious judge of Emma's affairs. She has been passed from one man to another; Sir William has, in effect, acquired Emma from his nephew, as though Emma were another fine piece for his collection. Far from disparaging her because she is a commodity, Sir William is excited by the way her value has increased with each new owner. As he puts it, she has sunk "lower and lower" in the eyes of society, and yet her stock has gone "up and up."

The movie gives a brief but faithful representation of Sir William the connoisseur and collector. Of Sir William, the Volcano Lover, there is almost nothing. But in this scene he refers to mud, a reminder to those who know his biography that he was not afraid to get his hands dirty and to muck about in order to acquire his Vesuvian treasures. After Sir William describes Emma's past, his colleague expresses astonishment that with a "past like that" she should be an ambassador's guest. "About the past," Sir William responds:

> Look at this statue. Two hundred years in a Greek temple. Then thrown into the mud by some barbarian soldier. Two thousand years of sinking lower and lower into the mud, then dug up by the plow of a peasant. Changing hands every year until at last it comes into its rightful place, into the hands of someone who understands the glory of its beauty, because, my friend, it is still beautiful, isn't it? Despite its past.

The equation of Emma and the statue is exact. Sir William's caress of the statue, his worship of art, is one with his appreciation of Emma.

Sontag's novel relishes the ironies of this kind of speech: the turns of phrase and the perspectives on art and life that Sir William sets up. The scene in which he gives his little lecture is itself an elaborate construction similar in spirit to Sontag's novel. Although *The Volcano Lover* is not a costume drama, it is very much influenced by film techniques, techniques that are not ancillary to the movie's message or merely illustrative of it; they enact the very art that Sir William and Sontag both adore.

As Sir William speaks of Emma sinking lower and lower only to ascend up and up, he walks toward a bust of what looks like a Greek goddess, and his colleague swings around to the other side of the sculpture. As the Neapolitan aristocrat pivots toward the sculpture, the camera captures his smiling face, intent on Sir William, but moving closer to the statue and then sliding the aristocrat's eyes and swiveling his head until he directly confronts its face. In effect, Sir William is making the aristocrat see the preciousness of this work. Just after the aristocrat's reference to Emma's past, Sir William places his left arm on the bust's right shoulder, so that he and the artwork are in profile. But as soon as the aristocrat speaks the word "past," the camera reverses its angle and the next shot is of Sir William's back as he faces the statue which is facing us, as though we are also a part of this argument about art and life. Then the camera reverses angles once again, in a shot that shows Sir William's right profile and the bust's left, as if the sculpture is looking at Hamilton while he looks at his colleague. For Sir William is, after all, in deep dialogue with the past. When he reaches the point of referring to himself as someone who understands the glory of the work's beauty, he momentarily closes his eyes as if dreaming of what he possesses—an idea that is emphasized by the way he shifts his resting hand from the bust's right shoulder to the left, which he grips a little more tightly and intimately. Having established rapport with the artwork, and having appropriated it as his own, he turns his eyes away from the sculpture and tells his servant that he will be dining alone with Miss Hart that night.

What makes the film's portrayal of Sir William Hamilton relevant to Sontag is that Sir William is all of a piece, no matter whether he is discoursing on art or women or politics. He is a man with an exquisite sense of form. What makes *The Volcano Lover* striking is its intellectual exuberance, which is so intense that it is erotic—no matter whether the subject is people, works of art, or history. The narrator is insatiably speculative, expressing an avidity akin to Sir William's. In *Vases and Volcanoes*, Ian Jenkins and Kim Sloan's exhibition catalog of Sir William's work, he is quoted as observing: "As one passion begins to fail, it is necessary to form another; for the whole art of going through life tollerably [sic] in my opinion is to keep oneself eager about anything. The moment one is indifferent *on s'ennuie*, and that is a misery to which I perceive even Kings are often subject."

As Sontag herself recognizes, *The Volcano Lover* represents the culmination of her life's work. In it she finally fuses in brilliant fashion the techniques of her fiction and her nonfiction. It is also her most deeply autobiographical work, finally releasing a pent-up Romanticism that she worked hard to mask in earlier books. Like Sir William, Sontag has been a collector and a connoisseur. In her autobiographical short story, "Project for a Trip to China," meditating on the objects that her fur trader father brought back from Asia, she remarks, "Colonialists collect." This is Sontag code not only for what her parents were but for what she is: a collector and connoisseur, fascinated yet revolted by her voracious effort to consume the world. In this respect she is like the photographers who are always appropriating the world in images, and like the Cavaliere (Sir William) with his immense art collection and his effort to "colonialize" Vesuvius by constantly traversing its circumference—and like her own crafted persona, frequently photographed beside her enormous collection of books.

The Volcano Lover can be read as a gloss on Sir William's hymn to art in *That Hamilton Woman*. The novel begins in the present, in a flea market. Things there are grimy, and the narrator thinks of all manner of reasons for not going in and handling the goods, but she cannot resist. "Desire leads me in," she confesses. This is just another version of the Cavaliere, who confesses he is "picture-mad."

The desire that Hamilton and Sontag express is what connects them to the world, but it is also what alienates them from it. Sir William is a rather lonely figure in *That Hamilton Woman*, especially when the second half of the film focuses on the love story of Lord Nelson and Lady Hamilton. In *The Volcano Lover*, Sir William is more fortunate, for Sontag maintains her interest in him. Yet his dying soliloquy, which Sontag performs brilliantly on a Dove audiobook, dramatizes his isolation in wheezing asthmatic breaths that the lonely child Susan Sontag knew only too well. In order to write the scene, she felt she had to "mark it off." She checked into the Mayflower Hotel on Central Park for three days, writing it straight out on a pad and ordering a BLT and a lot of coffee. She imagined herself dying and delirious, and the writing became like taking down her own last moments. Much of the novel was written abroad in Berlin, just after the wall came down, quickening Sontag's sense of historic events and of the world elsewhere that she and Emma and Hamilton and Nelson all sought.

The Volcano Lover is studded with parabolic passages that evoke the melancholy of Sir William's, and the artist's, inability to collect the world, to hold its attention:

> Collections unite. Collections isolate.
>
> They unite those who love the same thing. (But no one loves the same as I do; enough.) They isolate from those who don't share the passion. (Alas, almost everyone.)
>
> Then I'll try not to talk about what interests me most. I'll talk about what interests you.
>
> But this will remind me, often, of what I can't share with you.
>
> Oh, listen. Don't you see. Don't you see how beautiful it is.

The artist, the aesthete, the collector, become estranged from the world in the process of bringing it together. This paradox results, in *The Volcano Lover*, in a narrator who speaks to herself as much as to her readers—just as in *That Hamilton Woman* Sir William speaks to his sculpture and to himself when he addresses his colleagues.

The dialectical passages in *The Volcano Lover* are like those reverse-angle camera shots in *That Hamilton Woman* that constantly turn the argument in another direction: "Collections unite. Collections isolate." Each statement in *The Volcano Lover* elicits a counterstatement. In the flea market scene, the narrator, like Sir William, finally gives way to a worship of art. Just as he gazes at the glory of the sculpture's beauty, "because, my friend, it is still beautiful, isn't it?" Sontag's narrator exults: "Oh, listen. Don't you see. Don't you see how beautiful it is."

TWELVE

In America

(2000)

Eight years after the success of *The Volcano Lover*, Sontag published *In America*, another historical novel. This new work met with a mixed reception, but it won the National Book Award for fiction. *In America* has fewer essaylike elements than *The Volcano Lover*, but its view of human character, especially of the place of the will in human achievement, is reminiscent of her earliest published essays as well as her treatment of heroes in *Under the Sign of Saturn*.

SYNOPSIS

In America begins with an epigraph from Langston Hughes: "America will be!" It is a fitting start to the story of a group of Poles who travel to Anaheim, California, in 1876 to establish a utopian community. Their leader is Maryna Zaleska, Poland's greatest actress, who has forsaken her career in order to create a farming commune. She is aware of the likelihood of failure, but the romance of starting anew, the challenge of succeeding where communities such as Brook Farm failed, is too enticing not to pursue. She takes with her a devoted husband, Bogdan; a young son, Piotr; and a young writer, Ryszard, who aspires to win her love.

In a note on the copyright page, Sontag explains that her novel was inspired by the career of Helena Modrzejewska, Poland's renowned actress, who did indeed emigrate to America in 1876 and settle in Anaheim with her husband, Count Karol Chapowski; Rudolf, their fifteen-year-old son; Henryk Sienkiewicz, the future Nobel Prize–winning writer; and a group of friends. Sontag insists on the word "inspired"; since she does not follow the historical record too closely. She has allowed herself, she emphasizes, the freedom to invent.

The journey to the New World and the making of a new community are yoked to Sontag's effort to create a new story out of the material of history. She emphasizes her effort in the novel's preface, "Zero," in which she explores her personal relationship to her characters. Like Nathaniel Hawthorne, who describes in "The Custom House," his preface to *The Scarlet Letter*, how he "discovered" the story of Hester Prynne who wore the scarlet letter, Sontag dramatizes in "Zero" the creative process that led her to write her historical novel.

"Zero" explains who the writer of *In America* is. Sontag rehearses a good deal from the interviews she has given over the previous thirty years: she grew up in Arizona and California wanting to be, like Marie Curie, a great scientist and humanitarian; her grandparents came from Poland; at eighteen she read *Middlemarch* and "burst into tears because I realized not only that *I* was Dorothea but that, a few months earlier, I had married Mr. Casaubon" (i.e., Philip Rieff). She has been to Sarajevo (the novel is dedicated to "my friends in Sarajevo") and thinks of the Poles she overheard talking in a room (she has been magically transported to the past) as precursors of her beloved Bosnians—like the Poles, suffering occupation and partition. The Sontag narrator of "Zero" appears only once in the novel, and then very briefly.

Chapter One describes Maryna's disenchantment with her successful career. She sees herself as a prisoner of her fame and of the public's perception of her character. Thus she is wary of playing comic roles because comedy "isn't thought to be my strong point." She longs for release from these established opinions. She desires to recreate herself.

Chapter Two portrays Maryna's resolution to go to America. She is supported by her husband, Bogdan, and will be followed to the United States by Ryszard, the young writer who is in love with her. She offers many reasons for leaving—such as her desire to live in a free country that represents the future for her and her child and her husband who also wants to go, her simple curiosity, her sense of adventure, and her wish to be known as more than a Polish actress. But none of these reasons seems as important as her ambition to succeed in the terms of a New World, which will give her the opportunity to forge a new identity.

In Chapter Three, Ryszard and Julien (a friend of Maryna's) embark for America before her in order to scout out a place where she can settle in California. Aboard ship Ryszard meets many different American types who know nothing about Poland or its history of partition. He is told that if he is prepared to work hard, he can make a success of himself in America. He finds Americans to be extremely self-satisfied and certain of their freedom. In steerage he encounters a young woman, Nora, who has turned to prostitution in order to pay her way to America. Ryszard and Julien discuss the girl's plight, with Julien insisting that it is not as bad as being stuck in a loveless marriage. But then Ryszard realizes that Julien is thinking of his own troubled marriage with Wanda. Ryszard is sure that Maryna would approve of his interest in the steerage passengers. When the ship lands, he is astonished at the size of Manhattan, which he explores as a journalist. Unlike the confined microcosm of the ship, the city seems to contain elements of "everywhere." Preparing for the trip to California, he sees a poster promising it is the land of paradise for the laborer.

Maryna arrives in Manhattan in Chapter Four. She makes friends in the Polish community. She dines at famous restaurants such as Delmonico's. She attends performances of popular plays. She takes her son Piotr to the Centennial Exhibition in Philadelphia. It is all an effort that she must deliberately pursue because, as she reflects: "You men have it much easier. You are commended for recklessness, for boldness, for striking out, for being adventurous. A woman has so many inner voices telling her to behave prudently, amiably, timorously. . . . Each time I am brave, I am acting. But that is all that's needed to be brave. . . . The appearance of bravery. The performance of it." America exhilarates because it is unfinished and always "under way," she observes.

In the next chapter Maryna journeys to Anaheim to set up her "utopian household." She conceives of it as a community and family, "not a kind of place but a kind of time, those all too brief moments when one would not wish to be anywhere else." Is utopia a "very ancient instinct, for breathing in unison?" she wonders. It is like "sexual union . . . the desire to breathe more deeply, deeper still, faster . . . but always together." She conceives of the commune as a farm on which everyone will do their share in producing the food they eat. She does not miss the stage. On the contrary, she revels in the idea of "being stripped" and having to build herself up again.

Chapter Six recounts the phases of settlement in Anaheim for Maryna and her devoted following. After six months, Piotr is acclimated and wants to change his name to Peter. A reluctant Maryna finally grants his wish. She focuses on the "group enterprise," a familiar virtue to an actress who realizes that her achievement depends on a cast and crew working together. Although she is a queen who has abdicated her throne, she is surrounded by "those who knew her on the throne." Some of them begin to realize they are not cut out to be farmers. Even Maryna agrees to leave the commune for an excursion with Ryszard. By the end of this six-month chapter in Maryna's life, she decides not only to return to the stage but to hazard her career in America. As her husband realizes, she did not want the commune itself but a "new self," a new set of obstacles to overcome which would prove her worth.

In Chapter Seven, Maryna launches her career in San Francisco. She studies with a Miss Collingridge to perfect her pronunciation of English. She auditions for "bilious" theatre impresario

Angus Barton, who is skeptical that this foreigner can win over American audiences. "They don't want a steady diet of lady," he tells her. But she auditions so magnificently that she wins him over, and he profusely apologizes for his skepticism. Maryna is now in the process of transforming herself into an American "star," the requirements of which receive considerable attention. Apart from her husband at this point, Maryna finally confronts Ryszard's pursuit of her, confessing that she cannot say whether or not she really loves Ryszard. "I never know exactly what I feel when I'm not on a stage." The truth is, she tells him, actors just like to act.

By Chapter Eight, Maryna, now successful in America, remains restless and returns to Poland. Yet she seeks to renew her place as an American star and consents to a gruelling series of one-night appearances across America. In London she finds a more reserved reception and does not feel she is a success. America is more apealing because audiences revel in the sheer excitement of stardom.

In Chapter Nine, Maryna's American career is set against the ironic monologue of the great American actor Edwin Booth, with whom she will tour. A drunken Booth discourses on the nature of the actor: "First, he has to make himself interesting to himself. Then to other people." He dislikes the way P. T. Barnum has made a big show of everything, putting everything up for sale. Now actors have to sell themselves. Even though he calls Maryna an "abdicated Polish queen," he finds that she is too bland. She is not dangerous; she has not yet experienced her catastrophe. Booth is thinking, of course, of his brother's assassination of President Lincoln and how that act has marred his own career. He chides Maryna for making up some stage business (gestures) that she had not discussed with him. He prefers a traditional approach. If Maryna has to make up something new, he wants to be consulted beforehand. "An actor can't just *make it up*," he tells her. They must come to an understanding since they have a long tour ahead of them, he says in the novel's concluding line.

SONTAG READING SONTAG

Sontag told Christopher Hitchens in *Vanity Fair* that she had been considering a novel about a 1920s diva. She also had an idea about Slavic immigrants to America inspired by her friendship with the Russian emigré poet Joseph Brodsky. Then, as she explained to Bob Minzesheimer in *USA Today*, she was browsing in a Boston bookstore, picked up a biography of the novelist Henryk Sienkiewicz, and spotted a paragraph that mentioned his emigration in 1876 to Anaheim with the Polish actress Helena Modrzejewska (shortened in America to Modjeska). "What a fabulous story!" she thought. "I wanted to write about America, but with a foreigner's perspective. I like writing about foreigners. They're alive to the world; they take nothing for granted; they see the oddities." To Harvey Blume in the *Atlantic*, Sontag noted, "It's a privilege to be a foreigner, it's such an intensifier of experience."

Of the novel's structure—the opening that refers to herself and the ending with Edwin Booth's monologue—she commented that she wanted readers to realize: "Wow, that's a long journey." To her, a novel should be a "big trip that takes you a long ways from where you started and what you thought you know about the characters."

Sontag told Robert Allen Papinchak in the *Seattle Times* that historical novels are "like trampolines, giving me bounce." Yet she said she did not read the actress's memoirs (published in 1910) until after she had finished the novel. She wanted to take possession of Maryna's story, which to her was a story about a woman "who understands that to have a really big career, you can't really go all out on private life. Women don't have that luxury," she told Will Blythe in *Mirabella*. As an actress, Maryna is "nailed to her appearance, as women are." The real person, Sontag emphasized to Papinchak, "wasn't like my person at all." (She would later call the real actress a racist, among other things. See Chapter 1 for an account of the plagiarism charges against Sontag.) Her novel was not an effort to resurrect history so much as a way to discover characters—"their relationships, what they're doing and why America means something different to each one of them."

Sontag admitted to Dale Peck in *Book Forum* that she included some of her own memories of Arizona and Southern California in the novel: "The moment when the adolescent Polish maid discovers three eggplants in the back of the house, and tries to lift them up, and can't. That's a memory of mine, at seven. There were three eggplants in the back of this tiny bungalow in Tucson, and I'd never seen an eggplant before. I went to pick it up—and it was anchored to the earth, and I remember being so startled and entranced by that."

Part of the pleasure of writing *In America*, Sontag told Peck, was to discover what the past was like: "For instance, it's 1877 and Maryna's in the Palace Hotel in San Francisco. I find out that the earliest elevator—the hydraulic, invented by Mr. Otis—is shown in the exposition in 1876, in Philadelphia. So does the Palace Hotel, built right afterward, have elevators? It turns out it did. Discovering these things just makes you squeal with pleasure." Sontag asked Hitchens: "Do you know that in the 1880s there were more than 5,000 theaters in this country, and that more than half of their productions were Shakespeare? It was Bardolatry! Everyone knew at least some of the plays by heart."

As Sontag's comments suggest, she did considerable background reading for her novel. She told Joan Acocella in the *New Yorker* that she read about the 1870s in Kraków, New York, San Francisco, and Anaheim in crumbling newspapers, agricultural manuals, and old Baedekers (travel guides). She found a floor plan of the ship that Sienkiewicz (Ryszard in the novel) traveled on to America. She was "happy for a whole day" when she discovered that the elevators in the Palace Hotel had mirrors in them. She could use this detail to create a scene in which Maryna looks at herself while others are also looking at her—a perfect metaphor for the personality who is always on stage.

Sontag resisted a reading of the novel as autobiographical, even though in an interview with Elzbieta Sawicka in Warsaw in January 1998, Sontag confessed: "I am myself an actress, a closet actress. I always wanted to write a novel about an actress. I understand what acting is all about and what goes on in the profession." She had acted in school, and she really loved performing, but she herself had concluded that "this is not a life I want to live." Curious about the Polish connection, Sawicka wondered if Sontag's own ancestry figured in her feeling for Modjeska. Sontag said, "No, not at all." Sawicka countered: "The land of your ancestors doesn't have any meaning for you? Aren't you sentimental?" It was not a question of sentiment, Sontag insisted. "I'm not egocentric. I don't think about myself too much or about my roots."

CRITICAL COMMENTARY

Critics divided pretty evenly in their responses to *In America*. Elaine Showalter, in the *New Statesman*, praised the reminiscent tone of "Zero," the descriptions of California, the appearances of Henry James (Maryna has a brief scene with him) and Edwin Booth, but concluded that "overall" the novel is an "oddly plotless and inert chronicle of ideas and events in Maryna's career." On the other hand, the noted critic Sven Birkets, in the *Hudson Review*, faulted Sontag for resisting her natural bent—the novel of ideas. *In America* was not cerebral enough. Citing her famous statement about the erotics of art in "Against Interpretation," Birkets suggested that if Sontag could not fashion a truly sensual piece of literature, she should have concentrated more on a "hermeneutics" or interpretative mode. Similarly, Michiko Kakutani, in the *New York Times*, gave the novel poor marks for dealing in clichés about acting and America and for not raising the level of thought to at least the peak achieved by *The Volcano Lover*. Yet Mark Luce, in the *Atlanta Journal-Constitution*, admired the scope and style of the novel: "With charm, aplomb, variances of voice and her trademark wit, Sontag explores identity, nationalism, idealism and one woman's quest for transformation."

Writing in the *Irish Times*, Eamon Delaney observed that *In America* consisted of "boiled down historical research" and "banal psychological insights . . . dressed up to make a 'novel.'" In the *Guardian/Observer*, John Sutherland, one of England's most distinguished critics, was more damning: "Let's face it: if this was a first novel by a literary unknown it would have been lucky to make it into print."

Sutherland was fascinated with the resemblance between Maryna and her creator. He noticed that in "Zero" Sontag identified herself with Dorothea Brook in *Middlemarch*. Unlike Dorothea, Sontag breaks free of her Casaubon and creates a heroine in Maryna who will similarly refuse to bury herself in devotion to a great man and to private life. Maryna, like Sontag, will insist on taking center stage. "This heroine," Sutherland concludes, "did not follow her menfolk to America; they followed her. She made her career and achieved her stardom, even if it meant ditching the men in her life. It was, as Sontag says of herself and her luckless discarded Mr. Casaubon, 'morally right' to do so. The truly womanly thing to do, that is."

Scott McLemee, in *In These Times*, called "Zero" a "well-turned piece of metafiction," noting that it bore a distinct resemblance to Laura Riding's *Progress of Stories*, which, McLemee noted, Sontag had cited elsewhere and which included the conceit of a writer at a party introducing her characters to the reader. Yet the rest of the novel, McLemee added, was like the traditional realistic theatre, and Sontag's ability to draw human characters was fatally weak. She dealt in stereotypes except when her characters were intellectuals and artists. The America of the average person, the laborers and immigrants and "black folks," was lost on her. The novel was of a piece with her essay "What Is Happening in America."

Richard Lourie, in the *Washington Post Book World*, praised the novel's panoramic quality and its "full arsenal of narrative devices—standard third-person, omniscience, diaries, letters, snatches of dialogue, monologues both interior and spoken aloud." In the *New York Times Book Review*, Sarah Kerr admired the novel's construction but complained that for all its clever devices it lacked dramatic tension. Walter Kirn, in *New York* magazine, pointed out that it was America's energy, not its virtue, that Sontag admired and that her novel could be appreciative at precisely those moments when it was a conventional historical novel.

Michael Silverblatt, in the *Los Angeles Times*, provided one of the most sustained readings of *In America* as a "brilliant and profound investigation into the fate of thought and culture in America." He extolled Sontag's use of narrative devices, which he called "lenses," through which Maryna's career was presented. Rather than have Maryna explain herself, these lenses revealed "what she is becoming and what is actually happening to her." Both "Zero" and Edwin Booth's concluding monologue provided an "antisentimental" antidote to Maryna's "lacquered self-deception." Silverblatt thought "Zero" so good that it was an example of what "prose can achieve in our time." It evoked the "modern split sensibility," striving to integrate itself with the past. In Maryna, Sontag invested "everything she knows" about being an artist, activist, and performer. Attempting to rescue the novel from its growing reputation as a conventional work, the critic called *In America* an example of postmodernism built out of a "succession of microstructures" that link the "monuments of the past, the works of Stendhal, Tolstoy, George Eliot" to Maryna's nineteenth-century journey of discovery.

James Wood seconded Silverblatt's appraisal in the *New Republic*, suggesting that devices like "Zero" suspended the "characters in a fluid of modernity (or post-modernity)," signaling to the reader that they are "being watched by a contemporary writer; but inside this careful panopticon they live and breathe fully as free fictional characters." To Wood, the historical details meshed beautifully with the narrative. And he thought that Sontag had tactfully "subjugated her intelligence" to the demands of the novel's episodes. Yet he doubted whether the constraints of the historical novel could fully release the talents of contemporary writers, and he concluded: "Surely fiction has more primary duties than the recovery (even the enraptured recovery) of the past, and I wish that Sontag would release herself into the wide and even more unsettled straits of the palpable present-intimate."

For many critics, Sontag herself got in the way of interpreting the novel. In the *New York Observer*, Adam Begley, a sympathetic reviewer who enjoyed much of the novel, nevertheless put the questions that seemed to inform many other reviews of *In America*:

> No way to sweeten the pill: Susan Sontag is a powerful thinker, as smart as she's supposed to be, and a better writer, sentence for sentence, than anyone who now wears the tag "intellectual"—but she can't seem to write a great novel. . . . What's missing? Why can't she (like, say George Eliot) convert brainpower and word mastery into a knock-your-socks-off novel? Is it her reader's fault if the tale she's telling always seems less compelling than the ghostly presence of the teller, the scary shade of Ms. Sontag solemnly passing out her ideas? Does it seem so because when we read her we're on the lookout for evidence of her excellent intellect in action? What would happen if she vanished, if she erased the artful authorial intrusions and restrained the urge to share her pensees, if she let the story do its work? It's what she wants (sometimes)—I can tell.

Quite aside from Begley's judgment of *In America*, his review was characteristic of reviewers who were quite conscious of dealing with a writer who was an integral part of America's intellectual history. They could not help reviewing a monument, not simply the novel at hand.

The intrusive autobiographical elements of "Zero" also suggest that Sontag could not forget herself—that is, do without reminding readers of her unique standing in American intellectual life. "Zero" portends a grand link between past and present, between author and material, that the novel itself never delivers. In the end, "Zero" is important only because it is written in Sontag's own voice, and Susan Sontag must be noticed as the writer. In her interviews she is at pains to explain that she became a writer not to express herself but to contribute to the body of great literature. To be recognized as a writer means more to her than what she writes. Style predominates over content—to apply the terms of her famous essay "Against Interpretation" to herself.

Therein lies the problem. Sontag has never come to ground. She dreams of herself as a writer just as she dreams of an America that will be. The America that is has rarely appealed to her, and has usually merited her disapproval. In her essays she has dismissed most of American fiction, and her comments on American history are about as superficial and ill-informed as those of any writer who has achieved her prominence.

Reviews of Sontag's fiction often speak of a willed enterprise. She takes her cue from E. M. Cioran, who advocates a spiritual strenuousness that requires us to "sever our roots" and become "metaphysically foreigners." Her essay on Cioran perfectly captures her own *willed* existence. In it she embraces a thinker who counsels extrication from the world and from domestic commitments in order to experience life as "a series of situations" that leaves the consciousness free to explore its own labyrinth. What Sontag loves most about Cioran is his elevation of the "*will* and its capacity to transform the world." Not surprisingly, then, *In America* evokes the "power of the will." While acknowledging her utopian tendencies and her doubts that she will prevail in America, Maryna declares, "I must and I will!" She is reminiscent of the earlier Sontag who weighed the risks of idealizing North Vietnam but then insisted the country deserved to be idealized. Maryna writes to a Polish friend that with a "strong enough will one can surmount any obstacle." America, Maryna concludes, is a "whole country of people who believe in the will."

In America fails to achieve the success of *The Volcano Lover* because so much of it is declaiming without dramatizing. Even Sontag's fabled talent for epigram eludes her here: "Passion is a beautiful thing, and so is understanding, the coming to understand something, which is a passion, which is a journey, too." Only rarely does a character or a scene catch fire, as with Angus Barton, the theatre impresario. Sontag also achieves an amusing parody of Henry James's style in one brief scene.

The biggest disappointment is Maryna herself. Sontag mentions in "Zero" how taken she is with divas. She even describes a scene she witnessed between diva Maria Callas and the director of the Metropolitan Opera, Rudolf Bing, which occurred just as Sontag herself was beginning to establish a reputation in New York. But we learn little from Maryna or from the other characters about what it means to be a diva. Divahood, seemingly, would once have made an ideal subject for a Sontag essay, but she no longer seems willing to exercise the discipline demanded by the genre (see Chapter 13).

In America does not seem as deeply imagined as *The Volcano Lover*, and it lacks the tension between past and present that distinguished Sontag's earlier historical novel. In *The Scarlet Letter* the introductory Custom House section succeeds because Hawthorne takes on the burden of the past, establishing his link to the seventeenth century even as he would like, in some ways, to shed its influence. The past was unquestionably an ineluctable part of the novelist and his novel. History was palpable, and it suffused both his style and content. Sontag writes like an exile who believes she can through sheer force of will conjure up the past. The reader soon tires of the novelist as eavesdropper, one who never commits herself to her characters, who in fact seems to feel superior to her creations, since, after all, they are only products of her will.

THIRTEEN

Sontag Reading Sontag

For the last thirty-five years Susan Sontag has given hundreds of interviews broadcast on television and radio and printed in newspapers and journals around the world. She has often used interviews and the newspaper/magazine profile not only to comment on responses to her work but to shape how that work should be read. A fine selection of these interviews has been published in *Conversations with Susan Sontag*, which shows the development of a novelist, filmmaker, and essayist whose greatest impact on world culture occurred in the late 1960s through the late 1970s—a decade in which she produced classic essays that have become part of the canon of contemporary literature. Those interviews also show her yearning to be recognized as a creative writer, a novelist whose career was interrupted by certain issues of her time that demanded treatment in the essay form. But what Sontag viewed as an interruption, critics considered as her main achievement. Sontag strengthened their impression by publishing no novels for twenty-five years. And her production of short fiction was limited to one volume and some short pieces in magazines. Even with the success of *The Volcano Lover*, Sontag was treated as a critic who could also write fiction, if only sporadically and with mixed results.

By the mid-1980s Sontag began reorienting her career, publishing no major essays except *AIDS and Its Metaphors* and short forewords and prefaces to books she admired and wished to promote. Even when she published a new preface to a foreign edition of *Against Interpretation* (the preface was reprinted in the *Three-penny Review*), she reiterated that her early essays were not meant as part of a literary critic's program of study but rather as examples of her enthusiasm for works of art that she thought deserved a larger audience and more discussion. She was plainly irritated with critics who had taken her to be some kind of cultural arbiter. She insisted that she was speaking only to gratify herself.

Since the publication of *Conversations with Susan Sontag*, Sontag has participated in an important interview that once again attempts to transform readers' perceptions of her career. For the Winter 1995 issue of the *Paris Review* she gave what she called in one of her public readings "the interview of record"—acknowledging the honor that journal had bestowed on her by including her in its prestigious series "The Art of Fiction," which has featured interviews with many of the most important novelists of the twentieth century. In the same issue, under the heading "The Art of Criticism," there appeared an interview with George Steiner, whose essays rival Sontag's in sophistication and influence, and who also has written fiction.

Sontag's interview, conducted by one of her friends, the poet Edward Hirsch, explored her early reading of writers such as Jack London and Edgar Allan Poe. Before her teens Sontag had written stories, poems, and two plays. Writers such as André Gide inspired her with the idea of a career in literature. Her university education and early marriage are described as a detour on the way to becoming a writer. She explained that writing essays was laborious and often resulted in her changing her mind several times. Fiction, on the other hand, came quickly, and though she invariably revised, the first draft contained the "essentials." Essays represented the "constrained" part of herself whereas fiction represented "freedom." Of her work in the 1960s she said:

Obviously, I don't agree with everything in the early essays. I've changed, and I know more. And the cultural context which inspired them has altogether changed. But there would be no point in modifying them now. I think I would like to take a blue pencil to the first two novels, though.

Sontag's only real regret was writing theatre criticism for *Partisan Review*. She was not that kind of critic—one who goes to plays and passes judgment—and she felt she was being forced into the mold of Mary McCarthy, who had established her reputation writing theatre criticism in the same publication. After two pieces on the theatre, Sontag quit writing such reviews. "I am not a critic," she emphasized. "I thought of my essays as cultural work. They were written out of a sense of what *needed* to be written."

When Sontag said the cultural context had changed, she had in mind her assumption that the canon of great books would not be affected by her own enthusiasm for contemporary art that flouted the traditions of art or the conventions of society. What she called "playful," "transgressive," and "eccentric" art could be enjoyed without threatening what she called the "liberal consensus about culture." Now taste had become so "debauched" that Sontag believed that the very idea of seriousness had been undermined. It was a culture dominated by notions of celebrity and self-promotion. She doubted that the public would "understand what it means to talk about art as opposed to art projects." Perhaps realizing that she was sounding rather peeved, she added: "How tedious always to be indignant."

Describing her shift from essay writing to fiction, Sontag noted that most of her essays in the 1970s and early 1980s were requiems or tributes to the writers she admired. The essays amounted to self-portraits or fictions, she confessed, and she was coming "to the end of what the essay form could do for me." In *The Volcano Lover*, her Cavaliere was the "fully realized fictional form of what I'd been trying to say, in an impacted way, in the essay-portraits of Canetti and Benjamin."

And yet Sontag went through a crisis of confidence that prevented her from finishing another novel until *The Volcano Lover*. In retrospect, she told Hirsch, she realized that "I wasn't able to give myself permission to tell a story, a real story, as opposed to the adventures of somebody's consciousness." With *The Volcano Lover* she found not only characters but a great story she felt compelled to write. Although she did not deny Hirsch's suggestion that there were essay elements in *The Volcano Lover*, to her they seemed restrained compared with a "central tradition of the European novel" extending from Balzac to Proust and Thomas Mann.

The interview ended with Sontag's statement that she did not reread her work, except to check translations. She thought her best work was ahead of her. Although she acknowledged that all her work was unified by her temperament—most especially her ardor and melancholy—she liked to foster her "illusion of endless new beginnings. That's the most American part of me: I feel it's always a new start."

If the dialogue between Hirsch and Sontag in the *Paris Review* constituted the "interview of record," Joan Acocella's *New Yorker* piece, "The Hunger Artist," represented the profile of record. Acocella, another Sontag friend, paid her an enormous compliment by borrowing her title from Kafka's classic story. The *New Yorker* has over the years done classic profiles of writers such as Ernest Hemingway and Lillian Hellman. These pieces include a significant proportion of biographical material—which Sontag had always resisted making public. But with the eminent publication of her biography, Sontag began releasing material to glossy magazines such as *Mirabella* and *Vanity Fair*. Assured of a sympathetic hearing from Acocella, Sontag went well beyond her remarks in the *Paris Review* in an effort to refocus the reading public's view of her position in the culture and her significance as a writer.

The profile began in the exclamatory mode. When Acocella asked Sontag whether she missed writing the essay form, she replied: "Essays! Pooh! Forget essays! That was the past. From now on, I'm writing fiction. I have a whole new life. It's going to be terrific." She dismissed her early work—even suggesting it was the product of an illusion: "I thought I *liked* William Burroughs and Nathalie Sarraute and Robbe-Grillet, but I didn't. I actually didn't." Sontag had adopted these avant-garde artists largely because she believed that the realistic fiction and much of the art of that period (except for film) had lost its energy and had become shapeless. In her emphasis on form over content, Sontag was preserving her early essays as examples of good performances even as she was repudiating their meaning.

The encyclopedic quality of Sontag's essays has formed an indelible impression on the public mind that continues to influence reviews of her fiction. Few writers have dropped as many names and terms as Sontag has in her essays, and the writing about her is also suffused with the same name-dropping inclination that has always made her seem important and formidable. Reviews of *In America* and accounts of her recent public appearances invariably began by introducing her with epithets: "an intellectual Sherpa guide" (*St. Louis Post-Dispatch*), "America's intellectual bootgirl" (*Irish Times*), "the crown princess of American intellectuals" (*Atlanta Journal-Constitution*), "the onetime high priestess of the avant-garde" (*New York Times*), "the diva of New York intellectuals" (*Boston Globe*).

Sontag's latching on to names has to do with her irrepressible admiration for artists whom she believes deserve celebration. Inevitably, her habit of naming and celebration adheres to her, investing her with a kind of charisma. Like the old Gnostics, she seems to draw on a wisdom she only partially reveals by naming but not always explaining. Their power lay as much in what they chose *not* to reveal. They were "against interpretation." Sontag's desire to preserve some of the mystery of art—no matter that she apparently disowns some of her earlier work—means that the aura of mystery accrues to herself. Her catalog of names stands for a body of knowledge that most readers will find daunting and that some will find challenging. Those who are not irritated by her name-dropping will be grateful to her for cataloging areas of knowledge new to them. Even if no work of Susan Sontag's is likely to find a place in the canon of American literature, as a cultural figure and an impresario of the arts she is likely to prove an indispensable figure, both to those who wish to repudiate her influence and to those who cannot seem to start an argument, or defend a position, without invoking her name.

A Susan Sontag Glossary

Abbott, Berenice (1898–1991). American photographer. In *On Photography*, Sontag discusses Abbott's most important achievement: her recording of the history of New York City.

Abel, Lionel (1911–2001). One of the New York intellectuals, he is perhaps best known for his book *Metatheatre*, which Sontag discusses in *Against Interpretation*. She calls his book the "first American-style existentialist tract. His argument is clean-cut, pugnacious, prone to slogans, oversimplified—and, in the main, absolutely right." She finds it more reliable than George Steiner's *Death of Tragedy* and Martin Esslin's *The Theater of the Absurd*. Abel's thesis is that modern man struggles with the burden of his subjectivity. She does believe, however, that Abel makes too much of the liberal skepticism of Western culture. He relies on Montaigne, Machiavelli, and the Enlightenment and ignores Paul, Augustine, Dante, Pascal, and Kierkegaard, who were hardly liberal skeptics.

Adams, Ansel (1902–1984). American photographer celebrated for his stunning photographs of American landscapes, especially his shots of the national parks in the West and the California coast. In *On Photography*, Sontag calls him "Weston's best-known disciple."

Adams, John (1735–1826). Second president of the United States. In *Illness as Metaphor*, Sontag explains Adams's use of disease metaphors. In 1772 Adams wrote that the country seemed "worn out" by struggling and venality that was spreading "like a Cancer." Sontag's point is that such metaphors are deeply ingrained not only in discussions of physical illness but in the way people govern themselves.

Adorno, Theodor (1903–1969). German philosopher and student of Walter Benjamin. Adorno is best known for his writing on art and society. He presents an overview of his work in *Negative Dialectics*. Sontag discusses his views in "The Pornographic Imagination," taking issue with his belief that pornography does not have the structure of literature and is basically motiveless. Sontag refers to Adorno several times in her essay on Walter Benjamin in *Under the Sign of Saturn*.

Arbus, Diane (1923–1971). American photographer. Arbus is best known for her disturbing photographs of bizarre-looking people. Sontag devotes a chapter to Arbus in *On Photography* as well as mentioning her in different contexts throughout the book. In the main, Arbus is used as an example of the photographer who challenges the Whitman tradition of seeing America as a united country.

Arendt, Hannah (1906–1975). This German-Jewish political philosopher came to the United States in 1941 in flight from Nazi persecution. She became one of the New York intellectuals, publishing in the *Partisan Review* and in the *New Yorker* articles about totalitarianism and modern history. Her key work, *The Origins of Totalitarianism* (1951), established her international reputation. She was one of the few women in American intellectual life to command a respect comparable to that accorded to male philosophers. Sontag grew up in Southern California reading Arendt's articles and modeling herself, to some extent, on Arendt's formidable, controversial persona. In 1963 Arendt published *Eichmann in Jerusalem*, a book that questioned the passivity of Jews in the face of the Holocaust. The book caused huge debates, with New

York intellectuals such as Lionel Abel attacking Arendt, and others such as Mary McCarthy defending her. It is somewhat surprising that Sontag never published an intellectual portrait of Arendt. Indeed, all of her major essay-portraits in *Under the Sign of Saturn* are of men. Sontag briefly discusses Arendt's ideas about the Eichmann trial in "Reflections on *The Deputy*," included in *Against Interpretation*. Arendt's essay on Walter Benjamin is briefly mentioned in "Project for a Trip to China."

Aristotle (384–322 B.C.). Greek philosopher. Sontag is concerned mainly with the Aristotle of the *Poetics*. It disturbs her that his view of art still predominates, since his definition tends to subordinate art to the world; that is, art is a copy of the real thing, not a real thing in itself. Art is useful (it purges the emotions, for example), Aristotle argues. The problem with this approach, Sontag points out in "On Style," is that it confuses art with philosophy. Aristotle makes art into argument about the world rather than seeing it as an end in itself. Sontag comments on Aristotle's definition of metaphor in *AIDS and Its Metaphors*.

Arnold, Matthew (1822–1888). British poet and critic. In *Culture and Anarchy* (1873), he established the early modern idea of culture, which Sontag suggests in "One Culture and the New Sensibility" has been superseded: "Artists have broken, whether they know it or not, with the Matthew Arnold notion of culture, finding it historically and humanly obsolescent. The Matthew Arnold notion of culture defined art as the criticism of life—this being understood as the propounding of moral, social, and political ideas. The new sensibility understands art as the extension of life—this being understood as the representation of (new) modes of vivacity." In this passage from the concluding essay of *Against Interpretation*, Sontag is reiterating her position that art is not a comment on society but a fact of society, an entity in itself, a way of refreshing human vision rather than some kind of extra or adjunct to life.

Art Nouveau. An arts and crafts movement of the late nineteenth and early twentieth centuries. Artists worked on everyday objects—furniture, glass containers, pottery, textiles—to create curvilinear and brilliantly colored creations that sought to transform the domestic environment into a work of art. Sontag mentions such Art Nouveau figures as Tiffany and Gaudi in "On Style" as examples of experiencing the world as an "aesthetic phenomenon."

Artaud, Antonin (1896–1948). French actor, director, and theorist of the theatre. Sontag first wrote about Artaud in "Marat/Sade/Artaud." She also includes an essay on him in *Under the Sign of Saturn*. Sontag makes scattered references to him throughout her essays. She has been drawn particularly to his conception of the theatre's nonverbal aspects: physical movements, gestures, sounds, and a minimal use of words constitute what Sontag calls the "aesthetics of silence," which she used as the title for an essay in *Styles of Radical Will*. Artaud brought theatre back to a more elemental sense of itself, making it much less reliant on the conventions of realism that Sontag attacks in both *Against Interpretation* and *Styles of Radical Will*. Artaud's concept of the Theatre of Cruelty—a theatre that would emphasize the nonverbal and confront its audience more directly through gesture and movement—and its relationship to modern photography is discussed in *On Photography*.

Atget, Eugene Auguste (1856–1927). French photographer renowned for his documentary series on Paris. He photographed all aspects of city life—parks, cafés, markets, architecture, and the people in various trades and professions. His work is discussed in *On Photography*. Sontag notes that Atget's work was discovered and promoted by the American photographer Berenice Abbott.

Avedon, Richard (1923–). American fashion and portrait photographer. Sontag makes several references to him in *On Photography*, contrasting, for example, his statement that some of his best photographs are of people he met for the first time whereas painters have often relied on deep familiarity with their subjects.

Baldwin, James (1924–1987). African-American novelist and essayist. Sontag acknowledges Baldwin's passion, but like Camus, she finds him too rhetorical and oratorical. He is too concerned with conveying a message to create great art. In "Going to Theater, etc." (*Against Interpretation*), she reviews his play *Blues for Mister Charlie* and finds that it treats white people as inferior human beings.

Barthes, Roland (1915–1980). French critic and friend of Sontag's. She includes an essay on him in *Under the Sign of Saturn* and also wrote an introduction to his work in editions of *A Barthes Reader* (1982) and *Writing Degree Zero* (1968). Barthes was concerned to show how culture establishes its meaning in "texts." But texts for Barthes could mean not just books but almost any kind of cultural activity that had its own set of symbols and signs. He explored various aspects of popular culture, including photography. He became one of the models for Sontag of what an intellectual should be. "I had not read Barthes when I wrote *The Benefactor* or the first essays in *Against Interpretation*," Sontag told interviewers Eileen Manion and Sherry Simon. "When I discovered Barthes he was above all for me a model of density and passionateness. There is no waste in Barthes' writing."

Bataille, Georges (1897–1962). French novelist and critic. His fiction and criticism explore the erotic life. Sontag uses his work as an example of pornography as art in *Styles of Radical Will*. She affirms his view that pornography is not really about sex but about death.

Baudelaire, Charles (1821–1867). French poet and critic, considered one of France's greatest writers. Sontag refers to Baudelaire frequently, particularly in *On Photography* and *Under the Sign of Saturn*, where she discusses Walter Benjamin's writing about Baudelaire. Baudelaire was an inveterate commentator on art and photography, and Sontag often uses him as an authority in her writing. His most famous work is a collection of poetry, *Les fleurs du mal* (*The Flowers of Evil*, 1857).

Bauhaus. German school of design founded in the 1920s. Art should serve the needs of society, Bauhaus artists proclaimed. Artists and architects should emphasize the beauty of forms. Photographers such as Moholy-Nagy attempted to translate Bauhaus doctrine into photographs, although in *On Photography* Sontag argues that the Bauhaus approach to photography "has not prevailed." Photographers have not presented themselves as scientists of form but rather as the revealers of human content, Sontag suggests.

Beardsley, Aubrey (1872–1898). English artist whom Sontag alludes to in "On Style" in her catalog of artists whose work is defined by their style—in Beardsley's case, his work is distinguished by his violating the conventions of perspective and proportion. His elongated figures are uniquely Beardsley and not an imitation of "reality."

Beckett, Samuel (1906–1989). One of the masters of modern drama, Beckett is a touchstone figure in Sontag's essays. He is an example of the ascetic artist who uses words sparingly, favoring what she calls an aesthetics of silence (see *Styles of Radical Will*). An epigraph from Beckett's play *Endgame* is used at the beginning of *Under the Sign of Saturn*. In 1993, in Sarajevo, Sontag directed a production of his most famous play, *Waiting for Godot*.

Benjamin, Walter (1892–1940). German philosopher, social and literary critic. Sontag devotes an essay to him in *Under the Sign of Saturn*. His interest in photography is a major influence on *On Photography*, which includes an appendix of quotations that pays homage to "W.B." Benjamin had a surrealist sensibility, Sontag points out, and the "juxtaposition of incongruous quotations" is itself a surrealist act—related to photography's ability to incorporate discordant or contradictory elements in the same picture plane. Benjamin argued that both photography and the cinema subverted ideas of traditional art and challenged the very idea of the aesthetic. Sontag calls him "photography's most original and important critic." Benjamin's promulgation of avant-garde artists such as Bertolt Brecht is also reflected in what Sontag later called, in *Against Interpretation*, the "new sensibility."

Bergman, Ingmar (1918–). Swedish theatre and film director. He is one of the legendary figures of modern cinema, extolled for both his subject matter and technique in films such as *Wild Strawberries* (1957), *The Silence* (1963), and *Persona* (1966). Bergman's films are often full of Freudian symbolism and explorations of the supernatural. Sontag admires his technical proficiency (she often refers to him in *Against Interpretation*), but she dislikes his psychologism and praises films such as *Persona* that succeed in spite of his Freudianism.

Brady, Matthew (1823–1896). American photographer, most famous for his photographs that comprehensively documented the Civil War. In discussing the impact of photographs on the war, Sontag observes in *On Photography* that pictures of the "horrors of the battlefields did not make people any less keen to go on with the Civil War."

Brecht, Bertolt (1898–1956). German dramatist, the author of important plays such as *Mother Courage* (1941) and *The Caucasian Chalk Circle* (1948). Throughout *Against Interpretation*, Sontag refers to Brecht as one of the modern masters. In "The Death of Tragedy" she remarks that the playwright's didacticism and his anti-naturalistic techniques set him apart from other dramatists considered part of the "theater of the absurd." Far from not finding meaning in the universe, Brecht has a strong moralizing tendency. Sontag discusses Brechtian elements in "Syberberg's Hitler."

Bresson, Robert (1907–2000). Sontag includes an essay on the French film director in *Against Interpretation*. She praises films such as *Diary of a Country Priest* that negate the conventions of mainstream cinema. Bresson hired amateurs and purposely avoided the smoothly edited scenes of commercial film. His work embodies Sontag's call for art that abandons psychological realism and tight plotting in favor of probing spiritual and aesthetic issues. His sparing use of dialogue also exemplified what Sontag, in *Styles of Radical Will*, called the "aesthetics of silence." He made relatively few films but is considered one of the great directors of French cinema. Sontag includes an extended comparison of Bresson and Godard in her essay on Godard in *Styles of Radical Will*.

Breton, André (1896–1966). French writer, the author of *Nadja* (1928) and *Selected Poems* (1948). One of the most important figures in French surrealism, Breton attacked conventional and traditional art. He experimented with automatic writing and delighted in creating art by chance or accident. A forerunner of artists such as John Cage and Merce Cunningham, Breton is mentioned in several Sontag essays. In *On Photography*, for example, she refers to Breton's visits to flea markets and his efforts to find in them objects that could be considered art. *The Volcano Lover* begins with just such a visit to a flea market. In *Under the Sign of Saturn*, Sontag compares Breton and the surrealists to Artaud.

Bronzino, Agnolo (1503–1572). Italian Renaissance painter. His use of surface detail and angular figures provides Sontag in "On Style" with another artist who rejects the theory of art as imitation.

Brook, Peter (1925–). British director. Influenced by theorists of the theatre such as Antonin Artaud and Bertolt Brecht, Brook's productions have often been praised by Sontag. She includes admiring accounts of his productions of *King Lear* in "Going to Theater, etc." and in "Marat/Sade/Artaud."

Brown, Norman O. (1913–). Author of *Life Against Death*, the subject of an essay in *Against Interpretation*. Brown is important because he recognizes that "the truth is that love is more sexual, more bodily than even [D. H.] Lawrence imagined. And the revolutionary implications of sexuality in contemporary society are far from being fully understood." Brown, like Marcuse in *Eros and Civilization*, treats Freud and Marx not just as psychological or political thinkers but as agents in the "transformation of human culture" to a "higher consciousness." Sontag's film *Duet for Cannibals* is an exploration of the nexus between sex and politics which seems to have been inspired by Brown's work.

Burke, Edmund (1729–1797). British statesman and author, best known for his classic text *Reflections on the Revolution in France* (1790). Sontag cites Burke in *Illness as Metaphor*, noting that he said that the French during the revolution were in confusion, "like a palsy" attacking the "fountain of life itself." Burke is one of several political philosophers Sontag discusses in order to show how deeply rooted disease metaphors are in public speech.

Burke, Kenneth (1897–1993). Distinguished man of letters. His most important works include *The Philosophy of Literary Form* (1941), *A Grammar of Motives* (1945), and a novel, *Toward a Better Life* (1932). He taught Sontag at the University of Chicago. His interest in symbolic action, his attack on realism, and his attempt to combine the essay and the novel into a new form influenced Sontag's first novel, *The Benefactor*.

Burroughs, William S. (1914–1997). Novelist. Best known for his controversial novel *Naked Lunch* (1959). Burrough's work tends to be phantasmagoric and sexually explicit (he was charged with writing pornography). Sontag extols his fiction in "On Style" as an example of the artist who must be appreciated in terms of his form, not his content. In "The Aesthetics of Silence," she mentions his harsh, apocalyptic rejection of meaning.

Cage, John (1912–1992). American experimental composer. Cage is renowned for composing what might be called anti-music—in the sense that his compositions often rely on the ambient sounds around the audience and do not draw on traditional techniques of musical composition. In "The Aesthetics of Silence," Sontag uses Cage as an example of the modernist who builds silence into his work. She quotes Cage: "There is no such thing as silence. Something is always happening that makes a sound." Such statements provoke questions about what a work of art should contain; silence itself is used as a form of speech, Sontag concludes. References to Cage appear throughout Sontag's writing, and she wrote an essay about Cage, Jasper Johns, and Merce Cunningham for a book featuring their work. She compares Cage and Cioran in *Styles of Radical Will*. In *On Photography* she regards Cage's compositions as an example of "aleatoric" art—work that depends on chance for its performance and appreciation.

Callas, Maria (1923–1977). American operatic soprano, one of the great divas of the twentieth century. Sontag confesses her attraction to such figures in "Zero," her preface to *In America*. Sontag's attraction to opera is clear in her essays on Wagner and on several writers in *Under the Sign of Saturn*.

Camp. The term that defined Sontag's ability to draw on all the different levels of culture. In "Notes on 'Camp,'" Sontag defines the term as "love of the unnatural: of artifice and exaggeration." Camp is thus linked with her definition of art, which also includes the idea of artifice or construct—an alternative to or transformation of real life. Camp is also an aesthetic sensibility which accrues to itself a sense of exclusivity, of seeking an esoteric knowledge. In this respect, camp is a playful aspect of Gnosticism, which is also a form of knowledge shared by a select few. A whole book could be written explaining the plethora of references Sontag uses to describe camp. Among her references are certain favorites that are mentioned in other essays: *King Kong*, Tiffany lamps, Cocteau, Gide, Art Nouveau, Crivelli, Genet, and Wilde.

Camus, Albert (1913–1960). Author of *The Stranger* (1942), a classic modern novel, and journals, which Sontag reviews in *Against Interpretation*. His moral earnestness, in her view, prevents him from being a great writer. He is philosophical and illustrative; that is, his work is not substantial in its own right as art but seems to her "thin" and "somewhat skeletal." In *Illness as Metaphor*, Sontag discusses his novel *The Plague* (1948), which records the shock of modern man who finds himself susceptible to a calamity that seems out of place in the twentieth century.

Candide (1759). Voltaire's picaresque novel, a work Sontag taught at Columbia University and to which she refers in many interviews as one of the inspirations of *The Benefactor*. In his novel, Voltaire takes issue with Leibniz's belief that this is the "best of all possible worlds." Candide is a naive adventurer who travels the world in search of his lost love, Cunegonde. Like Hippolyte in *The Benefactor*, Candide is assisted by various older figures such as Dr. Pangloss, an eternal optimist whose doctrine is constantly challenged by a world of war, torture, and the dismemberment of human beings. Candide is irrepressible, but his journey is an outward one, whereas Hippolyte is persistent, but his adventure is internal. He retreats more and more into himself. Both Hippolyte and Candide reach, in a sense, the same conclusion. At the end of the novel, Candide resolves to cultivate his own garden. The problem for Hippolyte, however, is that at the end of the novel he cannot distinguish between himself and the world, between what is real and the novel he may have been writing.

Canetti, Elias (1905–1994). This Nobel Prize–winning writer has heavily influenced Sontag's work, particularly her early novels and essays. She includes a portrait of him in *Under the Sign of Saturn*, where she lauds his sense of literary tradition and his desire to model himself after great writers. Canetti's only novel, *Auto-da-Fe*, centered on a character who seems to relate only to the world "in his head," had an important influence on Sontag's first two novels.

Capek, Karel (1890–1938). Czech novelist and playwright. Capek was an arch opponent of fascism and the inhuman forces at work in modern life. In *Illness as Metaphor*, Sontag focuses on his allegorical play *The White Plague*, which, like Camus's novel *The Plague*, registers modern man's shock at a disease that overtakes and devastates society. Capek and Elias Canetti are discussed together in *Under the Sign of Saturn*.

Cartier-Bresson, Henri (1908–). French photographer. He is renowned for the exquisite composition of his photographs. Sontag quotes him in *On Photography* as wanting to "find the structure of the world—to revel in the pure pleasure of form." For him, photography finds the order in chaos.

Childs, Lucinda (1940–). Childs, a dancer and choreographer, has often been described as a "minimalist" because of her rather austere and spare style, which Sontag comments on in her essays on dance writing and in her television essay, "A Primer for Pina."

Cioran, E. M. (1911–1985). Romanian-born French essayist, one of the major influences on Sontag. She devotes an essay to him in *Styles of Radical Will*, emphasizing his vision of the writer as an exile. She also explores his notion that the writer must think against himself—that is, explore ideas in terms of their opposites. Discussing syphilis in *AIDS and Its Metaphors*, Sontag notes Cioran's youthful desire to contract the disease because of the myth that it induced hyperactivity and would help him to gain literary glory.

Cocteau, Jean (1889–1963). French poet, dramatist, novelist, and filmmaker. Sontag refers to him frequently in *Against Interpretation*. She compares Cocteau and Bresson in "Spiritual Style in the Films of Robert Bresson," and quotes Cocteau at the beginning of her essay, "Godard's *Vivre Sa Vie*." Cocteau's art and his statements about art second her theme that style and form *are* the work of art; that is, there is no meaning that can be extracted from art. Thus she quotes Cocteau: "Decorative style has never existed." In other words, style is not an "extra" or some value added to art; it is the substance of art. Cocteau is quoted in "Project for a Trip to China" (*I, etcetera*), and Sontag compares him with Paul Goodman in *Under the Sign of Saturn*.

Cornell, Joseph (1903–1972). American artist and filmmaker. He is most famous for his creation of boxes, in which he placed various incongruous objects. He often used photographs and old movie stills, pictures from magazines, and ordinary objects such as thimbles and parts of children's toys (a doll's head, for example). These three-dimensional collages are cited by Sontag in *On Photography* as a quintessential example of surrealism. Like photography, Cornell's boxes illuminate life in a "flash, fixed forever," Sontag observes.

Crivelli, Carlo (c. 1430–c. 1494). Italian painter noted for his sumptuous color and elaborate use of ornament on altarpieces and still lifes. Sontag cites him in "On Style" as an example of the artist who stylizes and embellishes objects that are meant to represent the world.

Cubism. A style of art often associated with Picasso and other early-twentieth-century artists who wished to consider the picture plane in terms of its own geometrical properties. Thus the space on a canvas becomes entirely a medium for the artist and not the artist's copy or mirror of the world. Styles such as cubism are essential to Sontag's argument in *Against Interpretation*, where she asserts that more attention must be paid to the aesthetic surface of works of art. Cubism forces readers to concentrate on the picture plane and not on its representation of something else. This is ultimately what art is, Sontag suggests, a presentation of itself.

Cunningham, Merce (1919–). Dancer and choreographer. Trained under the great American dancer and choreographer Martha Graham, Cunningham eventually rejected her psychological view of dance and her attempts to tell a story in her choreography. Cunningham prefers abstract movement and nonrepresentational dances. He collaborated often with avant-garde composer John Cage. Sontag often refers to both Cunningham and Cage as examples of artists who reject the mimetic tradition that holds art hostage to imitating or commenting on the world. Their works are about form, not content, but viewers and listeners who do not grasp their aesthetic position find their work "boring" or "confusing," Sontag observes in "On Style." She suggests that their work becomes fascinating when one realizes that they are exploring "principles of (and balance between) variety and redundancy."

Defoe, Daniel (1660–1731). English novelist and journalist. In *AIDS and Its Metaphors*, Sontag discusses Defoe's *Journal of the Plague Year* (1722), a fiction that purports to be an eyewitness account of the bubonic plague that devastated London in 1665. Like many accounts of plagues, Defoe's plague is regarded as a foreign import, a disease from abroad that infects the populace. This kind of historical association makes it possible to think of AIDS as a contemporary plague, she points out—though in fact, like any disease, it will become treatable and perhaps even curable.

De Kooning, Willem (1904–1997). Dutch-born American abstract expressionist painter. Sontag quotes him at the beginning of "Against Interpretation." He observed that content is an "encounter, like a flash." She uses him in support of her contention that art is about form and style, not content and meaning. Art does not represent the world; it is its own world—just as an abstract painting is not an imitation of reality but presents its own reality.

Delacroix, Eugene (1798–1863). French painter of the Romantic school, famous for his large canvases and violent colors. Sontag quotes him several times in *On Photography*, for he sensed that photography established a new relationship between human beings and their world, fostering a belief that the "photograph gives control over the thing photographed."

Deputy, The. A play by Rolf Hochhuth about the Nazi regime and the pope's support of it. In *Against Interpretation*, Sontag praises the playwright's faithful use of documentary appeals to present an authentic study of tyranny. He has produced both a moral act and a work of art. The play's outlandish length is justified, she believes, in order to capture the enormity of his subject.

Divine Comedy, The (1321). Dante's great poem, which Sontag calls in "On Style" a "morally objectionable work of art," and yet a work that remains great even if one cannot accept its values.

Doctor Strangelove (1964). Sontag reviews Stanley Kubrick's film about nuclear holocaust in "Going to Theater, etc." She finds the work full of liberal clichés and cartoonish characterizations.

Donne, John (1572–1631). English Renaissance poet. In *Illness as Metaphor*, Sontag describes Donne's treatment of illness "as an enemy that invades, that lays siege to the body-fortress." These kinds of military metaphors are so ingrained that it seems natural to use them, yet such metaphors distort what the individual needs to do to recover his health, Sontag argues. Metaphors of war excite the imagination when she believes it is necessary to calm it.

Duchamp, Marcel (1887–1968). French-born American artist with strong links to the cubists and surrealists. Duchamp made a distinction between "retinal art," which attempts to capture objects as they appear to the eye, and conceptual art, which is the art's imposition of the artist's vision on the world. Sontag makes much of this distinction in *On Photography*, noting that some photographers insist they are recording reality while others argue they are creating it. Sontag makes scattered references to Duchamp throughout her work. He is one of those modernists who is constantly challenging definitions of art. He pioneered the idea of "found art," that is, discovering "art" by chance in common objects. Photography comes out of a similar sensibility, Sontag argues, since it can potentially find beauty or interest in virtually anything that is photographed.

Dutchman (1964). Sontag reviews Leroi Jones's play in "Going to Theater, etc." Like Baldwin's *Blues for Mister Charlie*, *Dutchman* is marred by reductive characterizations, although it contains some "neat and powerful" scenes. The racial problems in both plays are filtered largely through sexual attitudes, which often overshadow what the playwrights are saying about the relationship between blacks and whites.

Evans, Walker (1903–1975). American photographer, most famous for his collaboration with James Agee on the book *Let Us Now Praise Famous Men*, one of the key texts of the depression. Sontag observes that like other photographers of the period, Evans strove to get a certain look from his sharecropper subjects. In other words, his photographs are by no means a literal representation of reality. Sontag regards Evans as the greatest exponent of the Whitman tradition, which she terms "euphoric humanism."

Feuerbach, Ludwig (1804–1872). German philosopher, a historical materialist who held that the individual's consciousness was shaped by the interaction of his sensory organs with the world. In *On Photography*, Sontag quarrels with his distinction between the "original" and a "copy." "It assumes that what is real persists, unchanged and intact, while only images have changed. . . . But the notions of image and reality are complementary. When the notion of reality changes, so does that of the image, and vice versa."

Feuillade, Louis (1873–1925). French film director, scenarist, and producer. Sontag treats this filmmaker of the silent era as a major influence on Godard in her essay included in *Styles of Radical Will*. Feuillade experimented with "hallucinatory, absurd, and abstracted" action tales, but while these aspects controlled the form of Feuillade's films, they are kept in tension by documentary and factual material in Godard's.

Fiedler, Leslie (1917–). Literary critic and novelist. Sontag takes issue with Fiedler in "What's Happening in America," suggesting that his criticism of young 1960s radicals for their rejection of the Puritan values of sobriety and the work ethic is an example of an older radical worried that the moral and ethical underpinnings of radicalism itself are being undermined.

Flaming Creatures (1964). Jack Smith's avant-garde film. In *Against Interpretation*, Sontag feels the need to defend Smith from charges of having produced pornography. The film depicts plenty of naked bodies and sexual acts, but it is not pornographic—if what is meant by that term is an intention to excite sexual feelings. Sontag finds the film by turns childlike and witty. It is not a film about ideas or characters; rather it is an example of what Sontag likes best in art: a profusion of direct and powerful images. The film contains no symbols to interpret, and it exhilarates because of its "freedom from moralism." Smith's film is an example of an aesthetic space, the "space of pleasure."

Frank, Robert (1924–). Swiss-born photographer inspired by August Sander. Frank sought to capture on camera the lives of everyday Americans. In Frank's work Sontag finds a randomness at odds with Sander's deliberate, highly organized project aimed to capture German social life.

Freud, Sigmund (1856–1939). Viennese psychiatrist born in what is now the Czech Republic. Sontag attacks Freud in "Against Interpretation" for his attempt to interpret art, to use it for psychological purposes. The problem with Freud's approach is that he restates or formulates art into something else—a message, a piece of content used to substantiate his theories. He does not recognize that art has its own coherence. She holds Freud and his followers responsible for treating the work of authors such as Kafka, Proust, Joyce, Faulkner, Rilke, Lawrence, and Gide as psychoanalytical allegories. This kind of psychological determinism now infects the work of directors such as Elia Kazan, she notes in

"Against Interpretation," who cannot stage a play like *Streetcar Named Desire* without overlaying it with notions of the decline of Western civilization. Sontag discusses Freud's cancer as an example of repressed sexual feelings in *Illness as Metaphor*. She compares Freud and Canetti in *Under the Sign of Saturn*.

Gaudi y Cornet, Antoni (1852–1926). Spanish architect. Sontag names him in "On Style" because his work has been loosely associated with surrealism—particularly because he favors irregular shapes and unusual textures. His curvilinear work confounds the Western tradition of straight lines and geometrically planned buildings. His buildings are projections of a singular artistic vision and not copies of the world he sees. His sense of style dominates his art.

Genet, Jean (1910–1986). Novelist and playwright. His most important works are *Our Lady of the Flowers* (1963), *The Maids* (1954), and *The Blacks* (1960). In "On Style," Sontag notes that Genet's characters might not be people his readers approve of, but that is beside the point, since a work of art does not exist in living rooms but in an "imaginary landscape." The work of art, in other words, contains itself; it is not contained or defined by the world. Sontag also discusses Genet's work in "Fascinating Fascism."

Giacometti, Alberto (1901–1966). Swiss sculptor and painter, invoked in "On Style" as an example of the artist who is concerned with pure form. His figures are not merely exaggerations or comments on the human figure, they are a "thing in the world, not just a text or commentary on the world."

Gide, André (1869–1951). French novelist and man of letters. His journals are a major influence on Sontag's conception of art. He is one of Sontag's exemplary figures, since he supported the primacy of literature and was engaged in politics as well. Gide makes the writer responding to literature and to his time a focal figure. Sontag refers to Gide throughout *Against Interpretation*. In *Illness as Metaphor*, she discusses his novel *The Immoralist*, whose hero contracts tuberculosis as a result of repressing his sexual nature.

Gnosticism. An esoteric religious movement prevalent in the second and third centuries A.D. From the Christian point of view, Gnosticism is a heresy, for it promises a revelation to the select few. The Gnostic believes that he is the repository of divine knowledge; that is, the divinity has entered the human being. The Gnostics wrote their own gospels and rejected much of the narrative of the New Testament about Christ's crucifixion and resurrection. They believed, instead, that he had simply returned to the Godhead, the source of spiritual wisdom. Modern thinkers such as Simone Weil have been attracted to Gnosticism because it preserves the quest for knowledge while forsaking what some moderns consider the incredible supernatural elements of Christianity. What Gnostics offer is a vision of God. Sontag often refers to Gnosticism in her writings and in her interviews. She has called *The Benefactor*, for example, a Gnostic novel, perhaps because its narrator seeks knowledge through his dreams and not through the rites and rituals of society and its institutions. She places E. M. Cioran in the "Gnostic-mystical tradition" in *Styles of Radical Will*. She probes the Gnostic strain in Artaud's thought in *Under the Sign of Saturn*.

Godard, Jean-Luc (1930–). Innovative avant-garde French filmmaker. Sontag considers him one of the giants of modern cinema and devotes a long essay to him in *Styles of Radical Will*, which also contains a comparison of Godard and Bergman in "Bergman's *Persona*." She is especially attracted to his use of documentary footage, posters, comic strips, and advertisements in order to present a complex and multi-layered art. Sontag often refers to Godard in *Against Interpretation*, especially in "Spiritual Style in the Films of Robert Bresson," and she includes an essay in Godard's *Vivre Sa Vie*. She discusses Godard's Vietnam film in "Trip to Hanoi" and his *Les Carabiniers* in *On Photography*, where she mentions Godard's surrealist side.

Goethe, Johann Wolfgang (1749–1832). German poet, dramatist, novelist, and scientist, and one of the great figures in German literature. Sontag deals with his work in *Under the Sign of*

Saturn, where she discusses Walter Benjamin's writing on Goethe. Goethe also appears briefly as a character in *The Volcano Lover*. The Cavaliere's wife, Catherine, reads Goethe's influential novel, *The Sorrows of Werther* (1774).

Goodman, Paul (1911–1972). American social critic. Sontag includes an essay on Goodman in *Under the Sign of Saturn*. She admires his wide-ranging work from essays to stories to novels to book-length criticisms of society. *Death Kit* was also influenced by Goodman's writing about gestalt psychology. In "The Pornographic Imagination," Sontag quotes Goodman: "The question is not *whether* pornography, but the quality of the pornography." In "What's Happening in America" (*Styles of Radical Will*), she supports Goodman's contention that the "whole character structure of modern American man . . . needs rehauling."

Goya y Lucientes, Franciso Jose de (1746–1828). Spanish painter. His portraits and paintings about war and human suffering have influenced many modern artists. Sontag writes about his book in *Transforming Vision: Writers on Art*. In "On Style" she also uses his portrait of Wellington to suggest that Goya is an artist who does make statements about the world, even though his art is more than just a representation of the world.

Great Dictator, The (1940). Sontag reviews Charlie Chaplin's film in "Going to Theater, etc." She judges it incommensurate with the importance of its subject. Chaplin's satire is puerile. She returns briefly to the subject of Chaplin's film in "Syberberg's Hitler."

Griffith, D. W. (1875–1948). Pioneering American film director. His important films include *Birth of a Nation* (1915) and *Intolerance* (1916). Sontag makes several references to Griffith in *Against Interpretation*. In "A Note on Novels and Films," she compares Griffith to Samuel Richardson, one of the originators of the novel. Her larger point is that the fifty-year history of cinema is a "scrambled" recapitulation of the two-hundred-year history of the novel.

Grotowski, Jerzy (1933–1999). Avant-garde Polish director.

Grotowski's unconventional rendition of theatre classics, in which he gave his acting companies considerable room to change the text, gained considerable attention in the 1960s and 1970s in Europe and America. Scattered references to his work appear in Sontag's essays, including a comparison with Artaud in *Under the Sign of Saturn*.

Guimard, Hector Germain (1867–1942). French architect. Renowned for his sinuous and sensuous details that make his buildings and structures rather lyrical, he is another good example of Sontag's argument in *Against Interpretation* that style, not content, is the major concern of art.

Happenings. The spontaneous "collages," assemblages of spontaneous performances, that occurred in the 1960s in Manhattan lofts and basements. Sontag wrote an essay about them, included in *Against Interpretation*. Happenings are full of surprises and have an alogical structure, Sontag observes. She is attracted to their "sensuous properties." They partake of the surrealist sensibility.

Hegel, Georg Wilhelm Friedrich (1770–1831). German idealist philosopher. References to Hegel occur throughout Sontag's work. For example, in "The Anthropologist as Hero" she observes that "Modern thought is pledged to a kind of applied Hegelianism: seeks its Self in its Other." Sontag is advertising to Hegel's idea of the dialectic, the process by which one idea encounters its opposite. In "The Pornographic Imagination" she devotes a paragraph to the failure of Hegel's "post-religious" thought. In her essay on Cioran, she discusses his philosophical system and Cioran's effort to replace it.

Hine, Lewis (1874–1940). American photographer. His brilliant documentary photography expressed his keen dedication to social justice. In *On Photography*, Sontag praises the "lovely composition and elegant perspective of Lewis Hine's photography of exploited children in turn-of-the-century American mills and mines."

Hobbes, Thomas (1588–1679). Political philosopher and author of the classic text *Leviathan*. In *Illness as Metaphor*, Sontag compares Hobbes to Machiavelli, noting that both men employed disease metaphors when discussing the condition of the state, and both believed that sickness of the body or the body politic could be cured by early intervention.

Hume, David (1711–1776). Scottish philosopher and historian. His most important work is *A Treatise of Human Nature*. He is associated with the schools of skepticism and empiricism—that is, an understanding of the world built upon the senses. In *Under the Sign of Saturn*, Sontag invokes Hume's comparison of consciousness to a theatre in her discussion of Artaud.

Ionesco, Eugene (1909–1994). Romanian-born French playwright. His important work includes *The Bald Soprano* (1956) and *The Chairs* (1958). He is often associated with "theater of the absurd," which depicts characters in a chaotic, meaningless, and unpredictable universe. Sontag attacks Ionesco's reputation in *Against Interpretation*, contending that his ideas are platitudes and that much of his work is repetitive. He has tried to make poetry out of banality and clichés. Compared with the masters of modern theatre—Brecht, Genet, and Beckett—Ionesco is "a minor writer even at his best."

James, Henry (1843–1916). American novelist who lived most of his life in England. James is celebrated for his treatment of the "international theme"—the conflict of American and European characters and values. Sontag finds James a touchstone figure because of her own Eurocentric sensibility. She draws examples from his novels—for example, in *Illness as Metaphor* she notes that in James's novel *Wings of the Dove*, Milly Theale's doctor encourages her to have a love affair to help cure her of tuberculosis. James himself makes a brief appearance in *In America*, where Sontag parodies his convoluted style.

Johns, Jasper (1930–). American painter who broke with postwar American abstract expressionism. Johns favored paintings concentrating on concrete objects such as targets and the American flag. He painted these items with great precision, encrusting the surface of his paintings so that the work of art seemed to be an object in itself and not merely a representation of a flag, a target, etc. The style and form of his paintings dominate their subject matter or content, making him a perfect example of Sontag's own writing on the primacy of style. Sontag quotes Johns in "The Aesthetics of Silence" and refers to him in many of her essays and interviews. Like John Cage and Merce Cunningham, who share similar artistic visions, Johns became a friend of Sontag's.

Kafka, Franz (1883–1924). Born in what is now the Czech Republic, Kafka wrote his stories and novels in German. His important work includes "The Metamorphosis" (1915), "In the Penal Colony" (1919), *The Trial* (1925), *The Castle* (1926), and *In Amerika* (1927). *Against Interpretation* contains scattered references to Kafka. Sontag regards him as exemplary of the modern artist. Kafka is interested in form, not content. And Sontag rejects efforts to interpret his work as an allegory of modern civilization. He is the pure artist concerned with fashioning all-encompassing fables of literature. Kafka's comments on tuberculosis are quoted in *Illness as Metaphor*. In *Under the Sign of Saturn*, Sontag compares Kafka and Walter Benjamin as well as noting Kafka's influence on Elias Canetti.

Keats, John (1795–1821). English Romantic poet, perhaps best known for his odes and his eloquent letters. He becomes the focal point in *Illness as Metaphor* for Sontag's discussion of tuberculosis as a disease that was thought to strike sensitive young writers.

Kierkegaard, Soren (1813–1855). Danish religious philosopher, author of important works such as *Fear and Trembling* (1846) and *The Sickness Unto Death* (1849). His first major work, *Either/Or* (1843), discusses the aesthetic and ethical views of life, a theme that runs throughout Sontag's work. He is mentioned several times in *Against Interpretation* as one of the progenitors of modern thought. Often called an existentialist, in Sontag's writing he appears to be exemplary of the writer who intensely examines his own life—a forerunner of writers such as Gide, Pavese, and Camus.

Kleist, Heinrich Wilhelm von (1777–1811). German dramatist, poet, and novelist. His most enduring work may be *Michael Kohlhass* (1808), a novella. In "The Aesthetics of Silence," Kleist becomes an example of the suicidal artist (he shot himself), of the artist who goes too far, seeking in silence an alternative to art or even an anti-art. Such writers resort to silence to express their distrust of words.

Kraus, Karl (1874–1936). Austrian writer, celebrated for his satiric plays, including *The Last Days of Mankind* (1922). Sontag discusses him in *Under the Sign of Saturn*, where he is treated as an important influence on Walter Benjamin and Elias Canetti.

Lange, Dorothea (1895–1965). American photographer. She produced one of the greatest documentary records of the depression. Lange also took photographs during World War II of the Japanese going to internment camps. But only later did Americans look at such photographs and consider the moral implications of internment. Sontag comments: "Photographs cannot create a moral position, but they can reinforce one—and can help build a nascent one."

La Tour, Georges de (1593–1652). French painter of dark interiors illuminated with candlelight. His subject matter is often religious. In "On Style," Sontag names him as an example of an artist who stylizes, that is, exaggerates certain features of a scene or figure in order to make a comment on his subject matter.

Lawrence, D. H. (1885–1930). English novelist and poet. His important works include *Sons and Lovers* (1913), *The Rainbow* (1915), *Women in Love* (1921), and a considerable body of short fiction and travel books. There are scattered references to Lawrence throughout Sontag's writing. In her review of Norman O. Brown's *Life Against Death*, she suggests that sexuality is even more important than Lawrence supposed it was. In *Illness as Metaphor* he is included in a list of writers who traveled the world seeking a climatic cure for his tuberculosis. In *Under the Sign of Saturn* she compares Paul Goodman to Lawrence.

Lawrence, T. E. (1888–1935). British soldier and author, famous for leading the Arabs in their revolt against the Ottoman Empire during World War I. His most important book is *Seven Pillars of Wisdom* (1926). Sontag refers to him in *Against Interpretation* as one of the modern figures who made the adventurer into a spiritual hero.

Leiris, Michel (1901–1990). French anthropologist, the subject of an essay in *Against Interpretation*. Sontag compares him to Norman Mailer as a writer who subscribes to the program of creating literature out of "self-laceration and self-exposure."

Levi-Strauss, Claude (1908–). French anthropologist, the subject of an essay in *Against Interpretation*. Like other literary figures of the 1960s and 1970s, Sontag was attracted to Levi-Strauss because he amalgamated language, behavior, and myth into an all-encompassing view of humanity. He argued against the distinction between "primitive" and "historical" societies, suggesting they shared common patterns. Thus he became an example of a writer who recognized what she called, in the concluding essay of *Against Interpretation*, "one culture and one sensibility." In *Styles of Radical Will* she compares Levi-Strauss to Cioran.

Lucretius (c. 98–55 B.C.). Greek poet and philosopher whose concern with death and pain is echoed in the work of Levi-Strauss, argues Sontag in *Against Interpretation*. For Lucretius, knowledge of the world, especially that based on science, provided man with a sense of "detachment and equanimity," observes Sontag. She identifies Levi-Strauss as a man "with a Lucretian pessimism" who finds in anthropology some consolation.

Lukács, Georg (1885–1971). Hungarian Communist writer, best known for his work in literary criticism and political theory. His major works include *The Theory of the Novel* (1920) and *History and Class Consciousness* (1923). Sontag writes about Lukács in *Against Interpretation*, acknowledging him as an influential figure but by no means the finest interpreter of the Marxist view of literature and history. She takes issue with his interpretations of realism—calling them crude—and she objects to the high place he accords the nineteenth-century realistic novel.

Machiavelli, Niccolo (1469–1527). Italian political philosopher, author of the classic text on government, *The Prince*. In *Illness as Metaphor*, Sontag explores Machiavelli's use of disease images and metaphors, pointing out that illness, whether of the body or of the state, can be cured, in his view, if early precautions are taken.

Mailer, Norman (1923–). American novelist and journalist. Sontag mentions his controversial novel *An American Dream* (1964) in "On Style," chiding critics who condemn Mailer for creating a hero who murders his wife but is not punished. This kind of moral response to a work of art seems inappropriate to Sontag, though it would undoubtedly be right if the same circumstance prevailed in real life. If art has moral properties, she adds, that morality stems from the form of the work of art, not only its supposed place in the world outside art. Sontag also devotes a few pages to Mailer's doctrine of writing as a "blood sport" in her essay on Michel Leiris in *Against Interpretation*. In *Illness as Metaphor*, Mailer is identified as a "cancerphobe" because of his many references to the idea that cancer is caused by repressed feelings. Sontag compares Mailer and Paul Goodman in *Under the Sign of Saturn*.

Malraux, André (1901–1976). Novelist, archaeologist, political activist, and public official. His major work includes *Man's Fate* (1933) and *Man's Hope* (1938). Sontag cites Malraux in "The Anthropologist as Hero" as an example of the artist/adventurer who makes of his career a "spiritual vocation."

Mann, Thomas (1875–1955). German novelist. His important work includes *Death in Venice* (1925) and *Doctor Faustus* (1948). Sontag describes visiting Mann in "Pilgrimage." His novel *The Magic Mountain* (1927), set in a sanatorium for tubercular patients, was one of the works of literature that inspired her to become a writer, and it is one of the key texts Sontag relies on in *Illness as Metaphor*. Mann wrote large novels that combine ideas and characters in a dramatic but also essaylike fashion that Sontag emulates in *The Volcano Lover* and *In America*. She also discusses Mann in "Syberberg's Hitler."

Mannerist painting. Associated with the sixteenth century, this style of painting flouts the conventions of realism and perspective. The artist is not attempting to imitate real life, consequently the human figure and the sense of space on the canvas are distorted and reshaped to express the artist's vision. Sontag prizes the Mannerist painters in "On Style," citing such figures as Rosso, Pontormo, and Parmigianino.

Mansfield, Katherine (1888–1923). British short story writer renowned for her subtle, poetic, and ironic fiction in collections such as *In a German Pension* (1911) and *The Garden Party* (1922). In *Illness as Metaphor*, Sontag quotes from Mansfield's journal to demonstrate how tuberculosis was considered a sickness of self that only the self could cure.

Marat/Sade (1964). Experimental play by Peter Weiss. The full title is *The Persecution and Assassination of Marat as Performed by the Inmates of the Asylum at Charenton under the Direction of the Marquis de Sade*. Sontag discusses the play in *Against Interpretation*, calling it a brilliant fusion of insanity and theatricality. Peter Brook's production deftly employs spectacle and sound and directs his actors with an intensity that appeals to all the senses. To her the production perfectly embodies Artaud's call for a theatre that is beyond psychology and concentrates on the "transpersonal emotions borne by characters." Ideas spring to life and are utterly devoid of the banality that deforms Arthur Miller plays such as *After the Fall* and *Incident at Vichy*. Objections to the cruelty and pornographic scenes involving the Marquis de Sade seem beside the point to Sontag, who argues that the playwright neither approves nor disapproves of such behavior but rather explores how the characters interact with one another.

Marcuse, Herbert (1898–1979). German-born American philosopher. There are many references to Marcuse in Sontag's work, including a comparison in *Against Interpretation* of Marcuse's

Eros and Civilization with Norman O. Brown's *Life Against Death*. In the early part of her career, Sontag was also influenced by Marcuse's Marxism and his criticism of the "repressive tolerance" of bourgeois society. She eventually rejected this concept but remained convinced of the defects of capitalism and the need to surmount it and acquire a higher consciousness, which she discusses in the essay on Brown.

Marx, Karl (1818–1883). German political philosopher. Sontag attacks Marx in "Against Interpretation" on the same grounds as she attacks Freud. In Marx's case, art, like all other phenomena, exists only so that he can impose his interpretation on it. Outside the realm of aesthetics, however, Marx has greatly influenced Sontag's thinking. In the 1960s and 1970s she described herself as a neo-radical who accepted Marx's theory of capital and of the rapacious, imperialistic aspects of the capitalist state. Even after she renounced Marxism as a form of thought in the 1980s, Sontag continued to repeat Marxist formulas about the iniquity and inequity of a capitalistic culture.

McCarthy, Mary (1912–1989). Critic and novelist. She is best known for her satirical novel *The Group* (1959). The only woman to find a prominent place among the 1930s New York intellectuals. Later Hannah Arendt and Elizabeth Hardwick would join her in New York City. She was known for her fierce criticism of both political opponents (the Communists) and her literary contemporaries—particularly in the American theatre, which she excoriated in *Partisan Review*, the primary venue of publication for the New York intellectuals. McCarthy's fiction, such as *The Company She Keeps* (1942), contains many thinly disguised portraits of her friends and enemies. But for Sontag, McCarthy was primarily important as an example of a woman who could hold her own with men and often best them—both in person and in her writing. When Sontag made a success with *Against Interpretation*, she was hailed as the next Mary McCarthy, with the literary critic Norman Podhoretz observing that there seemed to be only one place at a time in American culture for what he called the "dark lady of

American letters." Sontag refers to McCarthy briefly in "Nathalie Sarraute and the Novel," noting that Sarraute attacks McCarthy's essay "The Fact in Fiction" for its support of fiction that strives for realism and memorable characters.

Miller, Arthur (1915–). American playwright, author of the classic play *Death of a Salesman* (1948). Sontag's review of Miller's play *After the Fall* (1964) is included in *Against Interpretation*. She finds the play weak in both style and structure. Miller deforms the dramatic structure by giving the main character an ongoing garrulous monologue, and "Miller still writes on the level of a left-wing newspaper cartoon." All issues appear on the same level—whether they are Marilyn Monroe, the Holocaust, or McCarthyism.

Moholy-Nagy, Laszlo (1895–1946). Hungarian-American painter, designer, and photographer. In *On Photography*, Sontag quotes Moholy-Nagy's emphasis on "intensive seeing," which she links to poet William Carlos Williams's statement, "No ideas but in things." Photography's focus on the object has its corollary in modern painting, Sontag believes—especially in the work of artists such as Jasper Johns.

New York intellectuals. A group of intellectuals who, beginning in the 1930s, congregated around the *Partisan Review*, a progressive journal of literary and political opinion that greatly influenced liberal opinion in America. Sontag grew up reading the journal and hoped to write for it. She also got to know most of the New York intellectuals, including Lionel Trilling, Irving Howe, Clement Greenberg, William Phillips, Philip Rahv, Harold Rosenberg, Hannah Arendt, Mary McCarthy, Elizabeth Hardwick, Lionel Abel, and many others. A generation younger, Sontag was viewed by many of the New York intellectuals with some suspicion, especially since her work embraced popular culture and new forms of art that seemed to threaten (in their view) the canon of modern literature.

Nietzsche, Friedrich (1844–1900). German philosopher. He is one of the prophets of what Sontag calls in *Against Interpretation* "the new sensibility." In general, she looks to his writings to support her view of art. She quotes his book *The Birth of Tragedy* (1872) in "On Style": "Art is not an imitation of nature but its metaphysical supplement, raised up beside it in order to overcome it." The superiority—or at least the autonomy—of art is a constant theme in Sontag's work; art creates its own values, and this is what Nietzsche taught: modern man must create his own principles as the world of traditional (religious) beliefs disintegrates. Sontag relies on Nietzsche in "The Aesthetics of Silence" and in her essay on Cioran. In *Illness as Metaphor* she notes that Nietzsche's *The Will to Power* (1901) perpetuates many of the myths about tuberculosis. In *AIDS and Its Metaphors* she quotes Nietzsche's advice in *Daybreak* that it is necessary to calm the imagination of the person who is ill. In *Under the Sign of Saturn* she compares Nietzsche's attack on reason with Artaud's conception of "total theatre," one that involved all the senses and did not rely on language.

Nouveau roman (new novel). Sometimes called the anti-novel because the normal ingredients of the novel—plot, dialogue, and character development—are dispensed with. The point of such works is to focus on the nature of the universe, not on the peculiarities of individuals. The meaning of events is ambiguous because there is no center or core of meaning that can be relied upon to interpret existence. The new novelists claim to present the world as it is, not as it is symbolized or imagined by human beings. Alain Robbe-Grillet and Nathalie Sarraute are the practitioners of the *nouveau roman* Sontag discusses in *Against Interpretation*.

Novalis (1772–1801). German poet, one of the founders of Romanticism. His best-known work is *Hymns to the Night* (1800). Sontag evokes Novalis in "The Aesthetics of Silence" and in "'Thinking Against Oneself': Reflections on Cioran" in order to emphasize that there is no simple connection between words and things. "The nature of language," Novalis writes, "is to be its own and only concern, making it so fertile and splendid a mystery."

Ortega y Gasset (1883–1955). Spanish writer of literature, criticism, and philosophy. His best-known work is *The Revolt of the*

Masses (1930). In "On Style," Sontag alludes to Ortega y Gasset in making the distinction between aesthetic and moral values, but she believes there is also a moral pleasure in appreciating art which exists quite aside from approving or disapproving of the morality of characters or even of the work of art itself. She relies on Ortega for her definition of culture in "One Culture and the New Sensibility."

Paradise Lost (1667). Sontag cites Milton's epic poem to demonstrate that art does not depend on its message but on other intrinsic qualities that survive content that no longer appeals to or perhaps is not even relevant to later generations: "The satisfactions of *Paradise Lost* for us do not lie in its views on God and man, but in the superior kinds of energy, vitality, expressiveness which are incarnated in the poem."

Parmigianino (1503–1540). Renaissance painter and etcher renowned for his sensuous style. He is cited in "Against Interpretation" as an example of art for whom style is everything.

Partisan Review. The most influential literary and political journal of the late 1930s and 1940s. Sontag grew up reading the journal and longing to write for it. Some of her important essays, such as "Notes on 'Camp,'" first appeared in *Partisan Review*, though its editors, especially Philip Rahv, had many reservations about Sontag's arguments.

Pavese, Cesare (1908–1950). Italian poet and novelist, best known for *The Moon and the Bonfires* (1950) and *Death Will Stare Me Out of Your Eyes* (1951). Sontag devotes an essay to him in *Against Interpretation*. An anti-fascist who explored the problems of contemporary life with great intensity, Sontag sees him as an example of the "suffering self. For the modern consciousness, the artist (replacing the saint) is the exemplary sufferer. And among artists, the writer, the man of words, is the person to whom we look to be able best to express his suffering." She compares his journals to those of André Gide, Stendhal, Baudelaire, and Kafka.

Plato (c. 428–347 B.C.). Greek philosopher. Sontag refers to Plato at the beginning of "Against Interpretation," noting that his definition of art as an imitation or copy of this world has remained the basic theory of art for Western civilization—in spite of the fact that modern artists insist on art as subjective, as a form or structure with an intrinsic integrity. Even Aristotle, who challenges Plato's distrust of art, accepts the idea that art is mimetic. Sontag compares Plato and Artaud in *Under the Sign of Saturn*. Plato is also central to the argument of *On Photography*.

Poe, Edgar Allan (1809–1849). American poet, short story writer, and critic. Sontag has expressed her debt to Poe in many interviews. She describes his obsession with depression, melancholy, and wasting diseases in *Illness as Metaphor*. Sontag's first novel, *The Benefactor*, is influenced by Poe's evocation of the phantasmagoria of the individual mind. Sontag invokes Poe in *AIDS and Its Metaphors*: his story "The Masque of the Red Death" (1842), which describes a plague that kills everyone, is a foreshadowing of the kind of thinking that treats AIDS as a fatal plague—no one who comes into contact with it can survive.

Pollock, Jackson (1912–1956). American abstract expressionist painter. Sontag cites Pollock (famous for his massive drip-painted canvases) as eliciting a "purely aesthetic response to works of art." Viewers can have the same response to his work, Sontag argues in "On Style," as to a Greek vase.

Pontormo, Jacopo da (1494–1557). Italian Renaissance painter whose intensely emotional style strikes Sontag in "On Style" as an example of art that is not a mimetic but a subjective, transformative experience.

Realism. The term as Sontag uses it in her essays refers to a movement of literature that came to dominate the West in the nineteenth and twentieth centuries. Realistic dramatists and novelists captured the lives of ordinary characters, the "common man," and the social life of individuals in society. Characters on the stage and in fiction speak the language of everyday life, not the heightened, poetic words of Shakespeare and other classical writers. Realism also means constructing plots that seem probable, based on the actual experiences of people. Realism is also psychological—that is, a realistic work of literature develops the way particular characters think and act. Influenced by T. S. Eliot, Antonin Artaud, and many other European critics and artists, Sontag was arguing in the 1960s and 1970s for a more innovative and experimental kind of literature that did not imitate life but transformed it. This transformation might take place by severely limiting the vocabulary of characters, introducing pauses and silences found in the dramas of Samuel Beckett, for example. These plays were not about the psychological problems of individuals but rather about the complexity of existence itself. By the 1980s Sontag began to back away from her attacks on realism and began resorting to one of the most conventional forms of fiction—the historical novel—though she tried her own kinds of innovations through her use of self-conscious narrators who break the novel's illusion of exploring the past by referring to their own contemporary concerns.

Reich, Wilhelm (1897–1957). Austrian psychoanalyst. His most influential work includes *The Sexual Revolution* (1936–1945) and *The Function of the Orgasm* (1948). Reich's books have had a significant impact on writers who have adopted his view that sexual repression is the cause of illnesses such as cancer. Sontag attacks Reich's influence in *Illness as Metaphor*, pointing out that theories like his thrive only because the physical etiology of certain diseases is not yet understood.

Reinhardt, Ad (1913–1967). Sometimes called a minimalist painter, Reinhardt painted all-black canvases. He insisted on the separation of art and life. His work was not an interpretation or copy of the world; it was about form. Sontag cites him in "On Style" as one of the artists who are rejected by those looking for "content" in art.

Resnais, Alain (1922–). French film director. His important films include *Hiroshima My Love* (1959) and *Last Year at Marienbad* (1961). Sontag includes an essay on him in *Against Interpretation*. His work is united by a "search for an inexpressible past." While she finds his work beautiful, she also feels it lacks directness and vigor. She compares Resnais and Bergman in "Bergman's *Persona*."

Riefenstahl, Leni (1902–). Controversial German actress and director. She directed *Triumph of the Will* (1935), which celebrates Hitler's Nuremberg rallies and the ideology of the Nazi party. In "On Style," Sontag remarks that although Riefenstahl is a propagandist, she is also an artist, and to deny her genius is to reject her work "at our loss." Sontag would later reverse her position in "Fascinating Fascism," a fierce attack on Riefenstahl.

Rieff, David (1952–). Journalist. Sontag's son. His reporting on the war in Bosnia prompted Sontag to visit Sarajevo and direct a production of *Waiting for Godot*.

Rieff, Phillip (1922–). Sociologist. Sontag's first and only husband, whom she married while still an undergraduate at the University of Chicago. Sontag collaborated with Rieff on his masterpiece, *Freud: The Mind of the Moralist* (1959). The book contains some criticism of Freud's view of women, a view that reflected Sontag's thinking, though her name did not appear on the book, which was published shortly after the couple's divorce. Sontag comments rather negatively on Rieff's work in interviews. She finds it conservative. Her strongly anti-psychological bias also seems to derive, in part, from her work on the Freud book.

Riis, Jacob (1849–1914). Journalist and photographer. Riis became famous for his photographs of immigrants in tenements, published in *How the Other Half Lives* (1890), a pioneering work that established photography as a kind of social documentation. In *On Photography*, Sontag casts doubt on Riis's social activism, calling his photographs of slums "the most enthralling of decors."

Rilke, Rainer Maria (1875–1926). German poet, perhaps best known for his *Duino Elegies* (1923), which Sontag discusses in "The Aesthetics of Silence." She explores his belief that language must be purified to recapture the elemental aspects of human experience. In effect, language must be "cut back drastically" or peeled back, allowing "'things' themselves to speak." This emphasis on the "thing" itself is reminiscent of the Jasper Johns aesthetic that Sontag praises in the same essay. In *On Photography*, Sontag contrasts the rich texture of European civilization found in Rilke with "our paper phantoms, transistorized landscapes. A feather-weight portable museum."

Robbe-Grillet, Alain (1922–). French novelist and screen-writer. Sontag was influenced by his study *For a New Novel* (1965), and she lauds his screenplay for *Last Year at Marienbad*. There are references to him throughout *Against Interpretation*. He attacked the conventions of psychological realism. For Sontag he repre-sents the artist who is more concerned with the form than with the content of a work of art. He strives not to project a message but to create a work of art that is whole and consistent with itself. It is not an imitation of reality but a transformation of it. As she says of Robbe-Grillet's screenplay for *Last Year at Marienbad*: "What mat-ters . . . is the pure, untranslatable, sensuous immediacy of some of its images, and its rigorous if narrow solutions to certain problems of cinematic form."

Rosso, Fiorentino (1494–1540). Italian Renaissance painter. His use of odd perspective, harsh lighting, and clashing colors is another example of the artist who does not conform to the mimetic theory of art, which Sontag challenges in "On Style."

Ruskin, John (1819–1900). Highly influential art critic. His major work includes *The Seven Lamps of Architecture* (1849) and *The Stones of Venice* (1851–1853). In "On Style," Sontag notes that Ruskin wrote about the "moral aspects of the formal properties of painting." She is emphasizing that the shape of art itself carries its own moral authority, which is quite different from supposing there is a message or moral inside the work of art.

Sade, Marquis de (1740–1814). French writer best known for his erotic literature, especially *Justine* (1791), which Sontag dis-cusses in "The Pornographic Imagination." She argues that Jus-tine is "like Candide, who is also a cipher, a blank, an eternal naif incapable of learning anything from atrocious ordeals. . . . The personages in pornography, like those of comedy, are seen only from the outside, behavioristically. By definition, they can't be seen in depth, so as truly to engage the audience's feelings." De Sade's description of Italy is quoted in *The Volcano Lover*.

Sander, August (1876–1964). German photographer. He conceived of an ambitious project to photograph all classes and types in German society. His work was included in Steichen's "Family of Man Exhibition" in 1955. In *On Photography*, Sontag cites Sander as an example of the photographer who is looking for the typical, not the distinctive. As such, he is the opposite of Arbus.

Sarraute, Nathalie (1900–1999). One of the practitioners of the *nouveau roman*. Her novels include *Portrait of a Man Unknown* (1948) and *The Planetarium* (1959). Sontag discusses Sarraute's work in *Against Interpretation* and finds her ideas about the novel "exhilarating." Sontag is especially attracted to and quotes Sarraute's notion that the novel must foster "that element of indetermination, of opacity and mystery that one's own actions always have for the one who lives them." The quotation is apt for Sontag's first two novels as well as her first two films, in which the characters' motivations are opaque and mysterious not only to the readers and viewers but to themselves.

Sartre, Jean-Paul (1905–1980). French philosopher, novelist, playwright, and biographer. His most important work includes the novel *Nausea* (1938) and the play *No Exit* (1944). Sartre is celebrated as the founder of existentialism. His famous formulation "Existence precedes essence" evokes his view that human beings are always in process. An individual has no fixed identity, and there is no fixed meaning in the universe. This idea of the self that is constantly in flux and creating itself would naturally appeal to Sontag, who likes to think of herself as self-made. And she has been greatly influenced by Sartre, de Beauvoir, and other thinkers in his circle. Yet she has never devoted a major essay to him, and her references to him in works such as *Against Interpretation* are ambivalent. In her essay on his biography of Genet, she criticizes Sartre's verbosity even as she acknowledges his "cargo of brilliant ideas." She also praises Sartre as the "man who has understood the dialectic between self and other in Hegel's *Phenomenology* in the most interesting and usable fashion." She believes his masterpiece,

Being and Nothingness (1943), ranks with Dostoevsky, Nietzsche, and Freud in psychological perceptiveness. She especially likes the fact that Sartre does not "psychologize" Genet—Sartre does not reduce his subject to a set of psychological suppositions. Sontag compares Sartre and Paul Goodman in *Under the Sign of Saturn*.

Shaftesbury, Anthony (1671–1713). English philosopher. In *Illness as Metaphor*, Sontag discusses Shaftesbury's view that not every malady of the body politic ought to receive attention, because some cures are worse than the disease. "The body politic should not be overmedicalized; a remedy should not be sought for every disorder," Sontag summarizes, adding that he is making an argument for tolerance whereas Hobbes emphasizes reason and Machiavelli foresight.

Shelley, Percy Bysshe (1792–1822). English Romantic poet. Sontag cites Shelley several times in *Illness as Metaphor*, for in his letters to Keats he draws on the myth that poets are particularly susceptible to tuberculosis.

Smith, W. Eugene (1918–1978). American photographer. Smith was one of the originators of photographic essays, sequences of photographs that told a story or presented a setting in a detailed series of shots. In *On Photography*, Sontag singles out his photographs of a Japanese fishing village in Minamata, documenting people slowing dying from mercury poisoning. His work documents suffering, Sontag points out, which "arouses our indignation," yet the photographs also "distance us because they are superb photographs of Agony, conforming to surrealist standards of beauty." She argues that Smith's work conforms to Artaud's Theatre of Cruelty.

Snow, C. P. (1905–1980). British novelist. He is best known for a series of novels named after the first novel, *Strangers and Brothers* (1940). His controversial essay on "the two cultures" posited the idea that art and science were diverging in the modern world. Science had become recondite, and only scientists were capable of understanding and transforming the world—unless mutual understanding was fostered between scientists and artists.

Sontag attacked Snow in "One Culture and the New Sensibility," arguing that both science and art are united as instruments for "modifying consciousness and organizing new modes of sensibility." Like scientists, modern artists are "continually challenging their means, their materials and methods."

Steichen, Edward (1879–1973). American photographer. In *On Photography*, Sontag places Steichen squarely in the Whitman tradition. To her, Steichen's attempt to beautify the world, to find aesthetic pleasure in every object he photographed, ultimately led him to become superficial. Just to photograph something conferred on it an air of importance. Sontag is particularly critical of "The Family of Man" exhibition at the Museum of Modern Art, which she contrasts to the exhibition of Diane Arbus's work in 1972 at the same institution. Arbus's darker vision heralds, in Sontag's view, a cultural shift in the way photographs are viewed.

Stein, Gertrude (1874–1946). American writer celebrated for her experiments with language and form in *Three Lives* (1909) and *The Making of Americans* (1925). In "On Style," Sontag discusses Stein's "circular repetitive style," which is part of her effort to enhance the immediacy of her writing and to break down tenses that tend to deprive literature of its spontaneity. "Every style is a means of insisting on something," Sontag concludes.

Sternberg, Josef von (1894–1969). Austrian-American director best remembered for his films with Marlene Dietrich, including *The Blue Angel* (1930), *Blonde Venus* (1932), and *The Devil Is a Woman* (1935). Sontag discusses his work in "On Style," where she compares films from his early and later periods to show how an artist's work can vary stylistically. She also uses the term "stylization" to show how artists use style to indicate different attitudes toward their subject matter.

Stieglitz, Alfred (1864–1946). American photographer and gallery owner. One of the pioneering photographers, famous for his enchanting photographs of New York City and his riveting portraits of artist Georgia O'Keeffe. In *On Photography*, Sontag calls Stieglitz one of the "virtuosi of the noble image." He is also in the Whitman tradition of celebrating America and affirming life.

Story of O (1954). One of the main texts discussed in "The Pornographic Imagination." Sontag suggests that certain works of pornography, including this one by Pauline Reage, do have a psychology and pattern associated with literature; in other words, it is possible to conceive of pornography as a genre or branch of literature.

Strand, Paul (1890–1976). American photographer. He is noted for his exquisite sense of composition, whether the subject is the human figure or machine instruments. Sontag cites him in *On Photography* as one of those photographers who wanted to capture the world "out there."

Stylization. Sontag uses this term in "On Style" to distinguish between artists whose style is at one with their work and artists who "stylize" or use style to comment on their subject matter. Works that rely on stylization, she argues, often exhibit an ambivalence about their subject matter and include parts that do not cohere. Thus Orson Welles's film *The Lady from Shanghai* has a "visually brilliant denouement" that is at odds with the rest of the work.

Surrealism. A key term in Sontag's lexicon. In "Happenings" she defines surrealism as the "idea of destroying conventional meaning, and creating new meanings, or counter-meanings through radical juxtaposition ('the collage principle')." She employs the term "surrealism" throughout *On Photography* because of photography's ability to include or juxtapose contrary elements and unite them in a "realistic" frame. The surrealist sensibility "aims to shock," Sontag emphasizes.

Syberberg, Hans Jurgen (1935–). German filmmaker, the subject of an essay in *Under the Sign of Saturn*. Sontag admires the Wagnerian ambition of Syberberg's work. He makes epic theatre out of film, using puppets, various objects, and photographs, all of which resemble performance art. In terms of technique he is akin to director Robert Wilson, with whom Sontag has collaborated on a number of productions.

Talbot, William Fox (1800–1877). Pioneering English photographer. He made significant contributions to the way film is developed. In *On Photography*, Sontag quotes Talbot's observation that the camera has an affinity for recording the "injuries of time." She builds on this quotation to argue for the "link between photography and death."

Tiffany, Louis Comfort (1848–1933). Tiffany's extraordinary use of color in glassmaking, and the delicate curving shapes of his glass objects, make him a good example of style in art that requires no interpretation, according to Sontag in "On Style."

Trilling, Lionel (1905–1975). Literary critic, one of the New York intellectuals. Sontag often cites Trilling in interviews as a major influence on her. In his most famous book, *The Liberal Imagination* (1950), Trilling brought his formidable intellect to bear on modern literature and its place in society. He drew on Freud and other social thinkers to present a comprehensive view of literature heavily influenced by Matthew Arnold, who believed that literature in many ways provided modern man with a substitute for the values taught by religion. Sontag absorbed much of Trilling's earnestness, yet her early criticism reads like a rejection of his literary and political views. Sontag sounded much more radical than Trilling. Where he refused to commit himself to political opinions, finding considerable ambiguity in cold war politics and in the battles between Communists and anti-Communists, Sontag styled herself a "neo-radical" and launched attacks against her own country and against an earlier generation of critics whom she deemed philistine. Although her target in *Against Interpretation* is Matthew Arnold, it has occurred to several readers that she is attacking Trilling as well (without ever mentioning his name). Nevertheless Sontag has emulated Trilling's insistence that literature should be viewed within the widest possible cultural context. In her later years her view of culture has turned much more conservative, and it could be argued that she has returned to positions that are akin to Trilling's.

Trotsky, Leon (1879–1940). A leader of the Russian Revolution, a Marxist theoretician, and head of the Red army until he was expelled from the Soviet Union by Stalin. In *Illness as Metaphor*, Sontag points out that the Bolsheviks often used disease metaphors. Trotsky, for example, called Stalinism a "cholera, a syphilis, and a cancer."

Valéry, Paul (1871–1945). French poet and critic. His important work includes *Odes* (1923) and *Dance and the Soul* (1924). Sontag quotes Valéry in "On Style" to emphasize the supremacy of form over content. Form, Valéry contends, is the "sum" of a work's "perceptible characteristics." Form, he adds, "compels recognition." In other words, form is that term for a work of art that evokes its self-contained quality. Sontag builds on Valéry when she calls form "a plan of sensory imprinting." She also mentions him in "The Aesthetics of Silence" and in *On Photography*, where she takes issue with his contention that photography will usurp, in some ways, literature's powers of description.

Vertov, Dziga (1896–1954). Soviet film director and theorist. He edited several film journals and produced influential films such as *One Sixth of the World* (1926) and *The Man with a Movie Camera* (1929). An innovator in the documentary field, Vertov experimented with split screens, multiple exposures, the superimposition of images, and other techniques that challenged the conventional cinema. In *Under the Sign of Saturn*, Sontag compares him to Artaud as a "self-proclaimed revolutionary in the arts" and to Leni Riefenstahl in "Fascinating Fascism."

Wagner, Richard (1813–1883). German composer. His work includes *Lohengrin* (1848) and the four-opera *The Ring of Nibelungen*, produced from 1854 to 1874. His operas have been a major influence on Sontag. She wrote a piece on his work for the *London Review of Books*, and he is invoked several times in her essay on Syberberg in *Under the Sign of Saturn*, where she also compares Wagner and Artaud. Wagner appeals to Sontag because of his bold dramaturgy—his welding of music and stage movement, of ancient myth and romantic heroes and heroines. His use of arias and his obsession with the conflict between love and power are echoed in *The Volcano Lover*. His willingness to create monumental works of art lasting many hours longer than most operas is a virtue to her, and she praises other works like Syberberg's, which seem to break through the conventional limits of film and theatre. In "Theatre and Film," Sontag links Wagner, Artaud, and Cage as envisaging theatre as a "total art."

Warhol, Andy (1928–1987). American artist famous for his pop art canvases of Campbell's soup cans and of Marilyn Monroe. In *On Photography*, Sontag suggests that photographer Diane Arbus "lies within a Warhol aesthetic, that is, defines itself in relation to the twin poles of boringness and freakishness." But Sontag argues that Warhol was more narcissistic and that his work does not reveal Arbus's ambivalence about life in America.

Weil, Simone (1909–1943). French writer and activist, the subject of an essay in *Against Interpretation*. Weil is honored by Sontag for her involvement in the Spanish Civil War and in other causes on behalf of freedom. Weil's intense religiosity, especially her desire for martyrdom, disturbs Sontag. Although Sontag believes that humanity needs examples of selfless suffering (Weil starved herself in sympathy over those interned in concentration camps by the Nazis), she does not see how she could ever tolerate such behavior in her own friends or family.

Welles, Orson (1915–1985). Actor and theatre and film director, creator of the American masterpiece *Citizen Kane* (1941). In *Against Interpretation*, Sontag acknowledges Welles's innovative film techniques, but she criticizes him for never achieving a "rigorous narrative form" in "Spiritual Style in the Films of Robert Bresson."

Weston, Edward (1886–1958). American photographer. Weston is best remembered for his magnificent landscape photographs, many of them taken in the American West. In *On Photography*, Sontag suggests that his work expresses the "heroic vitalism of the 1920s popularized by D. H. Lawrence." She questions Weston's contention that photography enhances the human affinity with nature; on the contrary, she argues, the habit of "looking at reality as an array of potential photographs" estranges the viewer from nature.

Whitman, Walt (1819–1892). American poet. Whitman's great vision of America as a united land and people is constantly explored in *On Photography*. Sontag criticizes a number of photographers for sentimentalizing Whitman's vision and presenting a "family of man" portrait of humanity that too easily glosses over differences and obscures the complexities of history.

Wilde, Oscar (1854–1900). Irish playwright, poet, and critic. He is most famous for *The Importance of Being Earnest* (1894) and essays such as "The Critic as Artist." Sontag quotes Wilde at the beginning of her essay "Against Interpretation." She also invokes his name in "Notes on 'Camp.'" Wilde is a key figure for her because he rejected the convention of realism. Art for Wilde was not an imitation of reality. Indeed, he reversed the terms, declaring that life is an imitation of art. Wilde's emphasis on style over content and his attacks on moralizing literature appealed strongly to Sontag in her early phase, when she was emphasizing that art was about form, surface, and sensuousness and not merely the container of messages and meanings. To Chuck Ortleb, Sontag remarked that Wilde "is underrated as a serious presence in our culture. People are misled by the elegant smart-ass tone; they don't see his originality, much less the fact that some of his ideas parallel Nietzsche's."

Wilson, Robert (1941–). Theatre director and creator of performance art. Sontag has collaborated with Wilson on various projects, including an adaptation of an Ibsen play, *The Lady from the Sea*. Wilson combines the avant-garde music of John Cage and the choreography of performers such as Lucinda Childs and Merce Cunningham, both of whom are friends of Sontag and subjects of her commentary in her television essay on Pina Bausch. Wilson uses drawings and various kinds of installation art, including sculpture, in his theatre work, and his operas such as *Einstein on the Beach* combine so many different elements of the arts that he fulfills Sontag's vision of an all-encompassing contemporary art. Sontag compares Wilson's work with Artaud's in *Under the Sign of Saturn*.

Works by Susan Sontag

Against Interpretation. New York: Farrar, Straus & Giroux, 1966.
  Includes the following essays:
  "Against Interpretation"
  "On Style"
  "The Artist as Exemplary Sufferer"
  "Simone Weil"
  "Camus' *Notebooks*"
  "Michel Leiris' *Manhood*"
  "The Anthropologist as Hero"
  "The Literary Criticism of Georg Lukács"
  "Sartre's *Saint Genet*"
  "Nathalie Sarraute and the Novel"
  "Ionesco"
  "Reflections on *The Deputy*"
  "The Death of Tragedy"
  "Going to Theater, etc."
  "Marat/Sade/Artaud"
  "Spiritual Style in the Films of Robert Bresson"
  "Godard's *Vivre Sa Vie*"
  "The Imagination of Disaster"
  "Jack Smith's *Flaming Creatures*"

"Resnais' *Muriel*"

"A Note on Novels and Films"

"Piety Without Content"

"Psychoanalysis and Norman O. Brown's *Life Against Death*"

"Happenings: An Art of Radical Juxtaposition"

"Notes on 'Camp'"

"One Culture and the New Sensibility"

AIDS and Its Metaphors. New York: Farrar, Straus & Giroux, 1989.

Alice in Bed. New York: Farrar, Straus & Giroux, 1993.

"The Avant-Garde and Contemporary Literature." *Wilson Library Bulletin* 40 (June 1966): 930–932.

A Barthes Reader (editor). New York: Farrar, Straus & Giroux, 1982.

The Benefactor. New York: Farrar, Straus & Giroux, 1963.

"Dance and Dance Writing." *New Performance* 1 (1981): 72–81.

"Dancer and the Dance." *London Review of Books*, February 5, 1987, 9–10.

Death Kit. New York: Farrar, Straus & Giroux, 1967.

"Demons and Dreams." *Partisan Review* 29 (Summer 1962): 460–463.

I, etcetera. New York: Farrar, Straus & Giroux, 1978.

Illness as Metaphor. New York: Farrar, Straus & Giroux, 1978.

In America. New York: Farrar, Straus & Giroux, 2000.

"In Memory of Their Feelings," in Sontag, et al., *Dancers on a Plane: Cage-Cunningham-Johns*. New York: Knopf, 1990.

"The Lady from the Sea," in Robert Wilson, *RWWM*. Zurich: Memory/Cage Editions, 1997.

"Looking at the Unbearable: On Francisco Goya, *The Disasters of War*, 1863," in Edward Hirsch, ed., *Transforming Vision: Writers on Art*. New York: Art Institute of Chicago, 1994.

On Photography. New York: Farrar, Straus & Giroux, 1977.

"A Parsifal," in Trevor Fairbrother, et al., *Robert Wilson's Vision*. Boston: Museum of Fine Arts, 1991.

"Pilgrimage." *New Yorker*, December 21, 1987, 38–48, 50, 53–54.

Foreword to *A Place in the World Called Paris*, edited by Steven Barclay. San Francisco: Chronicle Books, 1994.

Styles of Radical Will. New York: Farrar, Straus & Giroux, 1969. Includes the following essays:

"The Aesthetics of Silence"

"The Pornographic Imagination"

"'Thinking Against Oneself': Reflections on Cioran"

"Theatre and Film"

"Bergman's *Persona*"

"Godard"

"What's Happening in America (1966)"

"Trip to Hanoi"

"Thirty Years Later . . ." *Threepenny Review*, Summer 1966, www.threepennyreview.com.

Under the Sign of Saturn. New York: Farrar, Straus & Giroux, 1982. Includes the following essays:

"On Paul Goodman"

"Approaching Artaud"

"Fascinating Fascism"

"Under the Sign of Saturn"

"Syberberg's Hitler"

"Remembering Barthes"

"Mind as Passion"

The Volcano Lover. New York: Farrar, Straus & Giroux, 1992.

"Wagner's Fluids." *London Review of Books*, December 10, 1987, 8–9.

Contributor to Toronto Arts Group for Human Rights, *The Writer and Human Rights.* New York: Anchor Press/Doubleday, 1982.

Preface to Roland Barthes, *Writing Degree Zero.* New York: Hill and Wang, 1968.

Works Cited in the Text

Note: For the biographical details of this study I draw on *Susan Sontag: The Making of an Icon*. Where I have used traditional print (hard-copy) sources, I have cited page numbers. For articles retrieved from websites, I have supplied the website address.

Acocella, Joan. "The Hunger Artist." *New Yorker*, March 6, 2000, 68–77.

Adams, Robert M. "Nacht und Tag." *New York Review of Books*, October 17, 1963, 19.

Akstens, Thomas. "Under Fire: Sontag, *Godot*, Sarajevo." *Assaph: Studies in the Theatre* 11 (1995): 75–82.

Arnheim, Rudolf. [Review of *On Photography*.] *Journal of Aesthetics and Art Criticism* 36 (Summer 1978): 514–515.

Banville, John. "By Lava Possessed." *New York Times Book Review*, August 9, 1992, 26–27.

Begley, Adam. "Sontag's High-Toned Tale: Her Brains Center Stage." *New York Observer*, February 28, 2000, www.observer.com.

Bell, Pearl K. "Literary Waifs." *Commentary*, February 1979, 67–71.

Bellamy, Joe David. "Susan Sontag." *The New Fiction: Interviews with Innovative American Writers*. Urbana: University of Illinois Press, 1974. Reprinted in Poague, 35–48.

Berek, Peter. "Susan Sontag's Private Line to the Absolute." *Commonweal*, October 10, 1969, 48–49.

Bernstein, Maxine, and Robert Boyers. "Women, the Arts, and the Politics of Culture: An Interview with Susan Sontag." *Salmagundi* 31–32 (Fall 1975 / Winter 1976): 29–48. Reprinted in Poague, 57–78.

Birkets, Sven. [Review of *The Volcano Lover*.] *Newsday*, August 2, 1992, www.newsday.com.

Blume, Harvey. "The Foreigner." *The Atlantic*, April 13, 2000, www.theatlantic.com.

Blythe, Will. "The Lioness in Winter." *Mirabella*, March 2000, 30–32.

Bockris, Victor. "Interview: Susan Sontag." *High Times*, March 1978, 20–25, 36–37.

Braudy, Leo. "A Genealogy of Mind." *New Republic*, November 29, 1980, 43–46.

Breslin, John. "Complexities of Consciousness." *Book World* (*Washington Post*), December 17, 1978, E3.

Brightman, Carol, ed. *Between Friends: The Correspondence of Hannah Arendt and Mary McCarthy, 1949–1975*. New York: Harcourt Brace, 1995.

Bromwich, David. "Large and Dangerous Subjects." *New York Times Book Review*, November 23, 1980, 11, 38–39.

Brooks, Peter. "Parti Pris." *Partisan Review* 33 (Summer 1966): 439–443.

Brown, Merle E. *Kenneth Burke*. Minneapolis: University of Minnesota Press, 1969.

Broyard, Anatole. "Styles of Radical Sensibility." *New York Times*, November 11, 1978, 21.

———. *"Good Books About Being Sick."* New York Times Book Review, April 1, 1990, 1, 28–29.

Bruss, Elizabeth. *Beautiful Theories*. Baltimore: Johns Hopkins University Press, 1982.

Burke, Kenneth. *Towards a Better Life: Being a Series of Epistles, or Declamations*. New York: Harcourt, Brace, 1932.

Byatt, A. S. "Love and Death in the Shadow of Vesuvius." *Book World* (*Washington Post*), August 16, 1992, 1–2.

Cady, Joseph. "Immersive and Counterimmersive Writing About

AIDS: The Archives of Paul Monette's *Love Alone*," in *Writing AIDS: Gay Literature, Language, and Analysis*, ed. Timothy F. Murphy and Suzanne Poirier (New York: Columbia University Press, 1993), 244–264.

Capouya, Emile. "The Age of Allegiance." *Saturday Review*, May 1969, 29.

Carvajal, Doreen. "So Whose Words Are They? Susan Sontag Creates a Stir." *New York Times*, May 27, 2000, www.nytimes.com.

Cawelti, John [Review of *Against Interpretation*.] *American Quarterly* 20 (Summer 1968): 254–259.

Christy, Marian. "Sontag Brought Personal Passion to Tale of Romance." *Chicago Tribune*, September 27, 1992, D5.

Clare, Anthony. "The Guilty Sick." *The Listener*, February 22, 1979, 294–295.

Clemons, Walter. "Mythology of Illness." *Newsweek*, June 12, 1978, 96.

Copeland, Roger. "The Habits of Consciousness." *Commonweal*, February 13, 1981, 83–87. Reprinted in Poague, 183–191.

Costa, Marithelma, and Adelaida Lopez. "The Passion for Words." *Revista de Occidente* 79 (1987): 109–126. Reprinted in Poague, 222–236.

Cott, Jonathan. "Susan Sontag: The *Rolling Stone* Interview." *Rolling Stone*, October 4, 1979, 46–53. Reprinted in Poague, 106–136.

Daniel, Max. "Tricky Nelson and the Lady." *Wall Street Journal*, July 30, 1992, A11.

Dawid, Annie. "The Way We Teach Now: Three Approaches to AIDS Literature," in *AIDS: The Literary Response*, ed. Emmanuel S. Nelson. New York: Twayne, 1992.

De Beauvoir, Simone. *The Second Sex*. New York: Vintage, 1989. First published in the U.S. in 1953.

Delaney, Eamon. "Sontag's Sagging Saga." *Irish Times*, June 17, 2000, www.irish-times.com.

Delany, Samuel R. "Under the Volcano." *Reflex*, October 6, 1992, 52–55.

Demott, Benjamin. "Lady on the Scene." *New York Times Book Review*, January 23, 1966, 5, 32.

———."Diddy or Didn't He?" *New York Times Book Review*, August 27, 1967, 1–2, 30.

————."Susan Sontag: To Outrage and Back." *The Atlantic*, November 1978, 96–99.

Dennis, Nigel. "Infirmary Blues." *New York Review of Books*, July 20, 1978, 18, 20.

Dideriksen, Patricia W., and John A. Bartlett. [Review of *AIDS and Its Metaphors*.] *New England Journal of Medicine*, February 8, 1990, 415.

Didion, Joan. "Goodbye to All That," in *Slouching Towards Bethlehem*. New York: Farrar, Straus & Giroux, 1968.

Dodsworth, Martin. "Uses of Literacy." *Encounter*, June 1970, 75–80.

Donoghue, Denis. "Sweepstakes." *New York Review of Books*, September 28, 1967, 5–6, 8.

————."Disease Should Be Itself." *New York Times Book Review*, July 16, 1978, 9, 27.

Drake, Sylvie. "Bearing the Pain of AIDS in 'The Way We Live Now.'" *Los Angeles Times*, February 24, 1989, Section 6, p. 8.

Dunning, Jennifer. "Pina Bausch and Susan Sontag." *New York Times*, August 11, 1986, C17.

Eder, Richard. "That Hamilton Woman." *Los Angeles Times Book Review*, August 16, 1992, 3, 7.

Elliott, George P. "High Prophetess of High Fashion." *Times Literary Supplement*, March 17, 1978, 304.

Ellmann, Mary. "The Sensational Susan Sontag." *The Atlantic*, September 1966, 59–63.

Feldman, Burton. "Evangelist of the New." *Denver Quarterly* 1 (Spring 1966): 152–156.

Fichtner, Margaria. "Susan Sontag's Train of Thought Rolls into Town." *Miami Herald*, February 19, 1989, 1G.

Frakes, James R. "Where Dreaming Is Believing." *New York Herald Tribune Book Week*, September 22, 1963, 10.

Freedman, Richard. [Review of *Against Interpretation*.] *Kenyon Review* 28 (November 1966): 709–710.

Fremont-Smith, Eliot. "Books of the Times." *New York Times*, August 18, 1967, 31.

Fries, Kenny. "AIDS and Its Metaphors: A Conversation with Susan Sontag." *Coming Up* (March 1989): 49–50. Reprinted in Poague, 255–260.

Garis, Leslie. "Susan Sontag Finds Romance." *New York Times Magazine*, August 2, 1992, 21–23, 31, 43.

Gates, David. "There Is No Crater Love." *Newsweek*, August 24, 1992, 63.

Gilman, Richard. "Susan Sontag and the Question of the New." *New Republic*, May 3, 1969, 23–26, 28.

Gitlin, Todd. "Sontag's Stories." *Progressive*, March 1979, 58–59.

Grondahl, Peter. "Sontag Laments on State of Literature." *Albany Times Union*, July 25, 1990, C3.

Grossman, Mary Ann. "Shaking Loose." *St. Paul Pioneer Press*, September 10, 1992, 14D.

Grossman, Ron. "At the C Shop with Susan Sontag." *Chicago Tribune*, December 1, 1992, 1, 2.

Grover, Jan. "AIDS: Metaphors and Real Life." *Christianity and Crisis*, September 11, 1989, 268–270.

Grumbach, Doris. [Review of *Death Kit*.] *America*, August 26, 1967, 207.

Guimond, James. "Photography as Myth/Photography as History." *Georgia Review* 32 (Fall 1978): 658–661.

Gurstein, Rochelle. *The Repeal of Reticence: A History of American Cultural and Legal Struggles Over Free Speech, Obscenity, Sexual Liberation, and Modern Art*. New York: Hill and Wang, 1996.

Halpern, Daniel. *Who's Writing This?: Notations on the Authorial I with Self-Portraits*. Hopewell, N.J.: Ecco Press, 1995.

———."A Win for Sontag, a Loss for Literary Culture. Trophy as Metaphor." *New Republic Online*, November 21, 2000, www.thenewrepublic.com/online/halpern112100.html.

Hassan, Ihab. "Negative Capability Reclaimed: Literature and Philosophy Contra Politics." *Philosophy and Literature* 20 (1996): 305–324.

Hayman, David. [Review of *Against Interpretation*.] *Books Abroad* 40:4 (1966): 461.

Hirsch, Edward. "The Art of Fiction: Susan Sontag." *Paris Review* 137 (Winter 1995): 175–208.

Hitchens, Christopher. "Signature Sontag." *Vanity Fair*, March 2000, 243–246.

Hoberman, J. *Vulgar Modernism: Writing on Movies and Other Media.* Philadelphia: Temple University Press, 1991.

Holdsworth, Elizabeth. "Susan Sontag: Writer-Filmmaker." Ph.D. dissertation, Ohio University, 1981.

Houston, Gary. "Susan Sontag." *Michigan Quarterly Review* 9 (Fall 1970): 272–275.

Hughes, Robert. "A Tourist in Other People's Reality." *Time,* December 26, 1977, 66–67.

Jacobson, Dan. "Sickness and Psyche." *Commentary,* October 1978, 78, 80–82.

Janes, Regina. "Illusions of Decisiveness in Susan Sontag." *Salmagundi* 55 (Winter 1982): 226–231.

Jay, Paul, ed. *The Selected Correspondence of Kenneth Burke and Malcolm Cowley, 1915–1981.* New York: Viking, 1988.

Jefferson, Margo. "Let Artistic Gray Areas Be, as Long as Truth Is Out." *New York Times,* June 12, 2000, www.nytimes.com.

Jenkins, Ian, and Kim Sloan, ed. *Vases and Volcanoes: Sir William Hamilton and His Collection.* London: British Museum Press, 1996.

Jonsson, Stefan. "One Must Defend Seriousness: A Talk with Susan Sontag." *Bonniers Littera Magasin* 58 (April 1989): 84–93. Reprinted in Poague, 237–254.

Judt, Tony. *Past Imperfect: French Intellectuals, 1944–1956.* Berkeley: University of California Press, 1992.

Justus, John. "Some New Criticism: Crotchets and Others." *Southern Review* 4 (January 1968): 252–258.

Kakutani, Michiko. "History Mixed with Passion and Ideas." *New York Times,* August 4, 1992, C16.

———."Love as a Distraction That Gets in the Way of Art." *New York Times,* February 29, 2000, www.nytimes.com.

Karnow, Stanley. *Paris in the Fifties.* New York: Random House, 1999.

Kazin, Alfred. *Bright Book of Life.* Boston: Little Brown, 1973.

———."Sontag Is Not a Camera." *Esquire,* February 1978, 50–51.

Kendrick, Walter. "Eminent Victorian." *Village Voice,* October 15–21, 1980, 44–46.

Kennedy, Liam. *Susan Sontag: Mind as Passion.* Manchester: Manchester University Press, 1995.

Kenney, Edwin. [Review of *Illness as Metaphor*.] *New Republic*, July 8–15, 1978, 37–39.

Kermode, Frank. "Alien Sages." *New York Review of Books*, November 6, 1980, 42–43.

Kerr, Sarah. "Diva." *New York Times Book Review*, March 12, 2000, www.nytimes.com.

Kiernan, Frances. *Seeing Mary Plain: A Life of Mary McCarthy*. New York: W. W. Norton, 2000.

Kirn, Walter. *New York*, March 8, 2000.

Koch, Stephen. "On Susan Sontag." *TriQuarterly* 7 (Fall 1966): 152–160.

Kolovakos, Gregory. "AIDS Words." *The Nation*, May 1, 1989, 598–602.

Kostelanetz, Richard. *One Million Words of Book Notes, 1958–1993*. New York: Whitston Publishing Co., 1996.

Krim, Seymour. "Susan Sontag: Shifting from High to Low Gear." *Book World* (*Chicago Tribune*), October 19, 1980, 3.

Kundera, Milan. *Jacques and His Master: An Homage to Diderot in Three Acts*. New York: Harper & Row, 1985.

Lahr, John. "Box Seat at the Theater of Ideas." *Book World* (*Washington Post*), October 26, 1980, 3, 14.

Leavitt, David. "The Way I Live Now." *New York Times Magazine*, July 9, 1989, 28–32, 80, 82–83. Reprinted in Ann Charters, ed., *The Story and Its Writer: An Introduction to Short Fiction* (Boston: St. Martin's Press, 1991).

Lehmann-Haupt, Christopher. "Susan Sontag and the Life of the Mind." *New York Times*, May 2, 1969, 41.

Leonard, John. "Susan Sighs in a Lonely Thicket." *Life*, March 28, 1969, 12.

———."Books of the Times." [Review of *Illness as Metaphor*.] *New York Times*, June 1, 1978, C19.

———."Books of the Times." [Review of *Under the Sign of Saturn*.] *New York Times*, October 13, 1980, C22.

Lesser, Wendy. "Interview with Susan Sontag." *Threepenny Review* (Fall 1981): 6–7. Reprinted in Poague, 192–198.

Lewis, Paul. "On Sontag." *Ten.8* 2 (Summer 1979): 3.

Lippman, Amy. "A Conversation with Susan Sontag." *Harvard Advocate* 117 (Fall 1983): 2–4, 26. Reprinted in Poague, 199–205.

Logan, William. "Exploring the Fantasies and Ritual Fears of Disease." *Book World* (*Chicago Tribune*), June 11, 1978, 1.

Lourie, Richard. "*In America*." *Book World* (*Washington Post*), March 5, 2000.

Luce, Mark. "Sputtering Finale Takes Wind from Sails of Sontag's 'America.'" *Atlanta Journal-Constitution*, March 26, 2000, www.accessatlanta.com/ajc/.

Ludwig, Arnold. *How Do We Know Who We Are? A Biography of the Self.* New York: Oxford University Press, 1997.

Mannion, Eileen, and Sherry Simon. "An Interview with Susan Sontag." *Canadian Journal of Political and Social Theory* 9 (1985): 7–15. Reprinted in Poague, 206–214.

McCaffery, Larry. "*Death Kit*: Susan Sontag's Dream Narrative." *Contemporary Literature* 20 (1979): 484–499.

McLemee, Scott. [Review of *In America*.] *In These Times*, May 1, 2000, www.inthesetimes.com.

Merkin, Daphne. "Getting Smart." *New Leader*, December 18, 1978, 12–13.

Miller, Laura. "National Book Award Winners Announced." *Salon*, November 16, 2000, www.salon.com/books/feature/20000/11/16/nba/print.html.

Minzesheimer, Bob. "Polish Migrants Lead Sontag to 'The Biggest Country.'" *USA Today*, March 9, 2000, 7D.

Mosle, Sara. [Review of *The Volcano Lover*.] *Newsday*, August 30, 1992, www.newsday.com.

Movius, Geoffrey. "An Interview with Susan Sontag." *New Boston Review* 1 (June 1975): 12–13. Reprinted in Poague, 49–56.

Nelson, Cary. *The Incarnate Word: Literature as Verbal Space.* Urbana: University of Illinois Press, 1973.

———."Reading Criticism." *PMLA* 91 (1976): 801–815.

———."Soliciting Self-Knowledge: The Rhetoric of Susan Sontag's Criticism." *Critical Inquiry* 6 (1980): 707–726.

———."Susan Sontag." *Thinkers of the Twentieth Century*, ed. Roland Turner. Chicago: St. James Press, 1987.

Nelson, Emmanuel, S., ed. *AIDS: The Literary Response*. New York: Twayne, 1992.

Newman, Edwin. "Speaking Freely." [Interview with Susan Sontag on NBC television, 1969.] Reprinted in Poague, 3–22.

O'Connor, John J. "Britain's Channel 4: Where Commerce Serves Culture." *New York Times*, June 22, 1996, Section 2, 27.

Ortleb, Chuck. "Susan Sontag: After the First Decade." *Out* 1 (April 1974): 32–34, 58.

Papinchak, Robert Allen. "Sontag Crafts a Journey of Discovery to America." *Seattle Times*, March 13, 2000, www.seattletimes.com.

Peck, Dale. "The Big Idea." *Bookforum*, Winter 1999, 24–25.

Perls, Frederick, Ralph E. Hefferline, and Paul Goodman, *Gestalt Therapy*. New York: Bantam Books, 1977. [Original edition published in 1951.]

Perrow, Charles. "Healing Words." *Tribune Books* (*Chicago Tribune*), January 22, 1989, 6.

Phillips, William. "Radical Styles." *Partisan Review* 36 (Summer 1969): 388–400.

Poague, Leland. *Conversations with Susan Sontag*. Jackson: University Press of Mississippi, 1995.

Poague, Leland, and Kathy A. Parsons. *Susan Sontag: An Annotated Bibliography, 1948–1992*. New York: Garland, 2000.

Polizzotti, Mark. *Revolution of the Mind: The Life of Andre Breton*. New York: Farrar, Straus & Giroux, 1995.

Prose, Francine. "Words That Wound." *Savvy Woman*, January 1989, 100–101.

Raban, Jonathan. "The Uncourtly Muse." *New Statesman*, December 12, 1969, 866–867.

Rabkin, Gerald. "Milan and His Master." *Performing Arts Journal* 9 (1985): 17–24.

Ray, Kevin. [Review of *The Volcano Lover*.] *St. Louis Post-Dispatch*. August 9, 1992, www.postnet.com.

Reynolds, Stanley. "Dreaming." *New Statesman*, April 26, 1968, 555–556.

Rollyson, Carl, and Lisa Paddock. *Susan Sontag: The Making of an Icon*. New York: W. W. Norton, 2000.

Rorem, Ned. *The Nantucket Diary of Ned Rorem, 1973–1985*. San Francisco: North Point Press, 1987.

Rosenbaum, Jonathan. "Under the Sign of Sontag." *Soho News*, November 12–18, 1980, 16.

Ruas, Charles. "Susan Sontag: Me, Etcetera . . ." *Soho News*, November 12–18, 1980, 8–9, 16. Reprinted in Poague, 175–182.

Sawicka, Elzbieta. "Ostatni Chorazy Oswiecenia." *Rzeczpospolita* [daily newspaper], February 24–25, 31, and March 1, 1998.

Sayres, Sohnya. *Susan Sontag: Elegiac Modernist*. New York: Routledge, 1990.

Scarf, Maggie. "A Message from the Kingdom of the Sick." *Psychology Today*, July 1978, 111–112, 114, 116.

Scarpetta, Guy. "Susan Sontag: Dissidence as Seen from the USA." *Tel Quel* 76 (Summer 1978); 28–37. Reprinted in Poague, 97–105.

Servan-Schreiber, Jean-Louis. "An Emigrant of Thought." *Questionnaire* [French television program, December 13, 1979.] Reprinted in Poague, 143–164.

Sheppard, R. Z. "Lava Soap." *Time*, August 17, 1992, 66–67.

Showalter, Elaine. *Sexual Anarchy: Gender and Culture at the Fin de Siecle*. New York: Viking, 1990.

———.[Review of *In America*.] *New Statesman*, June 5, 2000, www.newstatesman.co.uk.

Silverblatt, Michael. "For You O Democracy." *Los Angeles Times*, February 27, 2000.

Simon, John. "Looking into the Camera." *New Leader*, February 13, 1978, 17–18.

———."The Valkyrie of Lava." *National Review*, August 31, 1992, 63–65.

Span, Paula. "Susan Sontag, Hot at Last." *Washington Post*, September 17, 1992, C1–C2. Reprinted in Poague, 261–266.

Starenko, Michael. "On *On Photography*." *New Art Examiner*, April 1978, 12, 23.

Steiner, George. *Errata: An Examined Life*. New Haven: Yale University Press, 1999.

Stern, Daniel. "Life Becomes a Dream." *New York Times Book Review*, September 8, 1963, 5.

Stevens, Elisabeth. "Miss Camp Herself." *New Republic*, February 19, 1966, 24–26.

Stone, Deborah. [Review of *AIDS and Its Metaphors*.] *Journal of Health Politics, Policy and Law* 14 (1989): 850–852.

Stone, Laurie. "On Sontag." *Viva*, November 1978, 39–40.

Sullivan, Richard. "Appraisal of the Arts. *Books Today* (*Chicago Tribune*), February 20, 1966, 12.

Sutherland, John. "Excess Baggage." *The Guardian/The Observer*, June 10, 2000, www.sunlimited.co.uk/reviews/generalfiction.

Taliaferro, Frances. "Books in Brief." *Harper's*, January 1979, 90.

Tanner, Tony. *City of Words: American Fiction, 1950–1970*. New York: Harper & Row, 1971.

Taubes, Susan. "The Absent God: A Study of Simone Weil." Ph.D. dissertation, Harvard University, 1956.

Time. [Review of *Death Kit*.] August 18, 1967, 86, 88.

Toback, James. "Whatever You'd Like Susan Sontag to Think, She Doesn't." *Esquire*, July 1968, 59–61, 114.

Tyler, Anne. [Review of *I, etcetera*.] *New Republic*, November 25, 1978, 29–30.

Vidal, Gore. *United States Essays, 1952–1992*. New York: Random House, 1993.

Wain, John. "Song of Myself." *New Republic*, September 21, 1963, 26–27, 30.

Warner, Marina. "On Naples, Love, and Lava." *Vogue*, August 1992, 148.

Watney, Simon. "Sense and Less Than Sense About AIDS." *Guardian Weekly*, March 26, 1989, 28.

Weber, Bruce. "The Devil and the Commander." *New York Times*, February 19, 1993, B4.

Wood, James. "The Palpable Past-Intimate." *New Republic*, March 27, 2000, www.thenewrepublic.com.

Young, Vernon. "Socialist Camp: A Style of Radical Wistfulness." *Hudson Review* 22 (Autumn 1969): 513–520.

Index

A NOTE ON THE AUTHOR

Carl Rollyson is the author (with Lisa Paddock) of *Susan Sontag: The Making of an Icon*, and of biographies of Rebecca West, Norman Mailer, Martha Gellhorn, Lillian Hellman, and Marilyn Monroe. Mr. Rollyson has also written and edited a number of literary studies and reference works, including *Herman Melville A to Z* and *Critical Survey of Long Fiction*. He is professor of English at Baruch College of the City University of New York, and lives in Cape May County, New Jersey.